Values and ethics in the practice of psychotherapy and counselling

Values and ethics in the practice of psychotherapy and counselling

Edited by
Fiona Palmer Barnes
and
Lesley Murdin

Open University Press
Buckingham · Philadelphia

Open University Press
Celtic Court
22 Ballmoor
Buckingham
MK18 1XW

email: enquiries@openup.co.uk
world wide web: www.openup.co.uk

and
325 Chestnut Street
Philadelphia, PA 19106, USA

First published 2001

A catalogue record of this book is available from the British Library

ISBN 978 0 335 20475 5 (pb)   978 0 335 20476 2 (hb)

Library of Congress Cataloging-in-Publication Data
Values and ethics in the practice of psychotherapy and counselling/edited by Fiona Palmer Barnes and Lesley Murdin.
     p. ; cm.
   Includes bibliographical references and index.
   ISBN 978-0-335-20475-5 (PB) – ISBN 978-0-335-20476-2 (HB)
   1. Psychotherapy – Moral and ethical aspects.   2. Counseling – Moral and ethical aspects.   I. Palmer Barnes, Fiona, 1943–   II. Murdin, Lesley.
   [DNLM: 1. Psychotherapy.   2. Counseling.   3. Ethics, Medical.
WM 62 V215 2001]
RC455.2.E8 V34 2001
174'.2 – dc21

                                                                           00-050504

Printed and bound by CPI Group (UK) Ltd, Croydon, CR0 4YY

To Anne and Kenneth Knight
and Alfreda and Fredrick Milburn

Contents

Notes on editors and contributors

Mark Aveline (MD, FRCPsych, DPM) has since 1974 been a consultant psychotherapist in Nottingham running an integrated pyschodynamic and cognitive behavioural specialist clinical NHS service. He has held the posts of Chair of the Training Committee, South Trent Training in Dynamic Psychotherapy, Chair of the Psychotherapy Training Committee, Royal College of Psychiatrists, President of the British Association for Counselling and Vice-President of the Society of Psychotherapy Research. He is joint editor of *Group Psychotherapy in Britain* (Open University Press 1987) and *Research Foundations of Psychotherapy Practice* (1995) and author of *From Medicine to Psychotherapy* (1992).

Petruska Clarkson (MA, DLitt et Phil., CPsychol., FBACP, FBPS) is a consultant philosopher, chartered clinical, counselling and organizational psychologist, UKCP registered child, individual and group psychotherapist, recognized supervisor (BAPPS) and accredited management consultant (MIMC) with 30 years' international experience and more than 150 publications (in 22 languages) in these fields. These include the books *The Therapeutic Relationship* and *Ethics: Working with Ethical and Moral Dilemmas in Psychotherapy*. She is Honorary Professor in Counselling Psychology and Psychotherapy at the University of Surrey, Roehampton as well as at Westminster University and is based at 58 Harley Street, London, W1G 9QB.

Mary Anne Coate is a chartered clinical psychologist and has until recently been Head of Training at WPF Counselling and Psychotherapy. She is a fellow of the British Association for Counselling and Psychotherapy. Her origins are in mathematics and theology and among her publications are *Clergy Stress* and *Sin, Guilt and Forgiveness*.

Josephine Klein holds a doctorate and has worked as an academic social scientist. She is a fellow of the London Centre for Psychotherapy and is a full member of the British Association of Psychotherapists. She works in private practice and is the author of *Our Need for Others and its Roots in Infancy* (1987) and *Doubts and Uncertainties in the Practice of Psychotherapy* (1995).

Georgia Lepper (PhD) received her first degree in English and philosophy in the United States. Later, having become permanently resident in the United Kingdom, she undertook professional training, first as a counsellor, then in group therapy, at the Westminster Pastoral Foundation in London, and finally as an analytical psychologist at the Society of Analytical Psychology. Her research training in conversion analysis was undertaken at Goldsmiths College, University of London. She is currently Lecturer in psychotherapy at the Centre for the Study of Psychotherapy at the University of Kent.

Del Loewenthal trained as a psychotherapist with the Philadelphia Association. He is the founder of the MSc in 'Counselling and Psychotherapy as a Means to Health' and the MATER Project at the School of Educational Studies, University of Surrey, where he is a senior lecturer. He is also Chair of the Universities Psychotherapy and Counselling Association and editor of the *European Journal of Psychotherapy, Counselling and Health*. He is particularly interested in the implications of continental philosophy for practice and research. He works as an individual and group psychotherapist and has a small private practice in Wimbledon.

David Mann is a psychoanalytic psychotherapist and a member of the London Centre of Psychotherapy. He is a principal psychotherapist at the Invicta Community Care NHS Trust in Kent. He also works in private practice in Tunbridge Wells and south London. He teaches and lectures at a variety of training courses and runs workshops around the UK and Europe on 'Working with the erotic transference and countertransference'. He is author of *Psychotherapy: An Erotic Relationship – Transference and Countertransference Passions* (1997) and is the editor of *Erotic Transference and Countertransference: Clinical Practice in Psychotherapy* (1999). He is currently editing a new book, *The Desire for Love and Hate: Psychoanalytic Perspectives* (in press).

Edward Martin (MA psychoanalytic psychotherapy, MSc social policy) is a professional member of the Society for Analytical Psychology and Chair of the British Association for Psychodynamic Supervision. He has a private practice and is departmental consultant for individual work at the Westminster Pastoral Foundation where he teaches, supervises and lectures on these subjects.

Lesley Murdin (MA Oxon English literature, MA Sydney educational psychology) taught for the Open University and in the United States. She trained in psychoanalytic psychotherapy at the Westminster Pastoral Foundation (WPF) Counselling and Psychotherapy and now runs WPF's training. She has been Chair of the Foundation for Psychotherapy and Counselling and the Psychoanalytic Section of the United Kingdom Council for Psychotherapy (UKCP) and of its Ethics Committee. She is author of *How Much is Enough?* (2000).

Fiona Palmer Barnes (FBAC, BA) is a training analyst for the Association of Jungian Analysts and works in private practice in Herefordshire and London. She is a professional member of the Severnside Institute for Psychotherapy and the Foundation of Psychotherapy and Counselling and chairs the Ethics Committee of UKCP. She is author of *Complaints and Grievances in Psychotherapy* (1998).

Richard Rowson is a lecturer in moral philosophy and professional ethics at the University of Glamorgan. Since spending a sabbatical year in 1987–8 as research fellow at the Institute of Medical Ethics, he has worked in several areas of professional ethics, including consultant to the Home Office on police ethics, adviser to the Ethics and Nursing Committee of the Royal College of Nurses, tutor in medical ethics at St Mary's Hospital Medical School and contributor to television programmes on professional ethics.

Andrew Samuels is Professor of Analytical Psychology at the University of Essex and Visiting Professor of Psychoanalytic Studies at Goldsmiths College, University of London. A psychotherapist in private practice, he also works as a political consultant. His books include *The Political Psyche* (1993) and *Politics on the Couch: Citizenship and Internal Life* (2001).

Robert Snell is training as a psychoanalytic psychotherapist at the London Centre for Psychotherapy; his academic background is in the history of art. He works in the counselling service at the University of Sussex where his work includes co-facilitating therapeutic groups and running a mentoring scheme for student writers. He also teaches on the MSc in 'Counselling and Psychotherapy as a Means to Health' at the University of Surrey. He has a private practice in Brighton, and is book reviews editor for the *European Journal of Psychotherapy, Counselling and Health*.

Jan Wiener is Training Analyst for the Society of Analytical Psychology and the British Association of Psychotherapists. She is Senior Adult Psychotherapist at Thorpe Coombe Hospital, Walthamstow and works in private practice. She has published papers on analytical psychology and she is co-author with Mannie Sher of *Counselling and Psychotherapy in Primary Health Care: A Psychodynamic Approach* (1998).

Acknowledgements

We should like to thank all those who have helped us with this book: our contributors, our consultant editor Michael Jacobs and our colleagues who read chapters.

Above all, we should like to acknowledge the friendship that made the venture possible and to thank our husbands Neil and Paul whose comment and consultation helped us so much.

Editors' note

In this book we have tried to be sensitive to inclusive language and equal opportunities issues. Our contributors have chosen to use *patient* or *client* for those with whom they work and *therapist*, *psychotherapist* or *analyst* to describe practitioners.

The case material in this book is entirely fictitious, though it draws on our contributors' long experience in the field. Any resemblance in any detail to real persons is entirely unintentional.

Foreword

Jeremy Holmes

At first glance psychotherapeutic ethics is relatively straightforward. Therapists should be properly trained and belong to reputable professional organizations with well-developed codes of ethics. They should enter into clear contracts with the patients in which financial and practical boundaries are spelt out. Their practice, especially if publicly funded by third parties such as the National Health Servive (NHS), should be founded on scientific evidence, and clients should not be offered dubious treatments based on anecdote or charisma. Therapists should not impose their own values on patients, but respect their autonomy and choice. Patients should be safe-guarded against sexual, financial or informational (that is respect for confidentiality) exploitation by therapists. If unethical practice does arise, as with any profession it inevitably will, practitioners should be subject to disciplinary sanctions; their interests should be protected by adequate appeals mechanisms. All this should be conducted, as far as possible, with maximum transparency in the public sphere.

Yet these principles, however praiseworthy, will seem to most practitioners somehow to miss many of the key aspects of psychotherapeutic practice – not least, its confusions, uncertainties and mysteries. We aspire to be morally neutral, and yet constantly betray our values through our dress, speech patterns, facial responses and the decor and provenance of our consulting rooms and clinics. Like Freud we may wish to see ourselves as scientists, relentless in our pursuit of knowledge, yet we know that the evidence base for our practice is often flimsy, far removed from the narrative or, to use Freud's term, 'novelistic' concerns of day-to-day psychotherapeutic work. Further, in order to work effectively, analytic therapists must open themselves countertransferentially to the patient, becoming aware of all the positive and negative feelings including prejudice and sexual responsiveness that arise in their inner world as a result of the intimacy of therapy. At the same time they must cultivate an attitude of detached yet passionate curiosity about such feelings. They must keep clear goals for therapy in mind, but refrain from imposing on or controlling their patients. They must be able to accept the patient's destructive and self-defeating actions as aspects of necessary defence-mechanisms, while at the same time not condoning them.

This discrepancy between the ethical standards expected of a profession and the realities of psychotherapeutic work is a crucial theme for therapists. It does not mean that in order to practise psychotherapy one must have the ethics of a saint and the wisdom of a sage. Therapists are no less flawed than anyone else; indeed most have to a greater or lesser extent suffered and sinned, and the process of recovery has played its part in choosing their profession. There are however three interrelated qualities in therapists which go some way to ensuring ethical practice. The first is the capacity for self-reflection: the ability to see thoughts, feelings and actions as they arise, and to think about them. Second, the capacity to put those thoughts, feelings and potential actions into words rather than being drawn into enactment in the powerful interpersonal field which comprises the therapeutic situation. Third, the ability to attend closely to boundaries, and so to be aware of the dangers and possibilities created by therapeutic intimacy and its limitations. They must focus intensely on the patient, yet keep in mind the borderland between the ethical and the professional, the political and the personal, the private and the public.

Patients challenge therapists in ways that also raise issues that cannot be considered simply as technical. 'How do I justify going into therapy to friends who view it as mere self-indulgence?' 'Given my religious beliefs, does it matter if my therapist is clearly an atheist?' 'I came asking for some guidance about time-management, and I am being offered intensive and prolonged therapy: how do I decide what is right for me?'

The special contribution of this book is to explore the intersection of therapy and philosophical ethics. The therapists think clearly about such issues as how their values impact on their work, how they handle sexuality in the therapeutic situation, why firm boundaries are important and what to do when they transgress them, what to do about the need for confidentiality and the equally powerful human need to gossip, and where politics fits in with the privacy of therapy – to select a few from among those that are so admirably discussed in this volume – the better their therapeutic work is likely to be. It is not a question of imposing super ego-related standards. It is important to be clean – but to be squeaky clean can be too much of a good thing. We all fail from time to time. The crucial issue is to be able to think about failure and if possible put it to good therapeutic use, and if not to make adequate recompense.

I will end this brief and enthusiastic introduction to a book which manages to confront, challenge and uplift the reader, with a clinical anecdote. A schizoid young man who suffered from severe depression and had made several suicide attempts had been in therapy for two years. The circumstances of his life had improved dramatically during that time: he had had no hospital admissions, his relationship with his mother and estranged father had improved, and he had attained a reasonable job. However, he reported that he felt no better in himself, continued to see no good reason for living, and, as was his constant wont, challenged the therapist to put forward any good reasons why he should not kill himself.

The therapist responded, as he had done many times before, by pointing out how the patient had been subject to similar blackmail by his depressed mother (who had brought him up single-handedly) throughout his childhood, and that he was perhaps wanting to let the therapist know just how terrifying such threats could be, and how he had longed for a father who could help bear some of the brunt of her misery. The patient returned at the next session looking much better. The therapist privately congratulated himself that his interpretation had at last hit the mark. But when he commented on the apparent change in the patient, the response was that yes he had been feeling much better thank you, a change which he attributed entirely to having seen a television programme about philosophy through the ages and how philosophical insights could help make life more bearable.

This programme, he said, had helped him to discover that his own nihilism had a respectable philosophical pedigree, and that 'carrying on carrying on' was not such a bad way to live one's life. So, thought the therapist, perhaps ethics can be more powerful than interpretation, especially if it comes from powerful father-figures; but perhaps too, paradoxically, the humility to accept one's relative powerlessness is what makes psychotherapy a worthwhile enterprise, albeit one that is necessarily undervalued. He looked forward to the opportunity to discuss these thoughts with his colleagues. If books are forms of conversation, then a book such as this, like philosophy, will offer much consolation.

Introduction

Fiona Palmer Barnes and Lesley Murdin

Introduction

This book is about the values that underlie the theory and practice of psychotherapy. It is not about codes of ethics or techniques as such although, of course, these are the expressions of the very values that we wish to discuss. In recent years there has been a growth in interest and concern about the field of ethics and values for many reasons. In the second half of the twentieth century, after the Second World War, there was a consensus in which the common good was seen to be service to all citizens. In the UK this was expressed, for example, in the terms of the National Health Service and the Education Act 1944. In the 1980s, attitudes were changed and the emphasis moved from the practitioner who was offering the service to the rights of citizens receiving it. The language changed to stress the rights of consumers, thus patients became customers. Words like *accountability* acquired much greater importance in political and social life. Professionals who had assumed that they knew what was best for the patient began to have to explain what they were doing and why, both to their colleagues and to the public.

This book is the result of our concern to explore and debate the values that structure the professional and personal ethos of our particular world of work. This has required an exploration of the language that we use and the ideas and assumptions that lie beneath. We have therefore asked a number of authors to write about the values that inform the area of work that interests them and to consider how these values are expressed in theory and practice. One of these, Richard Rowson, has pointed out that there is no clear distinction to be made between ethics and morals. However, the main difference in common usage would be perhaps that morals are usually seen as the system adopted by an individual whereas ethics is the science of morality or of duty. Values are the expression of the esteem with which a person or society regards an object and it is with this esteem or valuing that we are mainly concerned. The terms *ethics* and *values* are often used interchangeably but the distinction that we make here is that the book deals with the assumptions that we make about value or worth and these may well be scarcely conscious for the therapist or for the patient.

The editors have both served on various professional ethics committees and are well aware of the complexity of the questions that may arise in the professional setting leading to a request for help or advice: what should I do in this or that situation? These sorts of questions are considered elsewhere, for example by Palmer Barnes (1998) *Complaints and Grievances in Psychotherapy*. We have, however, not asked the authors to deal specifically with what we should do. Rather, we have asked them to consider the processes by which we all come to ascribe value to people, things, behaviour, feelings and the ways in which these values will affect our professional theory itself and the way in which these theories are applied via technique. We hope that examining values will enable us each to make choices more freely.

The work that a psychotherapist does is of great significance. Though we have the power to do good, we also have the power to do ill. Most of the models in use today would place a high value on such concepts as awareness and choice, and perhaps increasingly also on responsibility and an attitude of concern for others.

Psychoanalytic theory and the forms of therapy that have grown from it, or in reaction to it, have not had a great deal to say explicitly about ethics and values. Nevertheless, every aspect of developmental theory or psychopathology implies a view of human nature and of the way in which we value some behaviours, character structures and states of mind as being better or worse than others. Therapists span a wide range in their views of the purpose of their work, all the way from the therapeutic zealot who sets out to heal and cure humanity to the freelance philosopher who has no intention beyond seeking to encourage learning and thinking. In the middle of this range would be those who take a developmental view and consider that they are facilitating forward movement that had become blocked in some way. Even the most minimalist of these views would require valuing one thing more than another.

Most therapists, if pressed, could come up with some aphorisms to convey the goals of their work: to make the unconscious conscious, to replace id with ego, to develop the capacity to reflect, to reach the 'depressive position' at least some of the time, to have better relationships with oneself or others. This is just a sample but it already introduces words like 'better', which raise the question: who decides what is better? If we pay some sort of homage to the overarching value of autonomy, then we would hope that the client or patient would be developing a personal view of what is good or better. This is an ideal that we might hold. It is not easy to sustain as the practice of

psychotherapy consists of a person who is vulnerable, in emotional difficulties, consulting someone who is supposed to know. As practitioners we
understand that everything we do or say constitutes a form of suggestion
and that our own value system is bound to be communicated to clients.

Each individual therapist must face his or her own values in the process of
theory making and technique building. In putting together the chapters for
this book we have also recognized the importance of the context in which
we live and work. Values are formed and hardened by the culture and
groups surrounding us and the outcomes of certain behaviour in contrast
with other sorts. In recent years therapists have been made aware of the
judgements that have been made by individuals and groups about the worth
of what we do.

The false memory debate for example has provided a school of particularly hard knocks. We have all had to face the uncertainty and limits of our
knowledge of the historical past. This is an area that we have not specifically covered because we are aware of a number of recent books that deal
well with these debates, for example by Sandler and Fonagy (1997). The
United Kingdom Council for Psychotherapy (UKCP) has issued a resource
document for practitioners (Murdin 1997), that emphasizes the importance
of agnosticism in dealing with questions of the accuracy of memories and the
problems that arise from lending particular weight to an account that is
given, at one particular moment in a therapy, about what happened in the
past. Therapists will of course take seriously the emotional needs of the
patient who is recounting any history and particularly one that involves
abuse or violence. Nevertheless, truth is a paramount value for most of us
and we cannot therefore ignore the warnings that a patient's accounts of the
past may change over time and cannot be relied upon to be totally accurate
at any stage.

A major area of value formation and influence is in the field of difference
and equal opportunities. Both of us have worked in this area and we know
that it is a subject of great importance and debate in psychotherapy. We have
not addressed it specifically in this book because we consider that it pervades
all questions of values and cannot be ignored in any aspect of our work.

Both outside and inside the profession, there is great concern about ethics
and standards. This ranges from an interest in moral philosophy to a deep
concern about the pressures that colleagues in the statutory and voluntary
sectors can find themselves facing in relation to ethics and values. Similarly
the commercial world, police, press and the churches have found themselves
the subject of scrutiny in these areas. As religious affiliation and practice
decline there is a countervailing growth in public interest in ethical questions
coming from every facet of society.

These concerns reflect and are reflected in a profound interest in the inner
and outer work of psychotherapists. There are, however, few books that
deal with this subject. Tim Bond (1993) has written on the practical aspect

of ethics in *Standards and Ethics for Counsellors in Action* and Jeremy
Holmes and Richard Lindley (1989) on *The Values of Psychotherapy*. The
popularity of both of these books indicates the need for a basis for discussion and thought about some of the more contentious and subtle aspects
of values in the work of psychotherapy. Alan Tjeltveit (1999) in *Ethics and
Values in Psychotherapy* considers the philosophical basis for establishing
values.

In this book, we are offering a broad spectrum of chapters which may be
used by individuals and groups to stimulate thinking and discussion on just
these questions. The authors have professional backgrounds in medicine,
philosophy, the social sciences and the arts. In this way, questions of value are
addressed from relevant but diverse perspectives. The first three chapters deal
with fundamental principles of ethics and morality. Richard Rowson gives
the philosopher's view of academic ethics as a study of morality and estab-
lishes some definitions. Del Loewenthal, Robert Snell and Petruska Clarkson
consider the therapist's responsibility to the other and the morality of intervening or not intervening, taking up or repudiating the bystander's position.

The next four chapters recognize that any attempt to consider the value
system of the therapist must pay attention to the way that the therapist's
values are expressed in the process and technique that is actually used in the
consulting room. Josephine Klein discusses the process of assessment where
subjective and value judgements are inevitably a part. She suggests ways in
which the values of the assessor may be recognized more openly and may be
more helpful to the patient. Once the process has begun other areas of
tension arise. David Mann writes about the values that are involved in dealing
with erotic transference and countertransference. Fiona Palmer Barnes considers the impasses that arise when the ordinary processes of therapy are not
enough to enable movement. Lesley Murdin's chapter is about the views of
success and failure held by therapist and client, arguing that these views will
need to converge during the process of therapy if there is to be a successful
outcome and ending.

Psychotherapists recognize that the work affects those in the immediate
and wider environment of the client. Psychotherapy does not take place in a
closed container. The social context will inevitably affect the way in which
we work in the sessions and also the kinds of constraints and demands that
we have to face both inside and outside the consulting room. The concluding chapters look at the tensions that third parties can bring. We have
responsibilities primarily to our clients but we must also face the fact that if
our work is effective at all, it will have much wider and further reaching
effects. Thus community and culture affect the patient, the therapist and the
work that we do. Questions arise over matters of confidentiality: when is it
appropriate or necessary to speak to someone outside or to write or carry
out research in this most private area of professional contact? Georgia
Lepper writes about the values involved in carrying out research projects.

Mark Aveline considers the dilemmas raised by such issues as confidentiality and the risk of harm and self-harm. Jan Wiener pursues the questions raised by our professional need for confidentiality when that imperative conflicts, as it often does, with safety or the requirements of other members of society.

The psychotherapist's relationships to society and culture and to his or her own spirituality are addressed in the final chapters. We all have to face the major questions about why we are doing this work. How and from what source do we derive our values and how do our own personal systems relate to the work that we are doing? Edward Martin discusses the area where private and public morality intersect. Mary Anne Coate writes about the moral imperatives in and for the therapeutic work. Andrew Samuels looks at the political context in which all psychotherapy takes place.

Taken together these chapters raise vital questions for practitioners and encourage them not only to examine their theoretical base for its moral and ethical implications, but also to consider their behaviour, technique, management and treatment of patients. For it is their value system that is being modelled with patients.

In conclusion, the European Association for Psychotherapy has stated in its definition of psychotherapy that it must be scientific, yet many practitioners would prefer to think of it as an art in which individuality and creativity are more important than predictability and standardization. As soon as we begin to address the work of psychotherapy and its definition, attitudes and personal values have to be added to the equation. Attitudes and values are implied in any discussion of the nature of psychotherapy and its location as a practice and as a discipline. Many practitioners spend a professional career without ever actually transgressing a code of ethics and yet treat clients in a way that could bring the profession into disrepute. There is a vast difference between keeping to the letter and keeping to the spirit of the law. We hope that this book will make a contribution to our positioning in relation to both the letter and the spirit of the needs of our profession.

References

Bond, T. (1993) *Standards and Ethics for Counsellors in Action*. London: Sage.

Holmes, J. and Lindley, P. (1989) *The Values of Psychotherapy*. Oxford: Oxford University Press.

Murdin, L. (1997) Guidelines on recovered memories, *The Psychotherapist*, 8: 1.

Palmer Barnes, F. (1998) *Complaints and Grievances in Psychotherapy: A Handbook of Ethical Practice*. London: Routledge.

Sandler, J. and Fonagy, P. (eds) (1997) *Recovered Memories of Abuse: True or False?* London: Karnac.

Tjeltveit, A. (1999) *Ethics and Values in Psychotherapy*. London: Routledge.

1 Ethical principles

Richard Rowson

Introduction

This chapter examines the assumptions that people make about ethics and the principles on which they base their moral evaluations. It explains the basic meaning of these principles and the different ways in which they are interpreted. As professionals concerned to clarify our own ethical perspectives and understand those of clients and colleagues, we need to know not only what broad and general principles we each hold but also what particular interpretations we give to them. We are then well placed to reappraise our own views, to identify where we disagree with others and to work towards mutually acceptable solutions.

The ethical principles to which we subscribe personally may or may not be compatible with our *legal* system, or the codes of our *profession*, since they are independent of them. They may, however, be dependent on any *religious beliefs* we hold.

In this chapter no significant distinction is given to the meaning of the words 'ethical' and 'moral': they are used interchangeably to refer to general ideas of right and wrong behaviour, good and bad states of affairs.

We begin with two questions concerned with assumptions that people frequently make about ethics.

Is ethics a matter of truths and facts, or of opinions?

For over 2500 years people have debated whether what is right and wrong is a matter of objective moral *truth*, or a matter of *opinion* – that is whether, when we judge someone's behaviour as right or wrong, we are

- *describing factual aspects* of their behaviour (just as we describe factual aspects of a person when we say they have a certain weight or height)
  or
- *expressing our feelings* about the person's behaviour
  or
- *reporting conventional social opinions* about it.

If Jane says to her colleague Sally: 'John was wrong to become sexually involved with his patient Mary', is she

- pointing out some *factual* quality of 'wrongness' in what John did
  or
- saying that *she disapproves* of his behaviour;
  or
- pointing out that such behaviour is *conventionally disapproved of*?

If you are the person who makes a moral judgement, you may see it as pointing out a moral fact or stating a truth. So Jane may see herself as saying that John's behaviour actually *is* wrong, not merely expressing her disapproval or claiming that his behaviour flouts convention. She may support her conviction by identifying aspects of his behaviour which make it wrong: he had deliberately encouraged the patient's dependency, knowingly allowed their mutual attraction to develop, not terminated the professional relationship once the attraction became evident, and so on.

On the other hand, if you are the person listening to a moral judgement, you may perceive the speaker as expressing an opinion rather than stating a fact – especially if, like Sally, you are uncertain whether you agree with what is said.

Imagine that, years later, when John is happily married to Mary, both Jane and Sally again reflect on his behaviour. By now Sally is clear in her view. She thinks John must have perceived the possibility of developing a fulfilling relationship with Mary and realized that the only way for it to evolve was by maintaining their professional connection. Since what he did has led to such a successful outcome, she sees it as the right thing to have done, even though she knows it flouted the conventional views of his profession. Jane, however, still sees John's behaviour as wrong because of its very nature, irrespective of its happy outcome: to her it is a moral *fact* that it was wrong, not a matter of *opinion*. She realizes, however, that Sally cannot see the truth of this since Sally looks at John's behaviour from a different perspective.

This example brings home the point that if, like Jane, we regard our ethical judgements as pointing out moral facts, we have to acknowledge that others may not be able to see them. So even if we are *correct*, and there *are* indeed moral facts, we may not be able to prove to others that there are. For what we see as evidence of them, others may not.

People who, by contrast, regard ethical judgements as expressing either the speaker's opinions, or the conventional attitudes of the culture to which the speaker belongs, will think that to attempt to prove moral facts shows a misunderstanding of the nature of morality. They consider that morality is not about facts or truths at all, but about values and principles which people happen to hold at a particular time in a particular culture.

Those who see judgements as expressing the speaker's opinions will regard Jane's conviction that she is stating facts about John's behaviour as simply indicating the strength of her attitude towards it: so strongly does she disapprove of what he did that its wrongness seems to be a matter of *fact* to her.

Those who consider that judgements express conventional attitudes will regard her conviction that she is stating a *fact* as evidence of how completely she has 'internalized' the attitudes of her culture.

An objection to the view that ethical judgements express social attitudes is made by pointing out that people often hold moral views which are at odds with the conventions of their society, as Sally did when she judged John's behaviour to be right, although she realized that it flouted conventional attitudes. A reply to this objection is to claim that in modern societies there are overlapping moral cultures and someone may be part of more than one. So, as a professional person Sally is part of one culture, with its views, but as an individual she is part of another, more free-thinking culture, the views of which are reflected in her judgement that John's behaviour was right.

As the debate as to whether morality is about facts, personal opinions or social attitudes has raged so long, we shall not pursue it further. It is important, however, to appreciate that there are these fundamentally different views about the nature of morality and about whether, when we make ethical judgements, we are identifying moral facts or are expressing opinions – either our own or those of our culture.

Is ethics concerned with aiming for the best consequences or with carrying out specific duties?

There are two other fundamentally different views about the nature of ethics. One – the *consequentialist* view – is that ethics is concerned with bringing about the best consequences. In its simplest form, this view is that our ethical obligation is to do whatever will bring the greatest benefits to everyone. So if everyone is likely to be happier if we tell a lie rather than tell the truth, we should tell the lie.

According to this view, actions such as telling a lie or breaking promises are *not intrinsically bad*, nor are actions such as telling the truth and keeping promises *intrinsically good*. All actions are *ethically neutral*, and whether they are right or wrong in particular circumstances depends on whether they lead to the best consequences. The end justifies the means, and since lying is not intrinsically bad, we have no obligation to avoid doing it.

Because the consequentialist perspective sees value in ends and not actions, it is often referred to as the *teleological* view of ethics, *telos* being the Greek for 'end' or 'objective'. People who hold this view base their ethical judgements on the *principle of utility*, which we look at in the next section.

The other view of ethics is the *dutiful* or *deontological* view – *deon* being Greek for 'duty'. According to this, certain types of actions are intrinsically good, and others intrinsically bad. Our ethical duties consist in carrying out the first and avoiding the second. The actions regarded as intrinsically good vary, but generally include respecting autonomy, telling the truth, keeping promises and being just. Those regarded as intrinsically bad usually include taking life and inflicting harm.

Not everyone holds either a teleological or deontological view. Some people – referred to as *ethical pluralists* – hold both, considering that ethical decision making requires us to bear in mind the demands of each perspective. So if keeping a promise would harm others, when deciding what to do they would weigh the ethical importance of keeping it against the importance of not harming others.

Teleological, deontological and ethical pluralist views are all compatible with both the 'fact/truth' and 'opinion' views of morality. Someone could regard it as a *fact* that ethics is concerned with seeking consequences or that it is concerned with being dutiful or that it is concerned with both. Others could regard it as a matter of *opinion* that it is concerned with one or the other or both.

Ethical principles

In this chapter 'ethical principles' means *the rules which people are committed to because they see them as embodying their values and justifying their moral judgements.*

When people make moral judgements we normally expect them to be able to justify them. When they do, it is usually apparent that their judgements are underpinned by one or more principles:

'I ought to go to the meeting tonight.'
'Why?'
'Because I promised the chairperson I'd be there.'

The speaker clearly holds the principle that promises should be kept.

Some people are committed to only one fundamental principle: *utilitarians*, for example, think that the principle of utility should be the sole basis for our judgements. *Deontologists*, on the other hand, subscribe to more than

one principle – such as tell the truth, respect autonomy and keep promises –
but they reject the principle of utility, while *ethical pluralists* accept several
principles, including the principle of utility.

Whatever principles people hold, they may see them as part of a 'fact' or
'opinion' view of morality. So someone may regard it as a *fact* that morality
is based solely on the principle of utility, or may consider that it is so *in their
opinion*, or in the *conventional opinion* of their culture. Similarly an ethical
pluralist or deontologist may regard it as a matter of *fact* or *opinion* that
morality is based on several ethical principles.

The principle of utility

The principle of utility underlies Sally's view. She judges the value of actions
by their *utility* in bringing about valuable consequences. For her it is the *consequences* of John's behaviour that make it right, irrespective of its *nature*.

Within professional contexts this principle is frequently interpreted as the
requirement to seek the best interests of our clients. However, its demands
are wider than this, and require us to bear in mind the interests of *everyone*
– including ourselves – who might be affected by our actions.

The principle of utility is applied in two basic forms.

- One, *act utilitarianism*, considers that before we act we should assess the
  likely outcomes of all options and choose whichever *act* we think will be
  the most beneficial in the *particular* circumstances.
- The other, *rule utilitarianism*, considers that we should formulate *rules* we
  think would lead to the most beneficial consequences if everyone were to
  follow them in *all relevantly similar* circumstances. We should then stick
  to the rules. If, for instance, we decide that the best consequences would
  be achieved if everyone always told the truth, we should adopt the rule to
  tell the truth and abide by it. In fact the rules we adopt are likely to be
  more complex than simply 'Tell the truth', and will incorporate qualifications such as: 'Tell the truth, except in circumstances of type X', where
  'type X' is, for example, 'when a lie might save a life'.

According to utilitarians, when calculating which actions or rules would be
most beneficial, we should consider the likely long-term effects. Many think
we should not consider the effects just on humans, born and unborn, but on
all sentient life – animals, birds, insects, fish and even plants. Moreover, since
most actions and rules are likely to cause some harm as well as benefits, we
should choose whichever we think will result in the *greatest net benefit over
harm*.

By accepting the principle of utility as the basis for our ethical decisions
we take on tremendous responsibilities. For, in order to calculate benefits
and harms as thoroughly as we can, we must be as *well informed as possible*,
not only about how our decisions might affect others, but also how they

might feel about these effects. In so far as our actions can affect clients and colleagues, we must therefore understand as well as we can their preferences, priorities and perspectives.

We must also be as *impartial as possible*. We must, for example, allocate resources – our time, professional expertise and money – solely on the criterion of what will produce the greatest net benefit, and not give priority to some people over others just because we have greater affinity to them. As utilitarians we must regard the well-being of people we do not know as just as important *ethically* as the well-being of those we do, even though they are less important to us *emotionally*.

Many people applaud this stance of impartiality. Because it regards the suffering and well-being of people and creatures who are *not* members of our particular group – our family, gender, age group, nationality, race, creed or species – as *important* as *similar levels* of suffering and well-being of those who are, it is anti-sexist, anti-ageist, anti-racist and anti-speciesist. However, some people reject the corollary of this, which is that we have as great an obligation to further the well-being and minimize the suffering of people we do not know as of those we do. Those who object to this consider we have a duty to give priority to the interests of our own family and clients over those of others.

Some people also find another aspect of this principle unacceptable. Since maximization of benefit is its only aim, we are obliged by it to ignore any wishes and interests of individuals which are likely to prevent us achieving the greatest net benefit over harm. We should therefore ignore clients' wishes and not seek their welfare if we are certain we can bring about better consequences by doing something else. We might, for instance, decide to provide no therapy for people over the age of 70, if research indicates that greater benefit for the whole population can be achieved by allocating all our resources to younger people.

Moreover, as utilitarians we should have no moral scruples in doing this, since we consider that fair allocation of resources has no intrinsic value. It has value only if it happens to lead to greater net benefit.

Considerations such as these lead deontologists to reject completely the principle of utility as a basis for moral judgements. Ethical pluralists accept that its demands have some ethical legitimacy, so include it as *one* of the principles on which they base their judgements, but they restrain its teleological demands by one or more of the deontological principles. So they may consider that although we have a prima facie obligation to seek the greatest net benefit overall, we should weigh the importance of this against the importance of carrying out such deontological principles as respecting autonomy, telling the truth, keeping promises, respecting confidentiality, treating people fairly and justly, and not causing harm.

A prima facie obligation is one we should fulfil *unless* the ethical value of doing so is outweighed by the ethical value of meeting some other obligation. In contrast, an *absolute* obligation is one we should *always* fulfil, come what may.

Respect autonomy

'Autonomy' means being *self-determining*, that is making one's own decisions about which ethical views and beliefs one will hold and about how one will live – for example, a patient deciding which therapies to pursue. We respect the autonomy of others, first, by *enabling* them to make such decisions, and second, by *not overriding* their decisions once made.

The principle of respecting autonomy underpins widely accepted views on human rights, which are primarily concerned to promote and protect the self-determination of individuals. A powerful strand in western culture is the view that a supremely valuable attribute of humans is their capacity to make moral choices and take moral responsibility for their actions. We achieve our full dignity and worth as human beings only when we exercise this capacity. Our ethical concern should therefore be to promote and protect this capacity in ourselves and others.

The principle of respecting autonomy forbids using people for our own ends. If we do this we treat 'persons', who are supremely valuable, as 'things', that is, as objects which are valuable to us only as tools to enable us achieve what *we* want. Even if what we want is admirable – such as to benefit others as much as we can – we should not manipulate other people to achieve it. In this way the demand that we respect autonomy is a bulwark against the paternalism of utilitarianism. Consequently, many people regard respect for patients' autonomy as vital in professional relationships.

To enable clients to be autonomous we should be truthful with them about their situation. If we have information relevant to a decision they have to make, we should give it to them as fully and impartially as we can. We should try to make their decision well informed and as uninfluenced by our values as possible and, when they have made their decision, we should not interfere with it.

There are, however, differing views as to whether we should always act in this way. Two questions are relevant here:

- Are we obliged to regard as autonomous *every* decision another person makes?
- Are we obliged to respect *every decision* we regard as autonomous?

Few would answer 'yes' to the first question, since we would then have to allow young children and severely confused people to do whatever they chose, even when we were certain they would harm themselves or others. So most people consider we are not obliged to regard every decision as autonomous, and are entitled to judge which are not. However, there is considerable disagreement as to the criteria we should use when making this judgement.

Should we, for example, regard someone's decision as autonomous only if we are certain that they have a full grasp of their situation, however complex it may be, have thought logically and unemotionally through all the issues and are free of all external and internal psychological pressures? Or are these criteria too demanding? After all, how often could we say our own decisions are made so scrupulously, even though we consider them to be autonomous?

We may adopt less rigorous criteria, and accept as autonomous decisions made by people who seem adequately aware of their situation, show no obvious signs of confused or deluded thinking, and do not appear to be subject to abnormal pressures. Although these criteria may be more easily met, they may also be open to more varied interpretations. What, for example, should we regard as deluded thinking?

> A young woman rejects therapy because she believes that her problems will be solved through prayer: she will rely on the intercession of the Virgin Mary. Someone else rejects help because she will rely on the intercession of her recently deceased aunt. Some people would be inclined to respect the first but not the second decision, but are we entitled to regard one as deluded and the other not?

There is clearly scope for debate on the appropriate criteria for judging decisions to be autonomous.

Consider now the second question:

> If we are satisfied that someone's decision *is* autonomous are we obliged to accept it, however misguided we think it is?

If, for example, after careful and – as far as we can see – accurate appraisal of the quality of his future life, a patient decides to end his life, are we entitled to prevent him? If we are not prepared to respect this or other autonomous decisions with which we may disagree, can we, indeed, claim to respect autonomy at all?

Some people conclude that we are not entitled to override autonomous decisions which affect only the person who makes them, although we may override other people's autonomous decisions if they would harm others against their will. Such interference is seen as justified because it protects the autonomy of those who would otherwise be harmed. However others challenge this, claiming that we have no moral obligation to ensure that *other people* respect the autonomy of third parties, only to ensure we respect it *ourselves* – even if this results in us not interfering with decisions which are likely to harm others. So if another psychotherapist does not respect her patient's autonomy, that is her moral failure, not mine. It would be *my* failure if I did not respect her decision about how to treat her patient.

Tell the truth, keep promises/respect confidentiality

Like respect for autonomy, these principles intimately affect the way we conduct professional relationships. Some people see them as *deontological principles* – that is, as prescribing actions which are *intrinsically* valuable – hence our duty to perform them.

Some see them as *utilitarian rules* – that is, as rules we should generally follow because, on the whole, abiding by them brings greater benefit than not doing so. On this view communities, human relationships and professional activities are more successful if participants can rely on each other telling the truth and doing what they say they will do. Equally, professional objectives are more likely to be achieved if clients communicate openly with psychotherapists and counsellors, and they will do so if they can trust that confidentiality will be kept.

People have different views on the relative importance of these three principles. Some, for example, consider we should keep information confidential whatever the circumstances, while others think that although confidentiality is valuable in itself, its value can be outweighed by other duties. So in certain circumstances – say an inquiry into professional misconduct – the duty of confidentiality may be less important than the duty to tell the truth.

Just as there are different views as to what is necessary to respect autonomy, so there are in relation to telling the truth, keeping promises and respecting confidentiality.

Some people think that to tell the truth we must give information about everything we know which may be relevant. Others think that we may choose what to tell and what not to tell and that, provided we have not uttered a lie, we have not flouted the principle to tell the truth.

> A practitioner is aware that her patient is adopted. He clearly does not know this, so he never raises the topic of his parentage. Does she have an obligation to tell him? If she does not, has she failed to be truthful?

There are similar variations as to what is thought necessary to keep a promise. Do we keep a promise so long as we carry out the minimum we have undertaken, or are we obliged to meet all the expectations which our promise is likely to raise in the person to whom we make it?

> A practitioner promises to see his patient every week for the next month. He does see him, but often it is only for half an hour rather than the hour the patient expected.

Finally, what is necessary to keep confidentiality? Must we not breathe a word to our consultant, supervision group or others, even on a need-to-know basis?

So we see there are different ways in which these apparently straightforward principles may be understood.

Do not take human life

Although for many people this is the most important of ethical principles, it is dealt with only briefly here as (we must hope!) it is unlikely to be a major consideration in psychotherapy and counselling.

Some people consider that we have an absolute obligation not to take human life – whatever the circumstances we are never justified in deliberately destroying it. Others see it as a prima facie obligation: it is wrong to take life but we may sometimes be justified in doing so, the onus being on anyone who takes life to justify it by citing exceptional circumstances. These may, for instance, be that the taking of life was the unintended but unavoidable result of acting in self-defence, or that it was the just punishment of a convicted murderer.

There is a spectrum of views as to what type of 'human life' is so supremely valuable that it should not be taken. At one end is the conviction that every form of life – from the fertilized ovum to the brain-dead body kept alive by artificial means – has the same supreme worth. At the other end is the view that the only humans who have this value are those who are self-aware, have expectation for their future and can relate to others.

There are also different perceptions as to what constitutes 'taking' life. For some we take life only if we deliberately do something positive to terminate it: say, administer a lethal injection. For others we take life if we merely withdraw life-prolonging treatment or if we fail to intervene when a life is under threat: if we do not, for example, give warmth and sustenance to a new-born baby.

Do not cause harm

The principle not to cause harm – known as the *principle of non-maleficence* – is seen by many as vital to professional care: before all else, we have a duty to ensure we do not harm our clients. Some who think in terms of a hierarchy of duties see the duty not to *cause* harm as one of – if not *the* – most important of all. Next in importance is the duty to *prevent* or *remove* harm, followed by the positive duty to *create* beneficial results. So we should not attempt to benefit anyone until we are certain we shall not cause them any harm. According to this view the duty not to cause harm is absolute and the principle of non-maleficence must overrule the utilitarian view that it is acceptable to cause harm if doing so will achieve the greatest net benefit over harm.

Of course what is meant by 'harm' varies enormously. It can be destruction of life, physical and psychological suffering, unjust treatment and failure to respect autonomy. The wider one's interpretation of 'harm', the fewer courses of action will be seen to cause no harm whatsoever. Consequently in professional situations many people find it difficult to accept the principle of non-maleficence as giving an absolute duty, and regard it as

permissible to balance benefits against harm. We may often feel more justified in embarking on a course of action which can cause harm to clients if
we have their permission to do so, and the more fully autonomous a client's
decision to accept the risk of harm, the more ethically comfortable we may
be. However, if a patient is not able to make an autonomous decision, we
may be faced with a dilemma arising from the clashing principles of non-
maleficence and utility. At this point we can only ask ourselves which we see
as the more defensible option:

- to cause some harm by doing whatever we think is likely to achieve the
  greatest net benefit (according to *our* views of 'benefit' and 'harm')
  or
- to withhold an action which might bring some harm to the patient, even
  though we know of no other action which would bring as much benefit.

Treat people fairly and justly

Fairness and justice have many meanings, but in relation to psychotherapy
and counselling we can interpret what is meant by treating people fairly and
justly as:

- we treat people *fairly* when we treat them alike unless some relevant
  difference between them requires us to treat them differently
  and
- we treat people *justly* when we treat each individual 'according to his/her
  due'.

Since to be fair we should treat people alike unless there is a *relevant* difference between them, we should not treat differently clients who have the
same problem but who differ in gender, race, sexual orientation, age,
religion or nationality unless these differences *actually* affect what treatment
is appropriate for them as individuals. We should not see people as *stereo-
types*, or decide how to treat them on the basis that they belong to a particular category, but should regard them as *individuals*, treating them in
ways that are appropriate to their individual attributes.

The problem, of course, lies in identifying which attributes of individuals
we should take into account when deciding whether it is fair treat them
differently and what is justly due to each person. Those aspects most frequently identified in relation to the provision of psychotherapy and counselling are *needs* and *deserts*: individuals who have greater needs, or are
more deserving, should be given greater resources or greater priority. But
to make just decisions on this basis we need impartial and agreed criteria
by which to compare needs and deserts, and these are hard to establish.

One suggestion is that certain things are fundamental to the well-being of
us all. These things – such as a sufficient amount of food and warmth – are our

basic needs, and those who do not have them are in greater need than those who do. The difficulty with this approach, however, is that it provides us with a basis for decision making only in the most extreme circumstances. For, beyond having common needs for enough food, clothing and warmth to keep us alive, we vary enormously as to what else is essential for our individual well-being. The ability to form loving relationships, for example, may be vital to the well-being of the majority of us, but can we safely assume that it is a vital need *for everyone*? Some intellectuals do not seem to need such relationships, but they do need calm states of mind to pursue their interests. So the self-sufficient intellectual seeking help to overcome panic attacks may be in just as great a need for therapy as someone who cannot form good relationships.

In view of such considerations some people do not see basic needs as *specific* things we *all* require, but as *whatever* is essential to the well-being of particular individuals. However, since what is necessary for the well-being of each of us can vary enormously, this can result in some people being entitled to disproportionate amounts of resources. Moreover, this approach also makes it difficult to distinguish 'needs' from 'wants', yet many people see this distinction as a useful way of separating more important desires (seen as 'needs') from less important ones (seen as 'wants'). Without such a distinction, we may feel obliged to meet those requirements of an individual which seem trivial or, again, disproportionately demanding. We are then faced with whether it is *fair* to give much more to some than to others. On the other hand, if we do make the distinction between needs and wants we can be accused of *unjustly* imposing our values on others by regarding some of their desires as 'mere wants'.

In the following cases individuals suffer similar levels of unhappiness and poor self-esteem because of disappointed expectations. They each ask for help in overcoming their difficulties. Can we justly regard some as having greater need than others or see some as having 'needs' and others mere 'wants'? Since the well-being of each is adversely affected to a similar degree, should we regard them as equally entitled to help?

- A woman whose parents communicated easily with each other, cannot communicate well with her husband.
- A woman brought up in an affluent household is unhappy because her current standard of living is vastly inferior to what she expected.
- A man feels inadequate because, despite many hours in the gym, he does not have the muscular physique he always longed for.

As already mentioned, treating people justly – giving to each his or her due – requires us to consider not only what individuals need or want, but also what they deserve. But just as there are practical and ethical difficulties in comparing needs, so there are also in comparing deserts. We may, for example, regard individuals as more deserving of our help if they are caring and considerate of others, contribute to their community, avoid reckless behaviour, pay for health insurance and strive to honour their commitments. But since the failure of some people to do these things may be the result of circumstances beyond their control it would be unjust to disadvantage them on these grounds. They may be no less deserving than others even though they have not met our criteria.

Whatever criteria of 'deservingness' we put forward, they are open to such challenges. Also open to challenge is the ethical acceptability of judging the deservingness of others according to criteria *we* decide upon. What is our entitlement to decide?

In these ways we see that, though the ethical demand to act justly is a powerful one, it can be difficult to know how to apply it in practice.

Live in accord with nature

The idea that we should live in accord with nature is similarly powerful: so much so that for some people merely to refer to something as 'unnatural' is enough to imply that it is wrong. But though powerful and pervasive, the appeal to nature is notoriously vague and so open to a variety of interpretations and questionable claims. For instance, by 'nature' may be meant 'nature as a whole' or 'human nature'.

One appeal to 'nature as a whole' as the arbiter of what is right and wrong is based on the idea that nature is a *system* in which the various *components* have *specific functions* to perform. By carrying out their specific functions the components enable the objectives of the whole system to be achieved. We should therefore use them only for their specific functions. If we use them for any other purposes, we misuse them – and that is wrong. For example, some people see human sexuality as a component of nature which has one specific function: the reproduction of the species. On this view we are wrong to engage in sexual behaviour – such as oral or anal sex – which cannot carry out this function.

Such a line of argument relies on the claim that specific functions can be clearly identified by looking impartially at the facts of nature. But can they?

If we look objectively at human and animal bodies we see that their physiology is suitably shaped for various sexual activities. We may also observe that members of most species take part in a wide variety of sexual activities, many of which cannot lead to reproduction. From an impartial observation of the *facts* of nature *alone*, we cannot claim that sexual activities have only one specific function since we see them used for a variety of functions: expressions of affection, as re-enforcements of relationships and as recreation. To justify the claim that sexual activity should be used for only one purpose we must, then, appeal to some *other* values or beliefs we hold. One such belief may be that nature is created by a mind – or God – who *intends* sexuality to be used in only one way. However, if this is the ground for our view we cannot claim it is founded on an *objective* observation of the 'facts' of nature alone.

Similar problems arise if by 'nature' people mean 'human nature', since how we see human nature and what we regard as the function of human beings are also influenced by the cultural values and religious beliefs we hold.

Furthermore, whatever our conception of human nature, we are likely to see it as complex, and this obscures any clear guidance we might seek by appealing to 'human nature'. For most people think humans normally have both emotions and the ability to reason and we act in accord with the former if we react emotionally and spontaneously, and in accord with the latter if we calculate what it is best to do before we act. But when emotions and reasons clash, which should we follow? The claim that either is the more fundamental part of our nature, and so the one we should always follow, is difficult to maintain. And if it is claimed we should follow whichever we think appropriate in the circumstances, we need values *other* than simply the principle 'live in accord with human nature' by which to decide which is appropriate.

Another interpretation of 'acting in accord with human nature' is 'doing what the majority does'. A difficulty with this is that 'what the majority does' varies from culture to culture and decade to decade. Consequently our guide to ethical behaviour turns out to be not what the majority does 'in nature', but what the majority appears to do when perceived from a particular culture at a particular time.

Moreover the claim that an activity is unnatural and wrong because only a minority do it is indefensible unless it is applied *consistently* to *all* minority activities. For anyone who regards only *some* minority activities as wrong must have *other* values or principles by which to judge some activities and not others as unacceptable. But, in fact, no one does apply the principle consistently, since no one regards *all* minority activities – collecting train numbers, being a concert pianist or psychotherapist, for example – as unnatural and wrong. People who, for instance, claim that homosexuality or interracial marriages are unnatural and wrong because only a minority engage in them, do not condemn all other minority activities. They must therefore have some *other* values or beliefs they hold to give plausibility to their condemnation of these particular activities.

In this section we have seen that the appeal to 'nature' as a guide to how we should live is understood in several ways. We have also seen that it is an appeal to be viewed with scepticism, since people interpret what nature is from the perspectives of the values beliefs they hold. So it is these, rather than an impartial observation of nature itself, which are the source of their moral views.

Be caring and loving

The principle that we should be loving and caring is seen by some as putting a welcome emphasis on *feelings* in ethics in contrast to other principles which seem to require the impartial application of *reason*. While this principle does indeed emphasize feelings, it does not – as some people imagine – enjoin us simply to act in accord with spontaneous emotions. On the contrary, it requires us to act in a caring and loving way to everyone, *irrespective of our spontaneous feelings towards them*. We should strive to cultivate positive feelings, and, whether we experience them or not, act caringly and lovingly to others.

Moreover, even when we already *feel* loving and caring we may need more than *spontaneous* reactions to actually *be* so. For unthinking responses, however loving, are not always in the best interests of others. To be truly caring we often need to *reflect* on their interests and on our abilities to further them in the best way possible.

The injunction to be caring and loving is not, then, necessarily antipathetic to other ethical principles. It may, indeed, be complementary to them. For when we pause to consider what is the most caring and loving thing to do we may well decide it involves consideration of consequences, fairness and justice, honesty or respect for autonomy. Deceiving people or ignoring their wishes may well be seen as lacking a loving and caring attitude towards them. So emphasis on the value of feelings in ethics does not rule out the importance of careful thought.

Respect rights

In the nineteenth and twentieth centuries, and especially since the United Nations Declaration of Human Rights of 1948, the concept of 'rights' has become increasingly important in ethical thinking.

There are different types of rights – legal, institutional and moral. How do they differ?

Legal and institutional rights are entitlements that people possess by virtue of living under, or belonging to, a particular legal system or institution. For example, legal systems may give people the legal right to travel on the public highway, and universities give fee-paying students the institutional right to use the library. Whether or not someone has such rights is a matter of *fact* which can be ascertained by checking the relevant laws and rules.

In contrast, *claims about moral rights, including human and natural rights, are based on moral viewpoints* which cannot be checked to be true or false like statements of fact. For instance, if people assert that women have a moral right to abortion on demand, their claim is based on their particular *ethical principles* and the way that they prioritize them. They may in this case consider that respect for autonomy is more important than respect for life in the form of the human foetus.

'*Natural*' and '*human*' rights are moral rights based on what people see human nature as being. John Locke, for instance, in his *Two Treatises of Government* (1690), claimed that the enjoyment of one's property is a *natural right*, because he thought it part of human nature to live in societies in which individuals own personal property. Others, however, have pointed out that there is no idea of personal property in some societies, and so the right to enjoy one's personal property can, at most, be claimed to be a right *in certain cultures*, not a *universal* natural right. Similar challenges are made to the claim that the United Nations Declaration of 1948 is a statement of *universal* rights.

Although claims about moral, human and natural rights express moral viewpoints, they are often assumed to be stating objective and unquestionable *facts* for two reasons. First, because statements about legal and institutional rights *are* about facts, many people who do not distinguish between different types of rights assume moral rights are also about facts. Second, because claims about all types of rights have the *linguistic form of statements*, they are often understood as stating facts.

'Jane has a right to healthcare'
has the same linguistic form as
'Jane has a high IQ'.

Both appear to be giving facts about Jane, even though only the latter (if true) is doing so. The former expresses a moral opinion as to what facilities *ought* to be accessible to Jane.

In this section we have seen that claims about moral, human and natural rights do not state objective facts. At most they express views as to what, if there are such things as moral facts, they are. But, as we have seen, many people question whether there are moral facts at all.

In some countries, however, statements of human rights have become embodied into legislation. In the UK, for example, the Human Rights Act now embodies the European Convention on Human Rights into law. Where this has happened statements of human rights reflect *legal* facts.

Obey religious authority

As mentioned at the beginning of this chapter, some people see their ethical principles as stemming from their religious beliefs while others do not. There is, however, no necessary ethical disagreement between those who do and those who do not, since most of the ethical principles discussed in this chapter appear in both religious and secular contexts. Realization of this can help break down partisan convictions that a particular religion or secular ideology is the sole possessor of sound moral views. It can also encourage people to respect the ethical perspectives of religious and intellectual traditions other than their own.

Conclusion

This chapter has set out the ethical principles to which we most commonly appeal. At different times and in different situations, most of us appeal to most of them. We may sometimes see several as relevant to a particular situation. If they clash, we find ourselves faced with an ethical dilemma. Sometimes we may be able to resolve it by weighing the ethical demands of the principles against each other and satisfying ourselves that one should be given priority over the others. Sometimes, however, we may find this impossible to do: we can neither decide which is more important nor find a compromise between them. Many people would not see this as an ethical defect on our part, since they consider it part of the nature of ethics that its demands are irresolvable in some circumstances.

This chapter has also pointed out some different interpretations given to ethical principles, and some difficulties in establishing what exactly the principles enjoin us to do. In so doing it has doubtless made the framework of our thinking about ethics more complex and less clear cut than many might have wished.

Unfortunately, that is the nature of current ethical thinking. It is this thinking which we are expected to take account of in our professional judgements, and which others may bring to bear when scrutinizing our professional conduct. As professionals, we are responsible for how we take these ethical principles into account in our decision making.

2 Psychotherapy as the practice of ethics

Del Loewenthal and Robert Snell

Introduction

It will be argued here that *ethics as practice* is not in any way separate from psychotherapy. Rather, if ethics is defined as putting the other first, as Levinas, the French phenomenological philosopher, defines it, then this is what all relationships should strive towards. Ethics is not extraneous to practice, or theory. To separate ethics from practice is fundamentally un-ethical. This has profound implications for the teaching as well as the prac-tice of psychotherapy. Psychoanalysis is crucially an examination of the ethics of relationships, and the primary place for this examination is the patient–therapist relationship. An essential question for the training of psychotherapists is therefore: 'What does it mean for the psychotherapist to put the patient first?' A corresponding question is: 'What does it mean for the patient appropriately to put the therapist first?' For when the patient is able to do this is he or she not ready to leave therapy?

'To be or not to be?' is the wrong question

If we start with questions of being, what seems to happen is that we slip into questions of *my* being, such that, should we then ever look at another's being, we do so only by taking ourselves as the measure. Levinas argues that ethics, as he defines it, must always precede ontology (the study of being). Yet for Hamlet, as for Heidegger and most of western thought, the question is 'To be or not to be?' Primacy is thus given to the ontological, with devas-tating consequences. This has formed the unquestioned basis of most psychotherapy, with its emphasis on autonomy, egocentricity, or notions of a bounded unitary self (Loewenthal 1996). Levinas was very interested in

Hamlet (Levinas 1985: 22). That ethical questions must always come before questions of being is, we argue, a phenomenological rather than a moral necessity. For Levinas, as perhaps for Shakespeare, Hamlet asked the wrong question, the result of which was that those he was closest to were killed off. This was because he put himself first rather than the other first. By asking the question 'To be or not to be?' Hamlet was concerned for himself before he was concerned for anyone else.

For Levinas there was also a related important reading, in that by asking this question it was as if Hamlet could be in charge of his own death: 'Hamlet is precisely a lengthy testimony to this impossibility of assuming death' (Levinas 1989: 42). The tragedy of Hamlet is that he tries to stay on top of that which he cannot. Do psychotherapists encourage a similar fate for their clients/patients?

Greek versus Hebraic: autonomy versus heteronomy

Levinas points out that 'Every philosophy seeks truth. Sciences too can be defined by this search' (cited in Peperzak 1992: 47). Psychotherapy is no exception in claiming it seeks the truth. Yet western culture contains two major philosophical traditions, the Greek and the Hebraic, each having its own underlying assumptions about the ways that truth, in terms of relationships, can be thought about and experienced. *Autonomy* places us first, *heteronomy* begins with putting the other first, recognizing the otherness of the other (their alterity). Furthermore, it is the Greek notion of *autonomy* that has, in western culture, assumed cultural dominance over the notion of *heteronomy*.

We shall first quote Levinas's reflections on heteronomy, before considering some of his ideas in more detail. We shall then look at autonomy in a similar way. Levinas describes the idea of truth in terms of heteronomy, as follows:

Truth implies experience. In the truth, a thinker maintains a relationship with a reality distinct from him, other than him – 'absolutely other' ... for experience deserves its name only if it transports us beyond what constitutes our nature. Genuine experience must even lead us beyond the Nature that surrounds us, which is not jealous of the marvellous secrets it harbours, and, in complicity with men, submits to their reason and inventions; in it men also feel themselves to be at home. Truth would thus designate the outcome of a movement that leaves a world that is intimate and familiar, even if we have not yet explored it completely, and goes toward another region, toward a *beyond* ...

Philosophy would be concerned with the absolutely other; it would be heteronomy itself ... Truth, the daughter of experience, has very lofty pretensions; it opens upon the very dimension of the ideal. In this way, philosophy means metaphysics, and metaphysics inquires about the divine.

(Levinas in Peperzak 1992: 47)

Let us examine the above quotation in more detail. Levinas's notion of heteronomy raises questions regarding notions of 'absolute' and scientific truth. He is saying that truth is not something outside experience and yet, although this may seem contradictory, it is beyond our nature. But this does not mean that one's experience is the yardstick for truth. We cannot claim to have the truth because it is our experience. Experience is that which gets us in touch with that which is other than what we are. It is not 'what we are', and it takes us beyond what we have been. So what we feel 'at home' with may stop us genuinely experiencing. We can conceive of and experience our environment as something complicit with us and submissive to our pre-conceptions, but genuine experience in the Levinasian sense is a reaching towards a beyond, beyond what familiarly surrounds us. Can it therefore only be in a relationship where the other is put first, in dwelling with the absolutely other, that truth is to be found? We shall not arrive at truth if we see the beyond as something to be colonized and incorporated. The truth will always be beyond.

This has enormous implications for ethics, ethical practice and so-called ethical committees. We cannot appropriate truth to our experience – it is outside us. Here Levinas's ideas parallel Wittgenstein's crucial insight, that knowledge is not arrived at through contemplation of our 'inner worlds' (Wittgenstein 1953). We have always to be prepared to go beyond our 'gut reactions'; only then do we have a chance, momentarily, to reach a truth with another. We tend, as Lyotard (1978) also points out, to delude ourselves as to what 'truth' is by forgetting that it is subject to our theories, to the place we are in, and to the position we take up. This delusion of truth we then tend to see as 'natural', as our nature. 'Truth' then becomes dependent on, for example, what school of psychotherapy we are in, and the danger is that this 'truth' must be upheld, as it shores up our place as psychotherapists and the therapeutic organizations that legitimize us. Truth must always be beyond that. Yet we jealously guard our position, in a way that can lead to per-version and injustice. For example, ethics committees looking at complaints rarely include members outside the particular training of the person com-plained against, let alone outside the world of psychotherapy. Levinas helps us to raise crucial questions about ethics and vested interest. Does our theor-etical orientation or club membership come before truth and justice? If we feel at home within the club might we be potentially perpetrating violence? Truth is leaving being at home. One cannot be at home with the truth. Some-times feeling things are 'right' is wrong.

Philosophy for Levinas is about putting the other first. If we are 'at home' it is always about me first, my place in the sun, in which case philosophy is needed to legitimize the corruption – to make us feel at home.

Levinas talks of truth as the 'daughter' of experience. Levinas is talking about the unknown, which he equates with the infinite, or the divine (although it has been argued, for example, by Grosz 1996, that he does not take appropriate account of gender).

In contrast to heteronomy, Levinas describes the Greek notion of autonomy as follows:

> truth also means the free adherence to a proposition, the outcome of a free research. The freedom of the investigator, the thinker on whom no constraint weighs, is expressed in truth. What else is this freedom but the thinking being's refusal to be alienated in the adherence, the preserving of his nature, his identity, the feat of remaining the same despite the unknown lands into which thought seems to lead? Perceived in this way, philosophy would be engaged in reducing to the Same all that is opposed to it as *other*. It would be moving toward *auto-nomy*, a stage in which nothing irreducible would limit thought any longer, in which, consequently, thought, non-limited, would be free.
>
> Freedom, autonomy, *the reduction of the Other to the Same*, lead to this formula: the conquest of being by man over the course of history. This reduction does not represent some abstract schema; it is man's Ego.
>
> (Levinas in Peperzak 1992: 47–8)

Levinas is speaking about the Greek/Cartesian scientific gaze ('I am a machine that thinks'), that claims disinterested, detached independence from the phenomena it surveys; a disembodied, supposedly free-floating, inquiring mind, Hamlet, who seeks the conquest of his own being. But there are many problems: we may all strive to be autonomous and in so doing not wish to consider that we reduce others to the same, existing only within our vision.

If we do have doubts about autonomy then do we seek a philosophy/ school of psychotherapy to reassure us? In autonomy one is subject to nothing, as if one were the subject. A problem for psychotherapists is that autonomy sells, and many psychotherapy trainings seem not to question, even to promote, the virtue of autonomy. The notion of 'disappointment guaranteed' is more difficult to market. The argument for heteronomy is always in danger of being incorporated into the philosophy of autonomy. For one way of retaining autonomy in the face of the argument for heteronomy is to *learn the language* of putting the other first – to pretend.

We have deliberately quoted Levinas at some length here, as the above is key to our argument that Hamlet and most of counselling and psychotherapy have wrongly chosen autonomy over heteronomy, encompassing every Other in the Same. The other becomes a bit player with at best a walk-on part on our stage. Thus the client/patient is a bit player on the therapist's stage and as a result of therapy everyone else becomes a bit player on the client/patient's stage.

Ethics, values and psychotherapy

'The face is exposed, menaced, as if inviting us to an act of violence. At the same time, the face is what forbids us to kill' (Levinas 1985: 86). As therapists what then are our values? There appears to have been a shift from earlier notions that psychotherapy and counselling can be or should be value-free enterprises (see for example Fruggen 1992). We are assuming that as psychotherapists we shall always be subjective – our values determining how we hear and what we say. That is in so far as we are able to say what our values are: for we are suffused with the values of our culture, which we can only ever partly step outside; and we are subject to our unconscious. Perhaps these are two different ways of saying the same thing. So it is vital for our practice that we attempt to consider what we regard as essentially human: under what circumstances is the world an alive and meaningful place for us as counsellors and psychotherapists? Is it when we can assertively go after that which appears important to us (autonomy) or does it begin with putting the other first (heteronomy) in a way that recognizes the otherness of the other (their alterity)? In this way our values and ethics are linked.

When speaking of ethics we do not mean codes of conduct. These in fact can be seen as unethical, since, however well intended in their systematization, they are putting the code rather than the other first. Levinasian ethics is not therefore about my right to exist (Spinoza), it is not even just about the other's right to exist, but can be seen as my responsibility for the other's responsibility to others. Why should we put the other first? Levinas says: 'my duty to respond to the other suspends my natural right to self survival' (Levinas [1981] 1995: 189). This 'right to exist' is in the face of the other, which asks us both 'do not do violence to me' and 'do not let me die alone', since to do so were to become an accomplice in his death. 'In the relation to the face I am exposed as an usurper of the place of the other' (Levinas 1981: 189).

But what, it might be asked, obliges me to put the other first? You are free not to, Levinas would answer – free to refuse the other. But this can never invalidate the other's prior claim upon you. On the other hand you can, as John Wild wrote in his introduction to Levinas's *Totality and Infinity*, make a free 'choice for generosity and communication' (Wild, in Levinas [1961] 1969: 14–15).

Before exploring 'ethical practice' we would like to examine some implications for current schools of therapy. Let us imagine a patient: a mother searching for the forgiveness of her estranged daughter. Would the person-centred psychotherapist encourage the mother to go in the direction that she appears to want to go in? Or would the therapist feel uneasy about this? Would the behaviourist devise a programme to help the mother assert herself and get what she wants? Would a psychoanalyst/analytic psychotherapist develop the mother's ego strength so she is more able to carry out her chosen task? All these approaches, which we have grossly caricatured and oversimplified, can be seen as unethical (and delusional) in that they attempt to promote an autonomy which is at the expense of the other. The mother would be putting her daughter first, if she gave a primacy to her responsibility for her daughter's responsibility; instead she is putting herself first in seeking her daughter's forgiveness.

Psychotherapy as an ethical practice

So who was Levinas? There is not much reference to him in the psychotherapy literature (and none in counselling). Levinas was born in Lithuania in 1905 of Jewish parents, moved to the Ukraine, where he was during the Russian Revolution, then went as a young man to France. He was to live most of the rest of his life in France, surviving a prisoner of war camp, dying in France in 1995. However, in 1928–9 he had gone to Freiburg where he attended Husserl's lectures. This was his decisive encounter with phenomenology and through this, Heidegger. While Levinas is now accredited with bringing phenomenology to France and greatly influencing Sartre, de Beauvoir, Merleau-Ponty and such postmodern thinkers as Derrida and Lyotard, it was not until he was 55 that he became a full professor. He gained his international reputation with the publication of *Totality and Infinity* in 1961. Besides his interest in philosophy he renewed in France his commitment to Talmudic studies, and was responsible for their academic revival.

Of the few texts found concerning Levinas and psychotherapy (O'Connor 1991; Schneider 1991; both cited in Gondek 1995) we wish to focus on Gans (1997) as providing a useful reading of the implications of Levinas for counselling and psychotherapy.

Rather than considering the implications of Levinasian ethics for practice we would subscribe to the notion put forward by Gans (1997) of psychotherapy *as an ethical practice.*

Gans describes his Levinasian-oriented ethical psychoanalysis as an 'endeavour to bring out the good of the Other by opening him/her to the between of responsible relatedness'. This responsible relatedness 'involves being able to enjoy, to dwell, to love intimately and to meet others face-to-face, and ultimately to realise that the face of the other is the aspect of divinity open to us'.

Drawing on Levinas's *Totality and Infinity* Gans describes how the therapist can help the client/patient with the blocks that prevent him or her being able to fully enter 'zones of relatedness'. To move from Levinas's 'there is' (the infinite void prior to experience, a continuous night of insomnia and fear of annihilation) by way of:

- 'living from' (we live from good soup through embodied love of life without which we can never enter into the between of genuine relatedness)
- 'dwelling' (for this to occur there must be a surrender to embodiment and finitude so that one moves from being only for oneself to dwelling where one can accept others and be touched by them)
- 'the face-to-face' (this is not reducing the other to the same, to a supporting role in one's own play, as with Hamlet, but instead recognizing and accepting the other's difference from the standpoint of difference rather than a comparison with oneself) and
- 'eros' (this is the realm of intimacy where the erotic as intimate loving is only possible).

Are not all the above points, albeit to varying extents, what should be aimed for in all relationships and crucially the psychotherapeutic one?

Conclusion

Gans (1997) notes that eros 'takes us beyond ethical analysis to ethical life' and it is this kind of value that we hope therapists, whatever their orientation, will find helpful in thinking about what it is that determines what they hear from their patients or clients and how they respond. A major criticism of Gans's exposition is that it too can be seen as a totalizing move – a charge that could be directed towards us too. Our intention is not to replace one framework with another. There are also criticisms of Levinas. Derrida (1995, 1997) argues that Levinas has been caught in a Christian conspiracy that developed the notion of ethics because Christians could not take life's rawness, and Grosz (1996), as we have mentioned, has argued that Levinas has ignored gender. For others what has been presented may appear like a form of humanism. If so then it could perhaps be considered as a postmodern humanism, since unlike Hamlet ethical practitioners try not to be at the centre of the world but always to be subject to ethics.

For Levinas, 'modernity will ... be distinguished by the attempt to develop from the identification and appropriation of being *by* knowledge towards the identification of being *and* knowledge' (Levinas 1989: 77–8). This is the enlightenment project which envisages that one day science will know. It leads to psychotherapeutic theories which are caught up with totalizing moves, to attempts to know rather than to accept who we are. This has enormous importance for how we train students of counselling and psychotherapy (and for the authors for the way that they examine the implications of the literature of phenomenology/existentialism, psychoanalysis and postmodernism with their students). Levinas can thus be seen to deconstruct the modernist project. For Levinas we are always subject to the other who is always an infinite mystery. We may think as psychotherapists that we sometimes get some idea of our clients'/patients' particular 'numbers', the repetitive ways they move in the world which are unhelpful to them, but we will never 'know' them. This recognition contrasts with various psychotherapeutic attempts at scientific certitude. Freud, for example, was often caught up in this way, when he hoped that physiology would one day vindicate his theories. If we cannot have this knowledge we cannot, for example, systematize Levinas. To systematize is to prevent ourselves from responding justly in the moment to our clients and each other.

Such systematizing is itself like a response to trauma, so that there is restriction and we cannot learn. Following trauma the world does not make sense to us. There is a war between ourselves and others rather than a rapport. The other is seen as threatening, locking us into an omnipotent grandeur which is empty. Bion ([1967] 1984), extrapolating from Freud, describes how no thinking is possible without a living link to the other. One can more easily *not* think through ethical codes, which can get us caught up in a type of knowing, with associated appeals and complaints procedures, which goes against accepting the other. It appears to be about the other but is not. The truth of the other is missed and in the process we do not learn in a way that enables us to make the right decisions. Levinas shows a way of thinking of ethics as practice in which one can appreciate the other's personal space and allow the other their otherness. As psychotherapists we can be ethical only if we see the other as someone we can serve and learn from. This is ethics as practice.

Acknowledgements

The initial ideas for this chapter were presented at the British Psychological Society, Division of Counselling Psychology, First International Conference, Stratford, UK, in June 1997, and a version of it has been published as a chapter: D. Loewenthal and R. Snell (1998) Teaching/learning and decision making: the face-to-face versus the interface, in P. Jarvis, C. Griffin and J. Holford (eds) *Learning in the Learning Society*. London: Kogan Page. Our thoughts were further developed in an article, D. Loewenthal and R. Snell (1998) Ethics as practice: Levinas and the postmodern therapist, *Journal of the Society of Existential Analysis*, December. Particular thanks for conversations over the years both with Dr Steven Gans and with our students.

References

Bion, W. ([1967] 1984) *Second Thoughts*. London: Karnac.

Derrida, J. (1995) *The Gift of Death*. Chicago: University of Chicago Press.

Derrida, J. (1996) *Archive Fever*. Chicago: University of Chicago Press.

Derrida, J. (1997) *Adieu à Emmanuel Levinas: le mot d'accueil*. Paris: Editions Galilee.

Fruggen, L. (1992) Therapeutic process on the social construction of change, in S. McNamee and K. Gergen (eds) *Therapy as Social Construction*. London: Sage.

Gans, S. (1997) Lacan and Levinas: towards an ethical psychoanalysis, *Journal of the British Society for Phenomenology*, 28(1): 30–48.

Gondek, H. (1995) Cogito and separation: Lacan/Levinas, *Journal of European Psychoanalysis*, 2: 133–68.

Grosz, E. (1996) *Space, Time and Perversion: Essays on the Politics of Bodies*. London: Routledge.

Levinas, E. ([1961] 1969) *Totality and Infinity*. Pittsburgh, PA: Duquesne University Press.

Levinas, E. ([1981] 1995) Ethics of the infinite, in R. Kearney (ed.) *States of Mind: Dialogues with Contemporary Thinkers on the European Mind*. Manchester: Manchester University Press.

Levinas, E, (1985) *Ethics and Infinity: Conversations with Philippe Nemo*, trans. R. Cohen. Pittsburgh, PA: Duquesne University Press.

Levinas, E. (1989) *The Levinas Reader*, ed. S. Hand. Oxford: Blackwell.

Loewenthal, D. (1996) The postmodern counsellor: some implications for practice, theory, research and professionalism, *Counselling Psychology Quarterly*, 9(4): 373–81.

Lyotard, J-F. (1978) *The Postmodern Condition: A Report on Knowledge*. Manchester: Manchester University Press.

Peperzak, A. (1992) *To the Other: An Introduction to the Philosophy of Emmanuel Levinas*. West Lafayette, IN: Purdoe University Press.

O' Connor, N. (1991) Who suffers?, in R. Bernasconi and S. Critchley (eds) *Re-reading Levinas*. Bloomington, IN: Indiana University Press.

Schneider, M. (1991) La proximité chez Levinas et le Nebenmensch Freudien, *L'Hern*, 60: 431–43.

Wittgenstein, L. (1953) *Philosophical Investigations*. Oxford: Blackwell.

3 Responsible involvement: ethical dimensions of collegial responsibility

Petruska Clarkson

Introduction

Counsellors, psychologists and psychotherapists are primarily engaged in the work of alleviating human suffering and facilitating desired development. Most psychotherapists work towards these goals with words ('the talking cure') within different kinds of therapeutic relationships (Clarkson 1997).

The United Kingdom Council for Psychotherapy has published the aspiration to have a statutory register. This desire for professionalism is reflected in its claims to the public that only legitimate practitioners of the profession will be represented in the relevant registers and that those who exploit or damage the public's trust will be subject at first to confrontation and, if necessary, to sanctions.

> The purpose of the codes is to clarify what is acceptable practice and what is not. If an organisation possesses the awesome power to remove a practitioner from its register, with all the consequences that will have on his or her life and livelihood, it should feel a compulsion to provide for that person a template against which to measure his or her conduct and practice.
>
> (Palmer Barnes 1998: 8)

Those practitioners who do not belong to the profession, usually represented by the relevant register, are commonly suspected of being 'quacks' or otherwise dishonest or incompetent. Most frequently a profession undertakes the duty of protection of the public by writing and implementing a code of ethics – the equivalent of a professional legal system which codifies appropriate and unethical conduct for members of that profession. (Employment law of course exists for handling disputes and grievances of *employees.*) All members of a *profession*, at least in principle, subscribe to their profession's published ethics code and agree to abide by its rules or submit to its sanctions – for the sake of 'protecting the public'.

Whether or not this is effective in protecting the public depends on many factors but particularly on

- whether clients know and understand the codes and standards of ethics and complaints procedures in our professions
- whether clients or students generally feel that they can effectively discuss their feelings about possible ethics violations with the practitioner concerned
- whether the complaints procedures are effective, just and fair
- whether the client can manage, or can get help in negotiating them.

The complainants' experience

According to POPAN (Prevention of Professional Abuse Network), complaints against psychotherapists are rare. However, only medical doctors of all the healing professions are more complained about than psychotherapists. It is only an estimate, but I would say that out of every hundred ethical violations which I, as a practitioner researcher, have come across, only one or two clients or students make a formal complaint. Many do not even make an informal complaint.

Pope (1989) found that clients and students who did not object to or may even at the time have desired sexual contact *subsequently* felt that such contact with a therapist or educator was coercive. Pope (1989: 171) reported that 'While 80% viewed such advances as ethically inappropriate at the time they occurred, 95% at the time of the study viewed the advances as ethically inappropriate.'

I have interviewed several clients who reported that they did not even know that a psychotherapist was not supposed to fondle them as part of their treatment. The likelihood that a client is going to be adequately alert to emotional or other abuse is very small since the person with whom she is having a very intense relationship and speaking about her deepest feelings is a trusted professional therapist.

The likelihood that she or he can effectively, clearly and rationally confront this person, and has the self-confidence to make a formal and official complaint, citing the proper causes of the relevant code of practice to the practitioner's professional body is even smaller. Jehu (1994) writes:

> In addition to self-blame for the abuse other sources of guilt include the perceived betrayal of the therapist by disclosing his abuse and perhaps instigating legal or disciplinary proceedings, infidelity to a regular

partner and engagement in sexual acts with the therapist that would normally be unacceptable to the victim.

(Jehu 1994: 107)

At the 1997 Universities' Psychotherapy Association Conference Thomas Szasz challenged psychotherapists with the question of whether professional psychotherapy organizations really exist in order to protect the professionals from the public? In fact people who try to make complaints are often left even more traumatized by the process. At the AGM of the UKCP in 1999, Frances Blunden of POPAN described such experiences as 'appalling'. POPAN (1998: 8) identified among core issues 'the punitive and distressing nature of complaints procedures . . . as well as instances of apparent organisational collusion in allowing abusive practices to continue, with pressure exerted on staff who try to speak out against it.'

The ethical duty confront/report colleagues

Clients are usually least informed and least resourced to act on their own behalf in such situations. Therefore we should rely on the professionals to deal with suspected abuses. If the professionals – who are most likely to hear about abuses – from clients and students – abrogate their responsibilities to and for each other these claims become flagrant misrepresentations to the public and professional self-regulation descends to an empty sham. The fact is that

> Many, if not most of the ethical violations by professionals come to the attention of fellow professionals when clients [or students] seek them out, sometimes to remedy the wrong that was committed, but more often because their original problem was not satisfactorily resolved. The clients [or students] may not even be aware that they were mistreated because they lack the requisite knowledge of professional standards [or accurate information]. Their current therapists can choose to ignore the matter, actively persuade the clients [or students] that no real wrong or harm was done, pursue the matter themselves (normally with the client's permission), or support their client's efforts to do so. Which course of action is chosen is crucial in the aggregate, in determining the effectiveness of the profession's self-policing.
>
> (Thompson 1990: 133)

The obligation to act appropriately by confronting and/or reporting colleagues when there is reason to suspect misconduct is enshrined in our codes of ethics. The BAC, BCP, BPS and UKCP all publish this undertaking to the profession and the public, thus fostering the legitimate expectation that professionals are ethically obliged to act in cases where they have reason to be concerned about their colleagues' unethical behaviour.

The *Ethical Guidelines of the UKCP* (1996) state:

2.11 (ii) Psychotherapists are required to take appropriate action in accordance with Clause 5.8 [initiate the relevant complaints procedure] with regard to the behaviour of a colleague which may be detrimental to the profession, to colleagues or to trainees.

(United Kingdom Council for Psychotherapy 1995–6: 1)

The relevant item from the British Association for Counselling (BAC 1992) *Code of Ethics* reads as follows:

B. 2.4.2 If a counsellor suspects misconduct by another counsellor which cannot be resolved or remedied after discussion with the counsellor concerned, they should implement the Complaints Procedure, doing so without breaches of confidentiality other than those necessary for investigating the complaint (see B.9).

(British Association for Counselling 1992: 4)

Various items in the British Psychological Society (BPS 1995) *Professional Practice Guidelines* read:

Psychologists shall conduct themselves in their professional activities in a way that does not damage the interest of the recipients of their services or participants in their research and does not inappropriately undermine public confidence in their ability or that of other psychologists and members of other professions to carry our their professional duties . . .

5.3 . . . not exploit any relationship of influence or trust which exists between colleagues, those under their tuition, or those in receipt of their services to further the gratification of their personal desires . . .

5.10 . . . bring allegations of misconduct by a professional colleague to the attention of those charged with the responsibility to investigate them, doing so without malice and with no breaches of confidentiality other than those necessary to the proper investigatory processes and when the subject of allegations themselves, they shall take all reasonable steps to assist those charged with responsibility to investigate them.

(British Psychological Society 1995: 453)

Comment

In research undertaken by Lindsay and Clarkson in 1999, 21 per cent of the 1000 sample of UKCP psychotherapists responded. The very fact of participation in any research demonstrates a willingness on the part of our respondent colleagues to think about, reflect on and do something to enhance the ethical understanding and practice of our professions. It shows good and effective collegial relationship manifesting as an enacted value of deep and serious concern about our own and others' conduct and the principles of our profession. It also provides us all – including government – with useful information for teaching, supervision and professional regulation. It is only by drawing on such confidential real-life responses from our colleagues that the published literature can be enriched and enlivened, contradicted or corroborated.

How prevalent are ethical concerns about collegial misconduct?

Concerns about the ethical conduct of colleagues emerged as the second highest aggregated source of ethical dilemmas mentioned in the 1999 study. Only the issue of confidentiality caused more concern to the random sample of 1000 UKCP psychotherapists. It is thus an issue of extreme concern (Clarkson 1999).

What are the kinds of ethical dilemmas experienced about collegial misconduct?

In order to answer this question – as best we could from our data – we then re-analysed all the items referring to ethical dilemmas about the *alleged misconduct of colleagues* (Clarkson and Lindsay 1999).

The most frequently mentioned ethical dilemma about colleagues concerned their competence to practice, for example:

I am afraid that she [a supervisee] might eventually be a very
damaging counsellor, but I don't seem able to let anybody know this,
even in the vaguest of terms, because I have no contact with her
course tutors. Am I right in thinking there's nothing I can do?

The second most frequently mentioned ethical dilemma about colleagues concerned the sexual misconduct of colleagues with clients or students for example: a practitioner expressed *'grave concern'* about a sexually abusing colleague who is 'still committing sexual misconduct'.

The third most frequently mentioned ethical dilemma about collegial conduct concerned attacks by colleagues on professional reputation for example:

I found that what I had heard seriously damaged my confidence in my
colleague's integrity as a psychotherapist. Yet there seemed to be no

appropriate place to take my concerns, especially as the source of my information was so informal.

Boundary violations and financial exploitation of clients and students ranked joint fourth; general misconduct (unspecified) and issues to do with moral competence (including lying about qualifications) ranked joint fifth. Issues to do with discrimination of various kinds and issues to do with the abuse of power over clients or students or members ranked joint sixth.

Reasons for avoiding this responsibility (bystanding)

Insensitivity to or disinterest about ethical dilemmas in psychotherapy

In the study about the experience of ethical dilemmas (Lindsay and Clarkson 1999) among UKCP psychotherapists, only 21 per cent replied to the questionnaire. Of these 20 per cent claimed that they had not come across ethical dilemmas in the last two years. One respondent wrote that in twenty years of practice he or she was fortunate enough never to have experienced an ethical dilemma. (Quotations from respondents in our various research studies used in this chapter are changed only for sense or the protection of identifying details. See reference section for details of other works.)

Ignorance of the ethics codes and processes

Among the responses to our questionnaires we found several examples of people apparently ignorant about ethical codes and how to use them. For example some respondents claimed that there was no appropriate place or process to take concerns, or that they did not know if there was. For example:

> It is not known, if this organisation takes third party complaints, but my colleague is unable to act, as she is bound by confidentiality to her client. However, she is gravely concerned that this counsellor is still practising and appears to have a poor sense of the difference between professional and social boundaries.

Marzillier (1999) reported his realization in 1992 'that clinical psychologists as a group had virtually no exposure to training in ethics and that was a serious deficiency both for ourselves and our clients'.

Ignorance of the duty to report

In some cases it was clear that respondents to our survey are working without adequate knowledge or training ethics codes and processes as far as their practice is concerned.

Do I have a moral duty to tell a trainee's training organisation that the trainee really needed several years of analysis to resolve this problem, before being ready to take on their own casework?

Some respondents appeared to be under the impression that collegial misconduct was not an ethical issue, but only a moral one:

Such a dilemma challenges my trust in myself. It is as I see it a moral, not an ethical matter. I won't collude with therapists and counsellors' bad practice on the grounds of professional 'ethics'. Ultimately my commitment has to be to my supervisee, not to my colleagues' egos.

'Unwritten protection laws'

So, although, as we have shown, there are quite explicit written professional laws which mandate practitioners to be responsibly involved in cases of suspected abuse by their colleagues, there appears (e.g. Bernard and Jara 1995) to be a comparative neglect of teaching and education about such responsible and ethical collegial behaviour. We suggest that all kinds of 'unwritten protection laws' have proliferated along with fear – justifiable or not – of the destructive consequences of becoming responsibly involved.

Pope (1989) also points out that psychotherapists, due to a defensive pride in their profession,

may believe that nothing should be done to bring discredit to the profession, especially if the consequent publicity should steer patients to another profession or should lead to additional regulatory measures by external organizations. They may use all the resources at their disposal to avoid airing dirty professional laundry in public.

(Pope 1989: 49)

One of our respondents for example described their greatest ethical dilemmas as to:

whether or not to remain belonging to UKCP and ensure my status is safe, for future (e.g. legislation), whilst at the same time believing it is creating a false position and status for the members (of safety and effectiveness) in the eyes of the public.

Concern with keeping insurance fees down

There are anecdotes about insurance companies which recommend that practitioners do not display their ethics codes in their consulting rooms – in case this should act as encouragement to making complaints. I also have correspondence in my possession citing the likelihood that complaints will increase insurance rates.

Fear of and actual experience of retaliation by colleagues

A good collegial working relationship is defined as one where there is a mutual commitment to working on the task – even if neither party feels like it (Clarkson 1995). Some practitioners seem to have the idea that any conflict, disagreement or criticism is evidence of a bad working relationship – instead of the fundamental requirement of a good working relationship, which is concerned with the benefit of those we serve rather than our own comfort alone.

Some of our respondents had also experienced this:

> The organisation was furious when we made the complaint . . . a colleague lost their job.

Of course any good respectful collegial relationship actually mandates the exchange of challenges as well as support and the engagement in mutual regulation as well as mutual affirmation.

Fear of being pathologized

From her UK experience Palmer Barnes (1998) writes:

> What must always be borne is mind is the bravery involved in making a complaint. It is much easier to close down on a bad experience. Pathologising the patient or colleague who has made a complaint is all too easy, and unfortunately it happens all too frequently.
>
> (Palmer Barnes 1998: 113)

A patient writes about the psychotherapist who had been sexually abusing her and the psychotherapist to whom he had referred her because he was 'safe'. This was defined as the new therapist undertaking not to divulge the unethical sexual relationship of his colleague to anyone else.

> He had reassured me that oral sex was not the same as full sex as he knew that I was confused . . . Later I held a belief that [her therapist/lover] had realised the stressful situation he had caused and therefore wanted to drop me. I also feared that the two men were in collusion. I feared that they were discussing my mental state . . . I expressed my fears to them both and they both denied this was true.

Perceived conflicts between ethics code items

Apart from explicitly self-protective agendas which prevented professionals from acting on their concerns about suspected collegial misconduct, we found cases where respondents felt that appropriate action was precluded by other items in ethics codes for example:

> The training system demanded that his therapy remain confidential; and if my supervisee had not found a way of conveying to the training committee her reservations, I would have felt compelled to contact them myself. (Competence issue) It concerns a junior colleague, but the problem seems to be the training committee's perceived rules which prevented proper access.

Concern for welfare of client took precedence

In many of the cases respondents reported considering taking action but did not do anything, for example:

> I chose to stay with my supervisee and actually did not signal my profound anger at what I consider a deeply immoral action on his part. And of course he still left.

Financial influences

Several of the respondents in our research made comments such as the following:

> I have difficulty reconciling . . . my own moral standards with that of the organisation I'm involved in at any given time and my need . . . to earn a living . . . I feel that the counselling and supervision network is quite a small network . . . therefore in order to pay myself OK I need to be on reasonable terms with most people who might . . . refer clients to me.

Bersoff (1995: 54) writes about the 'crisis' of 'diploma mills' along with serious concerns about incompetent and unsuitable students being allowed to qualify. Similar concerns also showed up repeatedly in our research. Do large income-producing member organizations get ethically judged with the same kind of promptness and severity as small organizations involved in similar misconduct but who produce less membership money or fewer donations?

> The professional project is above all aimed at achieving social closure in the realm of knowledge, credentialled skill and respectability . . . *vis-à-vis* the public, other professions and the state. Merely to describe these activities is to show how closely related the group's cultural assets are to their economic advantage, and therefore to their capacity for exploitation.
>
> (Macdonald 1995: 58)

Sense of belonging and 'smooth' working relationships

'This kind of difficulty can be very painful because the practitioners often know each other as colleagues or friends. It is often only after considerable heart-searching that such complaints are expressed' (Palmer Barnes 1998: 62). A recent article published by a psychotherapy organization recommended that 'talking about [*sic*] one's colleagues provides a way for better attachments both intra- and inter-psychically'?

There are so many benefits from claiming professional status while avoiding the responsibilities or accountability – not least maintaining falsely defined working relationships with colleagues who may refer clients, supervisees or teaching contracts. Given such extremely negative consequences of dealing with collegial misconduct professionals' reluctance to act ethically in this respect is very understandable, but at the same time very worrying.

Reinstate justice? A British Psychological Society example

It has been admitted that many professionals involved with ethics procedures lack the expertise, experience and competence to conduct complaints to proper standards (Collis 1998).

In some cases where complaints have been made, the process itself was experienced as inadequate for example:

> Many areas of this therapist's practice concerned me and other
> members of the panel – their advertising, failure to contact the GP
> [general practitioner], seek supervision, etc. We could not examine the
> emergent factors because that (apparently) did not form part of the
> complaint. The case was dismissed for lack of hard evidence. I was
> quite convinced, however, of malpractice.

The Peter Slade case attracted enormous media and professional interest with several letters published in *The Psychologist* objecting to the fact that a psychologist who had *for the second time* been found guilty of sexual abuse of patients was *not* removed from the Society's register. Pilgrim (1999: 41) called it 'an offence to natural justice'. Riley (1999) considered that the British Psychological Society had endorsed Slade's continued access to students where

> he will typically have more power than them, which he may well
> exploit. [Furthermore] . . . the general public is unlikely to be reassured
> by a judgement that its more cynical members might interpret as
> placing more importance on preserving the career of one of the Society's
> members than on protecting the public from future possible exploi-
> tation.
>
> (Riley 1999: 41)

Three Chairs of the Division of Clinical Psychology (Cohen, Guinan and Harvey) wrote:

> We have supported the policy of seeking statutory registration for the profession. The decision made by the Disciplinary Board not to expel Dr Slade, despite the seriousness of his behaviour, make us seriously doubt whether the Society can be trusted to handle its disciplinary processes in such a way that the protection of the public is ensured and the good name of our profession maintained.
>
> (Cohen *et al.* 1999: 5)

Finally, it may be as well to be reminded by a leading human rights lawyer that:

> A 'code of conduct' without any sanction, which does not even offer to pay the psychiatric bills of victims injured by its breach, is simply a confidence trick.
>
> (Robertson 1999: 117)

Responsibility: a UKCP example

A High Court judge ruled in February 1999 that the UKCP is accountable in law. As such the UKCP executive officers are responsible for the conduct of complaints procedures in fair, just and unbiased ways – without intimidation of a complainant or breaches of confidentiality.

This judgment was as a result of an application for judicial review which in this case ordered a body with responsibility to members of the public to follow their own procedures. Judicial review is the legal answer to the question: 'Who judges the judges?' It is the only resource when professional self-regulation fails. However, the process is extremely complex and expensive and highly unlikely to be within the resources of the average patient or student.

In fact, since the results of the February 1999 request for judicial review numerous other cases of intimidation of complainants and reports of organizational collusion with abuse have come to my notice. It is clear that what is published about complaints and ethics procedures may at times be at variance with the actual practice.

There are certainly grounds to conclude from these events and other studies (for example in Clarkson 1999) that there is a great deal of room for improvement in practitioners' understanding and appreciation of the role of ethics and our shared responsibility towards our colleagues within the profession.

Some explicit recommendations

Valuing responsible involvement

Palmer Barnes (1998: 64) acknowledges that: 'Whistleblowers are unusual in therapeutic organisations and agencies, but in the future there may need to be more if high standards and ethical practice are to be maintained.' Therefore, the appellation of professionals who behave responsibly toward their duties to protect the welfare of their patients (and the patients of their colleagues) may need to be much more respectful. Perhaps calling them 'responsible psychotherapists' instead of 'whistleblowers' might be better?

Pathologizing and accusing complainants for example of 'personal issues' must stop. Any ethical issue is both personal and political (see Clarkson 1999).

Breaching the confidentiality of ethics procedures should be treated as the ethical breach that it actually is and sanctioned severely – as it can make the unprejudiced hearing of any complaint impossible.

Concern for colleagues' welfare

We also believe that it is important to separate the ways in which we deal with misconduct from difficulties due to health problems. Psychotherapist impairment due to psychological dysfunctioning

> is not often remedied through either educative or disciplinary actions, but may succumb to psychotherapy and other rehabilitative efforts [of providing programmes] staffed by professional colleagues who volunteer to work for little or no fee on a limited basis.
> (Thompson 1990: 137)

Behaving responsibly towards our colleagues may in fact enhance our capacity for compassion. One of our respondents put it gently:

> I am not questioning the unethical nature of his action but would be interested in there being some thought about the ethics of depriving someone in their 50's of their livelihood for one such misdemeanour. I wonder if there is any possibility of a programme of 'rehabilitation' (including therapy and supervision) for such offenders.

Education and mediation as well as regulation

The desire for power and identity (of professional associations) may or may not be accompanied by a strong desire to serve the public and to do so in more effective ways, even though the profession espouses such goals. The immediate, often tangible, benefits of protecting and enhancing one's prestige and one's political and economic status may often be more powerful incentives than those of good service to the public. Should the two conflict, or appear to conflict, the latter is apt to give way (Thompson 1990: 129).

Therefore in my view education and mediation need to supplement genuine regulation. I have seen that *not* acting in cases of concern about colleagues' conduct is in itself a breach of ethics. Not acting responsibly is also a moral decision. Passivity is no defence when another's life or sanity or reputation is at stake. These are *human* rights. We are co-responsible for upholding them. 'This is a matter of their personal accountability as professionals; if they do not act they will be equally guilty of misconduct by not taking action' (Palmer Barnes 1998: 64).

Training and continuing education

Gawthop and Uhleman (1992), among others, showed that the recognition of ethical dilemmas and the ability to resolve them improves with training. Many of the studies done indicate that the teaching of ethics by osmosis, 'add-ons' or the introjection of 'rules' or group 'norms' without ongoing critical reflection or constant grappling with the complexities of ethical and moral decisions, is not enough. In addition philosophical training is essential since some research has indicated that the intellectual ability to deal effectively with complexity is a prerequisite for dealing intelligently, compassionately and competently with ethical issues (e.g. Pope and Vetter 1992; Pope *et al.* 1995).

> [It is a] good enough reason to make training in standards and ethics a formal part of every counselling course. There will be gains to clients in a greater sense of personal safety. Counsellors will also benefit because a sound understanding of standards and ethics is something which can unite counsellors from many different orientations.
>
> (Bond 1993: 208)

How can we foster such abilities and moral courage in training and supervision and our organizational life? Kant suggested the development of moral imagination. A 'learning by enquiry' research-minded and philosophically rigorous attitude to ethics and professional practice is more likely to keep us all questing and questioning than to lead to 'conformist obedience', cavalier carelessness or professional collusion. Or, in the words of Guggenbühl-Craig (1995):

> In medicine and psychotherapy, ethical behaviour means one tries to do whatever seems to be the most useful and therapeutic action at the time, realising that our knowledge is never absolutely sure. There is always room for new information and insight. Even more, it is our duty to question everything we are doing.
>
> (Guggenbühl-Craig 1995: x)

Using consultants/facilitators

There was no mention at all among the respondents in the 1999 study of informal attempts to resolve dilemmas with colleagues. Nor was there any evidence of attempts at mediation or use of consultants or third parties to resolve issues. Stone (1983) recommended the referral of a client, who has been victimized by a colleague, to consult a third party, an 'administrator' to reduce the dual role conflict of being both client's advocate and client's therapist. If the consultation goes ahead, the consultant assumes the responsibility of working with the client in proceeding with any legitimate complaint.

Ongoing research integrated with supervised practice

There is a lack of research on how complainants and complained against experienced our professional processes. As part of the ongoing research project Lindsay and Clarkson welcome anyone who would like confidentially to explore further their experiences in this regard. Indeed research in any one or more of its multitude of guises should be seen as part of any ethical psychotherapy practice and actively encouraged by professional bodies who want to improve their track record in terms of ethics and professional practice regarding educating, avoiding and improving procedures (Clarkson 1998).

From the review of the literature, researches and professional experience Lindsay and Clarkson have been concerned that many psychotherapists might not take action (even to establish what the possibilities are), even though all our ethics codes require that where there are reasonable grounds for doubt, confrontation and reporting should happen. Without the willingness to report, abuses will continue and perhaps proliferate as professionals experience a kind of protectionism born from ignorance or fear of retaliation – at the expense of the people we are supposed to serve.

Moving beyond the 'flag statements' of schoolism to individual registration of all psychotherapists

It is absurd to claim that complaints can be fairly heard by people whose livelihood depends on keeping the reputation of their organization good and preserving its financial welfare. This is what psychotherapy organizations claim that they can do. Even judgments of High Court judges (such as Lord Hoffman in the Pinochet case) are considered to be invalid – just for having historical sympathies with certain causes. Psychotherapists' judgements will be equally invalid if they are influenced by favours, the gaining of referrals, status and so on.

A most painful possibility is that our ethical codes are but hollow symbols of a myth of professionalism. As long as it appears to courts and to the public that psychology or counselling or psychotherapy is a cacophony of competing claims to workable procedures, the judgement of the members, regardless of the profession's highest minded ethical standards, will be open to challenge. Psychology is fragmented into many different schools each espousing its own theoretical orientation, a state of affairs which may motivate research and enliven the professional journals, but which may inspire little confidence in society. With the field so divided it is not difficult to explain why codes of ethics remain vague and abstract and a wide variety of specific behaviour is tolerated.

(Bersoff 1995: 104)

One possible way forward might be individual registration of all psychotherapists – independent of which 'school' they trained with or how they may be currently working. This is standard in all other *real* professions. Then complaints can be heard by genuinely independent professionals – who do not have vested personal, financial and professional interests in the downfall (or the protection) of certain of their colleagues or colleague organizations.

Educating the public

As Pilgrim wrote in 1992:

I am not satisfied that the discussion of abuse within the confines of a culture of therapists constitutes a genuine public airing. Equally, medical practitioners have researched and debated iatrogenic problems for decades but it has not stopped them plying their trade of prescribed dangerous drugs and surgical procedures. The lesson to be learned from this is that professions, including psychotherapists cannot be trusted to police themselves.

(Pilgrim 1992: 251)

The public needs to become familiar with what is dangerous and what is competent and ethical behaviour by psychotherapists, what to expect from complaints procedures, and what to do when professional self-policing does not work.

Bystanding

Bystanding occurs when someone does not get involved while someone else is getting hurt or suffering injustice. In most human situations I believe that responsible involvement is a complex moral obligation which can be understandably waived in response to all kinds of factors such as fear for oneself or one's family. Our ethics codes as they are published do not permit professionals to bystand the abuses of our colleagues where we become aware of them.

It is therefore an ethical obligation to come to the assistance of those whom we have reason to suspect are being harmed by our co-professionals or the organizations to which they belong. We may also owe it to our colleagues to help them if they are acting inappropriately or being maliciously slandered. Unfortunately as we know from bystander research, the larger the number of people aware of an atrocity, the less likely it is that any one individual will help.

As we have seen, acting on the profession's published claims to facilitate the confrontation of colleagues about their suspected misconduct is also very unusual. There may indeed be a few cases in which this would be inadvisable – for example if a patient's life is really in danger. There are many cases where time and consultation with peers can improve the ways in which all involved can be better protected. It is of course concerned with the very significant difference between an *avowed* value and an *enacted* value (Taylor 1954).

Wakefield (1995), a psychiatrist and Jungian analyst, writes:

> When I was a child, my family didn't know what to do when a member had problems; family members alternated between looking the other way and outbursts of judgmental anger. We in the helping professions can do better than that. We could help the wounded healer within ourselves and within our colleagues. Perhaps we are capable of being our brother's keeper.
>
> (Wakefield 1995: 89)

A plea for responsible involvement can easily be diminished by calling it evangelism. However, saying (or publishing) one thing and actually doing another can equally well be called hypocrisy. It is never possible to claim neutrality authentically when you know that someone else is being damaged. As the *Bystander* book (Clarkson 1996) explores in depth, neutrality in abusive situations always favours the aggressor. Anyone might choose to do that – and many psychotherapists do. Not to act is also an act. In an ethics of relationship, not being part of the solution makes you part of the problem.

As Thompson (1990: 133) points: 'The willingness to monitor and correct unethical and incompetent behaviour by colleagues is difficult to instil or to encourage. Yet without such willingness the entire structure collapses'. Are you willing? And shall we each start with ourself?

Bibliography

American Psychological Association (1992) Ethical principles of psychologists and code of conduct, *American Psychologist*, 47: 1597–611.

Bernard, J.L. and Jara, C.S. (1995) The failure of clinical psychology graduate students to apply understood ethical principles, in D.N. Bersoff (ed.) *Ethical Conflicts in Psychology*. Washington, DC: American Psychological Association.

Bersoff, D.N. (1995) Professional ethics and legal responsibilities: on the horns of a dilemma, in D.N. Bersoff (ed.) *Ethical Conflicts in Psychology*. Washington, DC: American Psychological Association.

Bond, T. (1993) Ethical standards and the exploitation of clients: the debate about sex with former clients, *Counselling*, 4(3): 2.

British Association for Counselling (BAC) (1992) *Code of Ethics and Practice for Counsellors/Counselling Skills/Trainers/Supervision of counsellors* (four leaflets). Leicester: BAC.

British Psychological Society (BPS) (1995) *Division of Clinical Psychology, Professional Practice Guidelines*. Leicester: BPS.

Clarkson, P. (1995) *The Therapeutic Relationship*. London: Whurr.

Clarkson, P. (1996) *The Bystander*. London: Whurr.

Clarkson, P. (1997) Integrative psychotherapy, integrating psychotherapies, or psychotherapy after schoolism?, in C. Feltham (ed.) *Which Psychotherapy?* London: Sage.

Clarkson, P. (1998) Writing as research in counselling psychology and related disciplines, in P. Clarkson (ed.) *Counselling Psychology: Integrating Theory, Research and Supervised Practice*. London: Routledge.

Clarkson, P. (1999) *Ethics: Working with Ethical and Moral Dilemmas in Psychotherapy*. London: Whurr.

Cohen, L., Guinan, P. and Harvey, P. (1999) News: division chairs voice concern over Slade decision, *Clinical Psychology Forum*, 123 (January): 4 & 5.

Collis, W. (1998) Report to AHPP AGM in AHPP newsletter.

Gawthop, J.C. and Uhleman, M.R. (1992) Effects of the problem-solving approach to ethics training, *Professional Psychology: Research and Practice*, 23(1): 38–42.

Guggenbühl-Craig, A. (1995) Foreword, in L.B. Ross and M. Roy, *Cast the First Stone: Ethics in Analytic Practice*. Wilmette, IL: Chiron.

Jehu, D. (1994) *Patients as Victims: Sexual Abuse in Psychotherapy and Counselling*. London: Wiley.

Lindsay, G. and Clarkson, P. (1999) Ethical dilemmas of psychotherapists, *The Psychologist*, 12(4): 182–5.

Lindsay, G. and Colley, A. (1995) Ethical dilemmas of members of the British Psychological Society, *The Psychologist*, 8: 448–53.

Macdonald, K.M. (1995) *The Sociology of the Professions*. London: Sage.

Marzillier, J. (1999) Training of clinical psychologists in ethical issues, *Clinical Psychology Forum*, 123: 43–7.

Palmer Barnes, F. (1998) *Complaints and Grievances in Psychotherapy: A Handbook of Ethical Practice*. London: Routledge.

Pilgrim, D. (1992) Psychotherapy and political evasion, in C. Feltham and W. Dryden (eds) *Psychotherapy and its Discontents*. London: Sage.

Pilgrim, D. (1999) The case of Peter Slade, *The Psychologist* 12(1): 71.

POPAN (1998) *Annual Report* of POPAN – Prevention of Professional Abuse Network. London: POPAN.

Pope, K.S. (1989) Teacher–student sexual intimacy, in G.O. Gabbard (ed.) *Sexual*

Exploitation in Professional Relationships. Washington, DC: American Psychiatric Press.

Pope, K.S. and Vetter, V.A. (1992) Ethical dilemmas encountered by members of the American Psychological Association, *American Psychologist*, 47: 397–411.

Pope, K.S., Tabachnick, B.G. and Keith-Spiegel, P. (1995) Ethics of practice: the beliefs and behaviors of psychologists as therapists, in D.N. Bersoff (ed.) *Ethical Conflicts in Psychology*. Washington, DC: American Psychological Association.

Riley, D. (1999) The case of Peter Slade, *The Psychologist*, 12(1): 71.

Robertson, G. (1999) *The Justice Game*. London: Vintage.

Stone, A.S. (1983) Sexual misconduct by psychiatrists: the ethical and clinical dilemma of confidentiality, *American Journal of Psychiatry*, 140(2): 195–7.

Taylor, H. (1954) *On Education and Freedom*. New York: Abelard-Schuman.

Thompson, A. (1990) *Guide to Ethical Practice in Psychotherapy*. Chichester: John Wiley.

Traynor, B. and Clarkson, P. (1996) What happens if a psychotherapist dies?, in S. Palmer, S. Dainow and P. Milner (eds) *Counselling: The BAC Counselling Reader*. London: Sage.

United Kingdom Council for Psychotherapy (1995–6) Ethical Guidelines of the UKCP, in *National Register of Psychotherapists*. London: Routledge.

Wakefield, J. (1995) Am I my brother's keeper? Impairment in the helping profession, in L.B. Ross and M. Roy (eds) *Cast the First Stone: Ethics in Analytic Practice*. Wilmette, IL: Chiron.

4 Assessment – for what? for whom?

Josephine Klein

Introduction

We may make our own assessment of a prospective patient, or a patient may be referred to us by a friend or organization after their assessment. What criteria for assessment ought we to use? What value judgements do we make, consciously or unconsciously? What leads us to decide whether this person would be well advised to undertake a course of psychotherapy, and why this particular kind? When a child is ill, we call the doctor, who says 'Measles'. Straight away we know, or we know the doctor knows, that there is a particular germ or virus or toxin that has made the child ill. We know what is going to happen from now on (more or less) if there is no intervention, and we know what intervention will help the sufferer. There has been a *diagnosis* – 'measles' – and everything connects to this: *etiology* or what caused the measles, *prognosis* or what is going to happen next, what usually happens with measles, and *therapeutics* or what will usually make it better. The thing to note is that diagnosis is inextricably tied up with etiology, prognosis and therapeutics. The four make up a single conceptual structure, like four variables in an algebraic equation. The etiology for a diagnosis of measles is nearly always 'It is caused by such-and-such', and then the prognosis is often 'This or that will happen next', and then the choice of treatment is limited and determined within that range.

This is not how it is in our field, nor, indeed, quite often in medicine, and I want a discussion about how it ought to be. From the beginning of psychoanalysis, we have resorted to diagnostic-sounding categories such as depression, obsessional states, anxiety states. Unlike medical diseases, however, these are states of the mind. They have no secure etiologies, or reliable prognoses, nor have we reliable therapeutics. There is very little that says we should treat borderline personalities one way, hysterics another. And so on. Ought there to be? If so, should we teach it? If not, should we say so?

First, I want to make a bow in the direction of a useful development which has been generated by the recent greater respect for countertransference information. The idea is that the well-analysed and sane assessor identifies something in the countertransference that characterizes the potential patient, and that the well-analysed and sane therapist understands something from this that guides the treatment. In making a diagnosis, we tend to rely on intuition, using unorganized unconscious knowledge in an intuitive rather than systematic way. We get some idea about the person before us because we are who we are, and the person before us is the kind of person to whom we tend to react in characteristic ways which we know and understand. With sufficient self-knowledge and humility, our reaction to the prospective patient gives us some understanding of their characteristic ways of being a person. I am *for* the use of countertransference, *for* the use of our professional experience in assessing patients and allocating them to the right therapist. But I do not think that we can leave it at that. In the long run I think that we need some commonly agreed and commonly understood categories to describe the potential patient which will tell potential therapists what kind of patient this person is likely to be, in a way which helps the therapists know what kind of treatment is appropriate.

All this is controversial. One friend, an experienced psychotherapist with an unusually incisive mind, is very clear about the uses of assessment. She says that its function is to uncover the phantasies, the object relations operating in the patient's mind to the patient's detriment. She holds that it may be possible to link the patient's symptoms to these object relations in the initial consultation, so that they can be taken into account. Listening for such object relations keeps her from focusing too much on the symptoms the patient reports or presents in the session. When my friend can see the object relations, the phantasies in the patient's internal world, the course of treatment seems to her to follow logically or inevitably: object relations are the focus of her understanding of the transference and of her interpretations.

Also if, in this interview, she finds it impossible to discern what is wrong in these terms, or if she can see that the patient has difficulty in understanding or making use of her way of looking at things, she recognizes that the patient may not be right for the treatment she has to offer and she does not recommend it. Difficulty in formulating an assessment in these terms may mean that the patient is not suited to this way of working, or that a further meeting with the assessor is needed.

This approach has great virtues of clarity and honesty. It leaves some people unhelped by the psychoanalytical method, but that is exactly what I would want, if the treatment is not going to help them anyway. Some may object that we would never have advanced our knowledge of psychotherapy if we took only the cases which can be helped by these limited means, but she, and I, and many practitioners, some very eminent, have in fact taken on what may still be called 'research cases'. We have done this both to help us understand how far tried and true methods would take us and to help us understand what modifications of conventional methods would be of benefit to particular categories of patients. (Later in this chapter we meet the point of view that reacts uncomfortably to the notion that there are 'categories' of patients at all.)

What I want is for every school of thought in psychotherapy to be able to state as clearly as my friend, how they assess, what their method of treatment is, and whom they cannot help because their method of treatment cannot be applied to them. She clarifies the role of the referrer in the more classical psychoanalytical orientation. A diagnosis is not aimed only at suitability for psychoanalysis. However, if we use the first encounter not for a diagnosis but to assess suitability for our kind of treatment, we reduce our function to the – admittedly important – one of gatekeeper. I think that now, at the beginning of the twenty-first century, we should take responsibility for making treatment recommendations in accordance with our understanding of what is wrong, of what the person needs to have treated. We need to do this much more precisely than we do at present; I know we do adjust the parameters a little, though usually we are shy of teaching about this at pre-qualification level.

Some interesting papers have been written about the role of the assessor not as diagnostician but as gatekeeper, standing between the distressed person and the treatment that is intended to alleviate that distress, someone who helps the distressed person be clearer about what is needed and what may be expected by them and from them as patients in treatment. But none attempts to tie etiology, diagnosis, treatment and prognosis together (Baker 1980; Shapiro 1984; Coltart 1988).

A second implication of using the first encounter, as my friend does, is that the first encounter is in effect likely to be the start of an analysis and has to be treated as such. You have to be careful not to break into the analytical space or spoil it in such a way that later analytical work will be impaired (Ogden 1989: 170).

Jane Milton (1992), in a paper that is more relevant than any other I have read, though I cannot agree with her, presents the interesting case of Mr D, which shows the psychoanalytically oriented approach at its best. An important part of her argument is that the assessor should try to remain a possible transference figure for the prospective patient, and not present a benign welcoming aspect to make the patient comfortable. She acknowledges that 'there is often a lack of knowledge among referrers and patients about the differences between different psychotherapeutic approaches'. If a psychoanalytic treatment is to be undertaken, it is 'important that a patient should leave the assessment interview having an idea about the nature of the process to be undertaken, its intrusiveness and its likelihood of exposing the patient to pain in the form of guilt and shame' (Milton 1992: 55). In contrast are the approaches that 'will allow the patient largely to retain his defences, and protect his privacy to a much greater extent'. It may be considered however, she continues, 'that paradoxically the patient is being subtly infantilised far more in such pedagogic procedures than in an analytic approach'. Yes, of course, she has a point, but I have some points to make too.

Jane Milton voices a common assumption that the psychoanalytic is really the only deep thorough treatment, all the others being what, on the same page, she calls *palliative*. She, and others, argue that some people need this palliative treatment because they or we believe that they cannot endure the psychoanalytic intrusion into their defences. Quite true. They cannot stand it. They do need a different approach. But where is the proof that other approaches are all palliative, that is do not remove the trouble in the long term? The evidence is not there, and the argument is weak. (The argument suggests that you have to have drastic intervention, a thorough clean-out for all troubles, always.)

Jane Milton's account of an interview with Mr D shows the psychoanalytic approach at its best. Mr D was a violent man who knew he was violent and did not want to be. He had been in prison for violent attacks during demonstrations and riots. He had asked his GP for help and had been referred on for psychotherapy.

> In the unstructured assessment interview Mr D quickly became white and sweaty with fear, and felt attacked and judged by the therapist. He wanted to leave the room but managed, with much active interpretative help from the assessor, to hang on to himself and have a conversation about what was happening. He was able to talk about his fears of violence and even acknowledge towards the end of the first interview, with fear and shame, when it was suggested by the therapist, a 'fascist' part of himself who was both a protector and a vengeful aggressor. In the second meeting, a week later, he reported much more anxiety in the intervening week, with impulses to violence to himself and others only just possible to resist. However, he remained adamant about wanting to explore things and try and change, and pointed out that nothing else had helped and that he felt at the end of the road.
>
> (Milton 1992: 53)

The paper makes it clear that Mr D has some good healthy ego processes and skills. He is able to hold on, though with difficulty, and not act on his impulses straight away. He is able, with help, to reflect on his behaviour; he is able to hold on to an 'image' of himself as behaving better than he does at present; he found that image desirable, it was his ego-ideal; he was happier when behaving well; and so on. He clearly needed help in that interview and will continue to do so, but he has some mental processes which will help him to contain and eventually modify whatever urges him to violence. He is capable of self-reflection. That word, self-reflection, is important but before we return to it, two points:

1 People capable of self-reflection are much more able to bear psycho-analytic treatment. But this does not mean that psychoanalysis is therefore the treatment of choice for all distresses that people with a capacity for self-reflection are prone to. This would need to be demonstrated, and so far it has not been.
2 Psychoanalytically oriented practitioners need more information about forms of psychotherapy which may suit people whose capacity for self-reflection is impaired, that is, what can be of use to people to whom *we* cannot be of use.

Evidence is building up to help sort out some of the connections between eti-ology, diagnosis, treatment and outcome. An excellent summary of material up to 1995 is provided by Roth and Fonagy (1996) in *What Works for Whom?* Meanwhile two lines of inquiry give us a foretaste of what eventual solutions might be like.

The use for diagnostic purposes of Kernberg's ideas about ego strength, and Fonagy's ideas about the capacity for self-reflection

Kernberg (1984, Part One) looks for certain characteristics. He does this by means of a well-worked-out theory which leads him to look for three sets of indications. Note that Mr D is a person who does well on these criteria.

- To what extent is there identity confusion? That is, how clear are the boundaries between self and other, and between inner and outer?
- To what extent is the person in touch with the realities that most of us share?
- To what extent is there ego strength? Particularly, (a) How well able is this person to control his or her impulses? (b) How able is he or she to toler-ate anxiety without too much upset? (c) How able is this person to react constructively to frustration?

According to these indicators Kernberg refers people to one of three types of therapy:

- Psychoanalysis if there is no identity confusion, and a good reality sense and plenty of ego strength.
- Expressive psychotherapy if there is no identity confusion, a good reality sense but not much ego strength. By expressive psychotherapy Kernberg means therapy of a psychoanalytically oriented kind which lets the patients talk ('express themselves' – so perhaps it could be by painting?

music? drama?) while the therapist elucidates and makes connections with the person's dynamics and inner life, but stays always experience-near and does not concentrate on the transference.
- Supportive psychotherapy if there is identity confusion and poor reality sense, as well as poor ego strength. Supportive therapy is of a more encouraging and advising nature, with minimal transference work and interpretation.

Fonagy and his associates, including Howard and Miriam Steele and Mary Target, build on attachment-based theory. Attachment theory started with the finding that tots between 1 and 2, left in the so-called Strange Situation on their own, with their mothers gone for a couple of minutes, show one of three main kinds of reaction, which have been named *securely attached*, *insecure avoidant* and *insecure resistant*. Later a fourth category was added: *disorganized*. Diagnoses that are made according to these categories at the age of 2 hold firm for the next three years at least. Please note, by the way, that here we have a bit of diagnosis that *is* connected to prognosis, though not as yet very securely to therapeutics. These findings have been combined with findings from a questionnaire administered to parents, called the Adult Attachment Interview, that asks people about their own history (George *et al.* 1996). You can predict the attachment reactions of the children from how the parents respond to the Adult Attachment Interview, with considerable success. A major finding.

The analysis of the Adult Attachment Interview does not focus on the substantive facts of the parents' story about their lives; the analysis is of the manner in which they responded to the interviewer's questions, the manner in which they talked. Were they interested in the interviewer's questions? Were they able to look at them calmly and able to take responsibility for them? (*Secure autonomous*, these parents were called, and you can guess what their children were.) Or were the parents mostly dismissive of any questions that had to do with feelings? Or were they mostly preoccupied with fears, angers and other feelings not very directly concerned with the interviewer's questions? Or even, just disorganized in their responses?

Fonagy and his associates used a slightly modified form of this interviewing schedule, not asking 'How do these people relate?' but concentrating on differences in the ability to take into account what another person is thinking or feeling (Fonagy *et al.* 1997). This would show in the way these adults had reacted to questions about their own parents, their children, other people mentioned, and also the interviewer. Were they able to reflect on what they were thinking or feeling? The hypothesis is that there is a process that becomes crucial in the years between 2 and 4 that gives the child what Fonagy called a 'theory of mind'. At that stage it occurs to the child that things go on in its mind, and that other people also have minds in which processes go on. Something crystallizes at this stage, and if the parents are too full of hate or disgust for their child, the child's propensity to pick up what goes on in the adults' minds shuts down, or is gravely impaired. And so is the developing personality's capacity for self-awareness, for a sense of one's own being in the company of others. Everything hinges on this capacity for self-reflection. It is, in its way, a revolutionary concept, at least in its implications, and one of its implications has to do with assessment for psychotherapy.

What kind of thing does the Adult Attachment Interview make manifest?

- Your awareness of your own and other people's mental states.
- Your capacity for reflecting on your own and other people's mental states – metacognition.
- Your sense that mental states underlie what you do and what other people do.
- Your sense that there is a developmental aspect or origin to mental states, something to do with earlier events and childhood.
- Your awareness that the interviewer has feelings too.

And so on. Conversely it shows up the people who have no such awareness, and who resort to clichés and conventional responses when asked about their lives; these people avoid thinking about themselves or other people.

This work is relevant to the process of assessment, because it demonstrates that if we listen to people in particular systematic ways, we may be able to predict quite reliably both the strength and the nature of some of their defences against understanding themselves. We can know how easy it will be for particular prospective patients just now to experience their therapist as a good object (relevant if we want them to stay in therapy), and how much they can at the moment cope with ambivalence, and be able at present to look honestly at their past and present thoughts and feelings, and how possible it is for them at present to distance themselves from the immediate here and now, have an observing ego, take the third position and other capacities of that sort – all very relevant to how one works with a patient, and all just the kind of thing that might help different therapists make sensible decisions as to whether a prospective patient will suit the particular type of treatment they offer.

This has implications for assessors. They might need to ask themselves first of all: 'Is there already a capacity for reflective functioning?' If not, the patient might need a therapy which helps to develop this. Fonagy, in his clinical work, seems to use slight modifications of classical psychoanalytical technique where this capacity is defective, and as he is a brilliant clinician, it works, but there may be other more pedestrian avenues to explore. Supportive group psychotherapy may be one. There may be a number of things that encourage the further development of a hitherto blocked capacity for self-reflection. Meanwhile, understanding the reasoning behind the use of the Adult Attachment Interview might be of considerable help to assessors.

Of course we have to be very cautious. These two examples, Kernberg's and Fonagy's, give us only hints as to the direction which the future of assessment might take: they are starting-points not end-points. But it is surely clear now that we should look for traits that give prospective therapists an indication of the kinds of opportunities and difficulties that particular patients might present, together with some thoughts on how to begin the therapy. Thus we get the beginnings of a diagnostic linked with a therapeutic.

A diagnostic that is thus linked with therapy might also be helpful for students and trainees. They need patients who can enable them to learn in not too dispiriting a way. More refined assessment techniques would help ensure that they do not get patients referred who are likely to have psychotic breakdowns or pernicious negative reactions – except, of course, for those students who want to learn to cope and who might do well with these under careful supervision.

Jeremy Holmes (1997) contributes an interesting hypothesis using attachment theory, linking diagnosis, etiology and treatment. As yet, however, it is a hypothesis, not yet tested in the field.

> Two basic patterns of insecure attachment have been described: avoidant and ambivalent (see Goldberg *et al.* 1995). The avoidant individual shies away from passionate contact with his attachment figure, hovering warily on the fringes of life, for ever keeping a safe distance. His childhood experience has been of unresponsiveness and rebuff in caregivers. When asked to give an account of his life he finds it difficult to remember or to elaborate. The ambivalent individual, by contrast, clings to attachment figures, fearful to let them go lest he be abandoned for ever. His caregivers have been inconsistently responsive, one minute ignoring him, the next intruding while he is happily playing. His narratives tend to be rambling incoherent affairs, bogged down in past pain with no structure or objectivity.
>
> (Holmes 1997: 167)

Holmes suggests that these two styles of attachment evoke different therapeutic strategies. People attached in an anxious avoidant way need a more flexible and warmer kind of holding before they can begin to put their painful thoughts into words and confide them to another person. Conversely, anxious ambivalently attached people need the holding of firmly maintained boundaries if they are to feel safe enough to express their negative feelings.

What works when?

Moreover, should we be confining our ideas of therapeutics as all to do with the talking cure, and one particular talking cure at that? Is it not odd that, whatever our diagnosis, the same therapy is recommended? Anyone who says that they have the cure for everything is commonly thought a quack.

We'll drink a drink a drink
To Lily the Pink the Pink the Pink
The saviour of the human race
For she invented medicinal compound
Most efficacious in every case.

Psychoanalysis, the talking cure par excellence, started us off in our profession. Since then it has kept its pre-eminence. But can the same treatment be right for everyone, however they may have been assessed or diagnosed or categorized?

How we talk in our talking cure depends on how we have been trained. There are variations in the strictness of boundaries, in the use of *holding* and the kinds of holding, in the use of silence, in the proportion and kind of transference work and of non-interpretative intervention. All this depends more on how we have been trained than on what may be appropriate for different states of mind. Of course, in practice we vary our technique according to what we feel the patient requires, but we are not helped much in our training in this respect. It is something we largely discover ourselves doing intuitively as we go along – and we depart from what we have been taught with some fear and trembling. We need to take these variations more seriously and with more respect. And we really need a diagnostic approach that will test these variations, commending and discouraging them as appropriate.

To this end I think some of us should be working toward understanding our colleagues who work in ways that are characteristically different from ours, who may have found themselves especially successful with certain kinds of patients, while finding others rather more intractable. This is already a formidable undertaking, given the history of psychoanalytically oriented psychotherapy and its conflicts and dissensions. But I think we should go further is the time ripe for meeting with different kinds of psychotherapists: Gestalt, Bioenergetics and other bodywork, group work, art therapy, music therapy, drama therapy? They may provide better help than we can, in circumstances which we can discover and define.

We could also learn from the fact that different therapies seem to indicate different kinds of desirable outcome. Psychoanalysis has defined itself as a technique only, increased consciousness being the outcome aimed at, which may be therapeutic or not, as the case may be. Other psychotherapies seem to go for increasing insight as the good outcome, or increasing capacity for growth and/or self-development, or increased resilience in adversity, and so on. Psychotherapists can usefully compare notes on this and also on how a wish for a particular outcome may affect assessment. And is it quite right to take so little notice of whatever patients may have in mind as a desirable outcome when they first come, and does their idea square with ours? Can we just ignore what people want, on the principle that we know better? (See Chapters 6 and 7 for further discussion of these points.)

An interesting book which helps to throw light on what different therapies have to offer is the rather ambitiously titled *The Art and Science of Assessment in Psychotherapy*, edited by Chris Mace (1995). It has an appealingly cool introduction by Digby Tantam to a great range of descriptions by British practitioners, as to what they look for in determining whether their particular perspective is appropriate in particular types of case: cognitive therapy, couple therapy, family, group, hospitalization, psychoanalytically oriented, among others.

Starting at the roots of practice, it would help if a variety of professionals could sit down together, and consider some real or invented descriptions of people in trouble who have asked for help. And if we could then each hazard a recommendation as to who needs what, and how we, in our particular corner, come to the conclusion as to what this person needs. We could talk about cases that seem similar. And we could tell each other what experience has taught us about our own particular techniques in which we were trained, in what kinds of cases they seem reliably useful, and when, or with whom, they do not seem so efficacious. How honest and liberating this would be. At present, we tend to behave as though everyone who comes to us will be most helped by the techniques in which we were trained.

In my experience, the current norm is that we send prospective patients to colleagues we know and trust, and these colleagues generally share our value systems and are engaged in the same kind of therapy as ourselves. These are the people we meet most and know best, whose published work we read, whose conferences we go to and with whom we share an ethos. But can this really be right? Should we not have assessors who can decide *which kind* of therapy is best suited to each particular person? Should people's symptoms decide to whom they should go? Their preferences as to outcome? Their financial situation? Their family's wishes? Their view of the problem? Our view of the problem?

Specialists in assessment and referral

We may need a new specialism, that of assessment consultant or referral consultant. These would be people to whom others can come in order to decide whether they would be well advised to undertake a particular course of treatment. I think there should be people recognized as having a special set of skills, which they should have studied and for which they should have had training. These skills will enable them to decide whether therapy is called for, and what kind. I believe our professions should be working toward a consultancy specialism, working towards having these consultants familiar with a wide range of possibilities for treatment, not just knowing good or bad Kleinians, Independents, Jungians or attachment-oriented people, or people working exclusively in the transference versus those giving more space for expressive and supportive work. I want something much wider, including knowledge of Gestalt, Bioenergetics and other body work, various types of group work, couple and family therapy, and so on. And all this based on the best available research information.

Several of my friends have not liked this. One writes that it smacks of a cognitive quick-fix approach to therapy. Another, fortunately very good friend, just says it is an omnipotent notion. Yet another, quoted below, condemns what he calls the bureaucratic approach. I agree that there is quite a bit wrong with the ideas as I state them here. But I believe I am facing in the right direction. I *believe* in the morality of outcome studies once we can get them right. (See Chapter 8 for discussion of research.)

Our profession needs eventually to find and agree on categories which tell the professional assessor what kind of therapist may be best for each client or patient. That is the therapist whose approach is more likely to be efficacious for this particular person, at least in the short run.

We should not expect to see too far in the future, given the present state of our knowledge. We are nowhere near the situation where we can look confidently into the future on the basis of one, or two, even three interviews with a prospective patient. Indeed the nature of our work may be such that we shall not always be able to make long-term recommendations. To look confidently into the future we need a reliable *prognosis* based on *diagnosis*, based on *etiology*, tied to *therapeutics*. Meanwhile, my suggestion which helps us to do better *now* is that referral consultants should not make recommendations that reach beyond, say, six months, at which point there would automatically be a reassessment. Let the consultants, in those initial interviews, find and categorize what strikes them about the person before them, and let them use this knowledge to make a decision about how that person may be best helped in the short run: bereavement talking cure, transference analysis, psychodrama, body work, whatever. Six-monthly reviews, incidently, are required in many NHS contexts and also by many medical funders. Malan's (1963) brief psychotherapy also has space for it.

There is another research element built into this system. Obviously, these well-trained referral consultants we are imagining are using the best predictive assessment categories and theories that are available to them at the time. At the end of six months they automatically get information about the relative success of their predictions. This will tell them what has proved a correct perception and what has not gone as expected. Feedback of this kind will eventually refine the diagnostic categories they have been using.

Some reservations

The friendly critic quoted near the start of this chapter, has another objection. She doubts whether it is fair to expect one person, one mind, to be able to understand the modus operandi of so great a variety of therapists and of the different conceptual frameworks which would enable them to discern, in the interview, the special personality configuration which would indicate a particular form of treatment. The consultant would have to have a number of different theoretical frameworks more or less simultaneously in mind, while at the same time staying vulnerable to the prospective patient's unconscious. Is this possible? She thinks not. I think perhaps it is.

An anonymous, very experienced and sophisticated retired social worker, raises exactly the doubts I would have voiced if I had been reading instead of writing this chapter:

> The whole concept of gatekeepers is, I think, suspect. It did not seem to me to work in the case of social-work intake-teams. In any event I think it's a bureaucratic 'solution' and creates a sort of bureaucratic tending structure, geared to 'efficiency' and, potentially, the needs of the system rather than that of the sufferer.
>
> Labelling is a big worry which could be damaging, both to patient/client and to psychotherapist/counsellor. We know that needs are far more complex than what is embraced by even the better conceptual categories, and the more you deem person X to need person Y because person Y is good at working with the X's of this world, the more you risk ignoring the complex whole and invoking the kind of shorthand categories as labels defining the total person, that has bedevilled work elsewhere in the mental-health world. Also the more therapists are deemed to be specialists in X, the more they are likely to rigidify the kinds of intervention they offer and you end up with a less flexible rather than a more flexible situation. There are also problems about selective perception that follow from this matching of 'categories', which can be very damaging because lots of things may not get picked up and you run the risk of creating a hierarchy of specialists, which acts as its own barrier to the greater flow and interaction you would like to see.
>
> The answer to more flexibility in referral lies in training and networking, both formal and informal. There have been significant shifts in the role and relationships of others in the mental health industry in these processes so why not among therapists?

We must keep these dangers in mind, but we must not give up trying to improve what we do. There is room for improvement and we must work at it.

References

Baker, R. (1980) The finding 'not suitable' in the selection of supervised cases, *International Journal of Psychoanalysis*, 7(3): 353–64.

Coltart, N. (1988) Diagnosis and assessment of suitability for psychoanalytic psychotherapy, *British Journal of Psychotherapy*, 4(2): 127–34.

Fonagy, P., Steele, M., Steele, H. and Target, M. (1997) *Reflective-Functioning: Manual for Application to Adult Attachment Interviews, Version 4.1* (unpublished). Address for correspondence: Psychoanalysis Unit, University College London, London, WC1E 6BT.

George, C., Kaplan, N. and Maine, M. (1996) *The Adult Attachment Interview*. Berkeley, CA: Department of Psychology, University of California.

Goldberg, S., Muir, R. and Kerr, J. (1995) *Attachment Theory: Social, Developmental and Clinical Perspectives*. New York: Jason Aronson.

Holmes, J. (1997) Too early, too late: endings in psychotherapy – an attachment perspective, *British Journal of Psychotherapy*, 14(2): 159–71.

Kernberg, O. (1984) *Severe Personality Disorders*. New Haven, CT: Yale University Press.

Mace, C. (ed.) (1995) *The Art and Science of Assessment in Psychotherapy*. London: Routledge.

Malan, D. (1963) *A Study of Brief Psychotherapy*. New York: Tavistock.

Milton, J. (1992) Why assess?, *Psychoanalytic Psychotherapy*, 2(1): 47–59.

Ogden, T. (1989) *The Primitive Edge of Experience*. New York: Jason Aronson.

Roth, A. and Fonagy, P. (1996) *What Works for Whom? A Critical Review of Psychotherapy Research*. New York: Guilford Press.

Shapiro, S. (1984) The initial assessment of the patient: a psychoanalytical approach, *International Journal of Psychoanalysis*, 11(1): 11–24.

5 Erotics and ethics: the passionate dilemmas of the therapeutic couple

David Mann

Introduction

The opportunity to contribute to a discussion on the ethics and values in psychotherapy gives me the chance to develop my ideas about the integrity of erotic material from a new point of view. In this chapter I explore the ethical dilemma of the erotic transference and countertransference highlighting two contradictory factors operating in therapeutic practice. The first is the way in which psychoanalytic theory and practice attempt to short-circuit the erotic processes in both patient and therapist. The second is the inherent erotic subjectivity of both participants which places eroticism at the heart of unconscious process. The dilemma thus posed is how to find an ethical solution to erotic subjectivity which neither sexually exploits the patient nor, equally abusively, denies their erotic subjectivity and respects the integrity of the psyche as a whole. I suggest that the therapeutic couple needs a sense of good enough incestuous desire in order for the therapist to maintain an ethical relationship with the patient.

The defence against the erotic

The process of psychoanalytic treatment, both in theory and practice, has evolved largely in order to deal with the passions of the erotic transference and countertransference. Almost all the techniques of psychotherapy have their origin in an attempt to defuse the possibilities of the therapist and patient developing a sexual relationship. Placing the therapist's chair behind the couch was Freud's response to an earlier incident to avoid the patient throwing her arms around him. A prohibition on any physical contact was introduced after Freud realized that pressing the patient's forehead during analysis was sometimes experienced as sexually exciting for the patient; he does not tell us if it was also sexually exciting for the analyst; presumably it could be. The therapist's 'rule of abstinence' was largely concerned with helping the analyst abstain from a sexual entanglement with the patient. Later developments in object relations theory introduced ideas of 'secure boundaries', 'containment', 'reverie', 'safe space', 'therapeutic frame' and 'the holding environment'. All these concepts are united around the central notion that the intense feelings and phantasies in the analytic encounter need some sort of limit set. While the theoretical justifications for these ideas are various, they can be seen as further underpinning the taboo on sexual passion and activity in the analytic couple. These procedures and concepts have found expression in the one public statement to which therapists of all persuasions adhere: the psychoanalytical couple, the therapist and patient, should refrain from any physical sexual activity with each other. This point of principle has taken on equivalent status of an incest taboo.

While many of Freud's original theoretical ideas have been challenged and developed, the technical procedures for the practice of psychoanalysis have remained mostly unchanged and unscrutinized. If changes have occurred, such as Ferenczi's 'mutual analysis' technique (allowing the patient to act as analyst in certain circumstances), they are seen as having departed from the definition of psychoanalytic practice (Dupont 1995). Most psychoanalytic practitioners have adopted Freud's procedure for analytic therapy without question or a second thought. Though it is uncommon to reflect on the meaning of these procedures, generations of therapists since Freud have followed Freud's practice for the same reasons: to prevent the passions of the erotic transference and countertransference getting out of control.

The history of the psychoanalytic movement suggests that both patient and therapist need as much protection as they can get from the fires of the erotic transference and countertransference. Psychoanalysis was borne out of the abortive treatment between Freud's mentor, Joseph Breuer, and his patient, Anna O. This lovely young patient infatuated Breuer to the extent that his wife became jealous and morose. When the treatment was suddenly terminated, Anna O declared that she was pregnant with Breuer's child. This was a phantom pregnancy but was, psychologically if not physiologically, a true reflection of the passion that had developed between them. The whole case made a deep impression on Freud (1915) and, as I have argued elsewhere (Mann 1999), shaped much of the psychoanalytic discourse about the erotic as a resistance, or as 'erotic horror', to use Kumin's (1985) apt phrase, for the next hundred years.

Other eminent (and not so famous) psychoanalysts have fared little better in the erotic transference and countertransference: Jung, Ferenczi, Rank and many others found themselves in sexual relationships with patients. Freud admitted to being tempted on several occasions.

It has been only in recent decades that the sexual involvement between a patient and a therapist has come to be seen by the general public and therapy organizations themselves as abusive. Until recently such sexual relationships were tolerated in many analytic societies. We can see this change of attitude within the general work environment where there has been a reflection of a shift in society's view about sexual relations between professionals and their patients or clients. Therapists were also calling for a reappraisal of the therapeutic encounter; this drew attention to the problem created by such sexual relationships and encouraged a fresh look at the transference and countertransference implications of erotic material: why it might be a hindrance or a help, 'a minefield or a gold mine' in the phrase of Spector-Person (1985). (See Mann 1997a and 1999 for a fuller discussion of the literature on the erotic transference and countertransference.)

Little wonder, then, that the common view inside the psychoanalytic profession for most of the twentieth century was that the erotic transference and countertransference is, essentially, a form of resistance, a negative therapeutic reaction, that it is an attack on the therapeutic process and that it is utilized by the patient's defences to avoid psychological change. Since it is impossible to discuss the erotic in a way that is entirely judgement free, it is my opinion that the old formula, erotic transference = resistance, is essentially a moral judgement, loaded with unconscious negative assumptions and anxiety about the erotic unconscious. To see the erotic transference solely as resistance is, more than anything else, indicative of resistance in the therapist, expressing their anxiety about having to deal with the nature of the erotic unconscious.

For Freud, both the transference and countertransference were seen as essentially erotic phenomena. He also proposed that the father was the central figure in the development of the child's psyche. He never fully worked out what function the mother might have in the child's mind apart from administering bodily needs and playing a fairly passive role in the Oedipal triangle and the child's experience of the primal scene (the parents having sexual intercourse). Gradually, as psychoanalysis developed, particularly with the British object relations school, the focal point shifted from father/child to mother/child. The mother and infant relationship not only came to dominate the developmental theories of how the child develops, but also became the model for analytic practice which was largely viewed as repeating or replicating the psychological functions of the mother.

The mother reigned supreme as the influential figure for the child, the father (if mentioned at all) became a more distant, shadowy figure. For example, in the work of Fairbairn ([1941] 1986), the father became 'the mother without breasts', a castrated figure defined by lacking something, a curious reversal of Freud's construction of women as lacking a penis.

One point of contention I have with the development of psychoanalytic theory and practice is that it is rarely able to maintain the importance of the knowledge that the conception of a child takes two parents, the mother and father, the egg and sperm. Psychoanalysis seems to find it very difficult to keep the balance of the child having two significant parents. While I locate my own psychoanalytical perspective very much in the British school of object relations, especially the ideas of Klein, Fairbairn and Winnicott, my appreciation of them is in part critical. That said, I need now to indicate what seems to me a serious problem in the object relations mother and child model.

The shift in the theoretical paradigm entailed not only a dethroning of the father, but also a foreclosure of the erotic. The transference and countertransference were no longer seen as essentially erotic in character. Indeed, the idea of the transference and countertransference as essentially erotic was now reversed to the extent that the mother/baby relationship was also sterilized and de-eroticized. Whatever else mothers and babies might feel (aggression, hate, envy, greed, love), erotic experiences were not among them. This was especially true of the mother. What the psychoanalytic construction of the mother contained was a woman with no sexual or incestuous desires. It was as though motherhood had nothing to do with sex, sexuality, erotic desire or phantasy. This is an absurd position given that sex, sexuality and erotics has everything to do with how babies are conceived.

The reason why I mention the development of what I call *the de-eroticized mother* is because, along with the other technical procedures I described above, I think theoretical developments can also be viewed as manoeuvres to limit the erotic passions in the analytic couple. I am not suggesting a conscious process or a conspiracy here, nor would I say that defusing the erotic was the only reason for developing object relations theory! What I would like to suggest is that psychoanalysis is subject to the same unconscious processes as those we encounter in clinical work and in everyday life. In that respect, we might anticipate that psychoanalytic theories show the same tendency to represent both a form of resistance in the thinker and a desire for a new transformational experience. In other words, while object relations theory had the transformational effect of bringing the mother into the psychoanalytical picture of the child's psyche, it could do this only by foreclosing the mother's erotic desire.

In a sense we see these two extremes, sexual acting out and erotic denial, as typical of the Oedipal dynamic in the dysfunctional family. Typically in families where incest occurs the active abuser is the father. The mother usually denies knowledge of what is happening in the family, but we can invoke the idea that this is the mother's passive contribution to the sexual abuse, a denial, the act of turning a blind eye to the erotic in the family. Certainly the children who have been abused and now seek therapy as adults tend to be confused and incredulous about their mother's professed ignorance. In the psychotherapeutic profession most, but by no means all, the active sexual misconduct is by male therapists. Yet can we draw the parallel with the dysfunctional family and say that if female therapists abuse their patients it is more likely to be by turning a blind eye to the erotic subjectivity in the thera-peutic process? In that sense, if male therapists run the risk of identifying themselves with the *active* abuser/father (Mann 1989) then female therapists run the risk of identifying themselves with the *passive* abuser/mother. In suggesting this I would also couple this idea to what I said earlier about the trend in psychoanalytic theory and practice to defuse the erotic undercur-rents in the therapeutic couple.

Turning a blind eye to the erotics of the transference and countertrans-ference is another aspect of de-eroticization. I would add that I do not think these two forms of abuse are always gender specific: male and female thera-pists are capable of either abusive action. When I make the connection between therapeutic practice and the dysfunctional family, I refer only to the symbolic equivalence.

I am aware that such a description of the historical development in psychoanalysis may not appeal to every reader. What I would like to high-light is that whatever the reason for the shift in the paradigm from that of Freud to that of object relations theory, it is nevertheless largely indisputable that the move from a paternal to maternal based theory of the mind and analytic practice saw a concomitant shift in the perception of the transfer-ence and countertransference: from essentially erotic to entirely (or mostly) non-erotic. In my view, the de-eroticization of the mother is connected to the de-eroticization of the transference and countertransference. In that respect, the de-eroticization of the transference and countertransference via the de-eroticization of the mother in psychoanalysis may be viewed as another of the defences against the erotic; another way in which the analytic encounter attempts to short-circuit the erotic undercurrents in the analytic couple.

Stanton (1999) describes the process of 'stalling', indicating shifts in the transference associated with the primal scene. I would like to use this term more generally to refer to the loss of energy, a cutting out of power and momentum, rather like a car engine that stalls, when the erotic is split off and dislocated from the transference and countertransference so that it becomes either ego-alien (not recognized as part of the self) and/or demo-nized (seen as resistance and destructive rather than as reproductive and transformational). But the process of stalling the erotic transference and countertransference shifts it from being normal and universal to pathologi-cal and rare.

The erotic, then, has generally been experienced as threatening to the therapist in particular and psychoanalysis generally. That such elaborate pro-cedures and theories have been unconsciously invoked to short-circuit and stall the erotic is testimony to the power of erotic phantasy. There would be no need for such defences if what is protected against were not a temptation.

In summary, psychoanalysis has struggled against the sense of engulfment of erotic passions from its inception. Many of the developments in both therapeutic procedures and psychoanalytic theory can be viewed as attempts to short-circuit and stall the erotic transference and countertransference in the analytic couple.

The erotic unconscious

This model of the de-eroticized mother has increasingly come into question with later generations of writers after Klein, Winnicott and Fairbairn. Searles ([1959] 1965), while concentrating his discussion on the father–daughter relationship, also draws attention to the mother–son dynamic, whereby the mother gives the son a sense of being erotically desirable during Oedipal love.

The most systematic exploration of the erotic processes between mother and child has been developed by Wrye and Welles (1994) and transmuted into therapeutic practice in the concepts of the maternal erotic transference and maternal erotic countertransference. In my own work (Mann 1997a), I have advanced the idea of the erotic pre-Oedipal mother and the erotic Oedipal mother, with related transference and countertransference implications. Other writers such as Raphael-Leff (1984) and Schaverien (1995) have also described how psychoanalytic theory and practice have defended themselves against the erotically alive mother by hiding behind a mother = nurturer model.

Sex, sexuality, gender, love and erotic phantasy are so integral to psychological development that, as I have emphasized, the erotic is at the heart of unconscious processes. These include the sensual and love components of both the erotic pre-Oedipal and erotic-Oedipal relationships, 'body loveprinting' (Wrye and Welles 1994); homo- and hetero-eroticism; conscious erotic fantasy and unconscious phantasy behind expressed desire of what an excited individual does with another person; the importance of the primal scene and what I have previously termed 'good enough incestuous desire' (Mann 1999).

So powerful is the function of erotic phantasy in the psyche that it exercises a structuring influence on non-erotic issues, whereby the erotic constellates other conscious and unconscious issues around the erotic core of the unconscious. This remains the case throughout life, from infancy to old age. In particular, the erotic relationship inherent in the mother and baby dyad sets the foundations for later adult expression of both erotic fantasy and actual sexual activity. From infancy onwards the erotic brings people into relationship with others. In that sense, the erotic provides the motivation for our psychological need for others. In this way, our desire for the other and our desire to be desired by the other sets the stage for the erotic to be the principal source of both pleasure and frustration throughout the life cycle. In other words, the erotic leads to opportunities for growth, transformation and learning from experience. The erotic bond, our desire for others (an 'other'), inevitably draws us into human relationships with their ensuing highs and lows.

Part of the reason why I am drawing attention to the centrality of erotic phantasy in the clinical situation (Mann 1989, 1994, 1995, 1997a, 1997b, 1999) is because outside the therapeutic encounter in everyday life (the 'real world' for want of a better term) it is that very erotic experience which is one of the most transformational forces in the life of most individuals. Humanity at large, in most cultures, epochs and geographical locations, has placed a particularly high prestige on erotic fantasy and experience, often as offering the greatest possibilities for psychological growth.

There is a clinical issue here of considerable importance. On the one hand, it is not possible to demarcate clearly infantile and adult erotic experiences as totally distinct from each other. Adult erotic expression in the transference and countertransference will always be suffused with infantile erotic components. On the other hand, the adult erotic expression cannot be totally reduced solely to an infantile foundation. The erotic development of an individual throughout life means that new experiences enable the individual to evolve, change and mature with successive stages of development. Transformation has a cumulative effect: one transformation alters the preceding foundation; further transformations have effects on the previous transformations and so on. By binding our desires to those of another, the erotic unconscious propels us into relationships all the way from infancy and, eventually, as we break away from parents, into the 'mature dependency' (Fairbairn [1941] 1986) of adult relationships.

The erotic unconscious can be thought of in terms of what I described elsewhere as the individual's erotic subjectivity (Mann 1994, 1997a). This erotic subjectivity is not something from which any individual can opt out. It has nothing to do with whether a person is sexually active or celibate either through sexual inhibition and anxieties or sublimated energies. We all have erotic processes whether we want them or not. Erotic subjectivity is the sum knowledge of our desires and experiences of the other's desire. That is to say, erotic subjectivity is our subjective experience of how we see ourselves in erotic relation to others and contains all our feelings and fantasies about ourselves as erotic subjects and erotic objects. We do not stop being an erotic individual in a manner of a detached, objective outsider to our own erotic experience. We cannot put our erotic subjectivity to one side when relating to others as we could, say, put issues of our gender out of our mind when exploring the structure of blood molecules through a microscope. Our eroticism has no significance in our dealings with microbes, but cannot be separated out in our dealings with other people and their eroticism. We may be able to stand back, subject passion to reason (some of the time!) and get a deeper understanding of the erotic phantasy life of ourselves and others, but this 'objective' or 'rational' process must in itself be rooted in a subjective relation.

Clearly the importance of the erotic unconscious and erotic subjectivity is centrality to all that is human in the patient and therapist. Sexuality, gender and erotic phantasy life are thus fundamentally important in the recognition of the whole person. If the erotic is not part of the process, the integrity of the psyche is mutilated, amputated and disfigured.

In the analytic encounter both participants bring their erotic subjectivity into the therapeutic setting. The therapeutic encounter is designed to activate powerful unconscious processes so it should be no surprise that sex, desire, pleasure, bodily sensations, in a word the erotic, will be present in a strong form. Each has his or her own erotic phantasy life and this will impact on the other. The erotic unconscious ensures that both partners will get into each other's fantasy/phantasy life in the deepest layers of the unconscious.

Clinical example

I wish to describe the following clinical material by way of illustrating the twists and turns of the ethics of the erotic transference and countertransference. The patient, whom I shall call Jane, is in her mid-thirties. She is married with children under school age. She was originally referred to me by X because the recent deaths of two grandparents had initiated a problematic bereavement reaction. When I first met her it was clear that the bereavements, though distressing, were not the real issue. Her difficulties were with her husband and the effects of her childhood.

Jane reported that, as a child, she had often witnessed her father's violence towards her mother. She would take her mother's side but repeatedly experienced a confused message from her mother, who would make Jane apologize for upsetting her father. She said that she loved her mother but did not respect her for staying in the marriage.

Her father was seldom physically violent with Jane though he would often be verbally abusive. She recalled with pain how several times he had said to her: 'You're the bastard that stops me doing what I want to do and keeps me stuck here with that cunt' – indicating Jane's mother. In her adolescence she recalled telling mum confidential things about when her periods began and needing her first bra, only to discover that mum told dad, who then opened it up for public ridicule in the form of a family joke. At other times, dad would humiliate her in a different fashion at family gatherings: he would pretend to make a grab at her big breasts. She eventually called his bluff on one occasion pushing her chest forward saying, 'Go on then, have a feel', for which he called her a 'trollop', a nickname that subsequently stuck in the family. I was struck that as she told me this particular incident the tone of her voice conveyed embarrassment and shame but also a proud, satisfied triumph. I commented on this contrast, but aside from this acknowledgement at the time, there seemed little further significance.

I have become accustomed to recognizing these discrepant pieces of material as important unconscious dislocations. When such unconscious dislocations appear it is usually difficult to know initially what they represent other than the fact that something important is being represented. Usually the meaning of such dislocated material becomes apparent only after a period of time and after further experience and reflection in the countertransference.

Jane set about creating an image for me as of someone who was sexually demure: she would dress in baggy jumpers to hide her curvaceous figure; she wished she was tall and thin, indicating with her hands the desire for a stick-like figure; she did not like wearing skirts, especially if they were short; she did not enjoy sex; she would walk down the street avoiding eye contact with men and would never stop and exchange words with strangers. She put this in the context of her humiliating experiences with her father.

Later she told me her primal scene experience and fantasy. She recalled entering her parents' bedroom, seeing her father lying on top of her mother, and dad shouting at her to get out. On many occasions she said that she and her siblings would lie and listen to the noises coming from their parents' bedroom. Because the noises that mother made were similar to these she made when father was hitting her, Jane and her siblings assumed something violent was occurring. In addition, she told me that she felt very sexually inhibited with her husband. She would undress only in the dark, was careful not to make a noise during sex in case her children heard and wanted the whole thing over as quickly as possible in case one of the children were to interrupt.

Given her history and sexual difficulties, Jane consciously saw herself as sexually inhibited and clearly wished that I would also see her that way too. She was so successful in this that, for a while, she convinced me. However, a series of unconscious dislocations put that conscious image into doubt. The most compelling of these was the off-hand remarks made in passing. For example, she told me that her sex life between leaving home and having children had been good. Both she and her husband would hurry home from work so they could go to bed early. At this time she enjoyed wearing sexy underwear and garments bought at Ann Summers parties. This information did not tally well with what she had previously said; I was further struck that, whenever she discussed her erotic subjectivity, she would tell me she was embarrassed, especially in saying this to a man, but always looked me in the eye and appeared to be enjoying the conversation. This last point was dislocating in the light of what she had previously told me, that she would often avoid eye contact with men.

There was also something about Jane that I find difficult to describe. I call it *sexual energy* or *erotic vitality*: people either have it or they do not – most do. Erotic vitality is not the same thing as being attractive, and the two do not always go together. I can explain it no better than to say it is the sense you have about somebody that they are erotically viable, you can imagine that they have intimate relationships with others: possibly even with you if the circumstances permitted it. In struggling to describe this I am reminded of a comment by the jazz trumpeter, Louis Armstrong, when asked, 'What is rhythm?' He replied, 'If you don't know you ain't got it'. With erotic vitality I think it is possible to know it without having it, but that does not make it any easier to describe. I can say that Jane had plenty of erotic vitality.

I began to question her portrayal of herself as inhibited and demure. It was apparent that she found many situations sexually exciting; these included offering her breast to her dad, sex before she had children and discussing sexual matters with me. I added that I suspected she had found that listening to her parents' sexual activity had also been exciting, as well as disturbing.

She then began to describe two recent events. The first was on the London Underground with a man trying to sell her a second-hand ticket. Despite not wanting to talk to him she was giving him enough appropriate signals to keep him persisting in talking to her, thus breaking her rule about talking to strange men. The other event concerned a family social event when a cousin, several times removed, sought to exploit their obvious mutual attraction and to encourage her into having an affair. She resisted 'going all the way' but gave enough positive signals to keep him talking to her for the whole evening. I said clearly there was a side of her that was not inhibited: the inhibition was in recognizing the side that enjoys the erotic 'zing'. Jane was very thoughtful at this; she said that she stopped enjoying sex with her husband after having children because the thought that the children would hear her during intercourse made her feel her husband was like her dad. She added that it had always been a characteristic of her husband subtly to humiliate her sexually as her dad had done, her husband justifying himself against her objections by saying, 'It's my body, you just carry it around'. I said that if it is as if your husband becomes your father then it is also as if you become your mother during sex. Jane was upset but nodded, adding that her mother had once confided in her that dad was very good in bed. This had confused Jane even more, especially reconciling the similarities of sounds when mother was being hit and having an orgasm. Among other issues, neither parent had worried about the children hearing them. This had left Jane confused about whether she could enjoy sex. In her unconscious she was identifying herself with her own children while she and her husband were in bed.

After this discussion Jane arrived in a mini-skirt, though she was self-consciously half-hearted about this and sat with her coat across her legs. The effect was both to display and hide herself simultaneously. Though she was not mentioning it, it was, none the less, a significant issue as she had previously mentioned that she did not like wearing short skirts. I hesitated about making a comment: should I say something and run the risk of being inappropriate, like her father. After thinking about this for a while I said: 'We seem to be talking about everything and nothing at the moment, so I thought that I had better mention what we are not talking about, namely that I have noticed you are wearing a short skirt and that seems significant'. Jane blushed but was also noticeably relieved I had said something. I had intended my remark to break the silent denial without being open humiliation, that such a comment would thus avoid a direct enactment of an identification with her father in the countertransference. I had hoped that what I said was an acknowledgement of her erotic subjectivity, without attempting to undermine her in the process. She went on to say that she had spoken to her husband about some of the sexual matters we had discussed and this seemed to improve the situation between them. She felt more relaxed and was able to have sex with the light on.

What I focus on in this case material is the ethics of the erotic transference and countertransference. An overt sexual relationship with this patient was never going to be a possibility and therefore not an ethical concern. Even if I had wanted to make this relationship more sexual and exploit her seductiveness, and I did not wish to do this, I am sure that Jane would not have allowed it to happen. Her teasing behaviour with her father, the man on the London Underground and her cousin, while exciting and tempting, was never so tempting as to draw her into totally transgressing either the incest barrier or her marriage vows. She might go close to the line, but would not overstep it.

In many respects, the more serious ethical problem was whether to and how to acknowledge Jane's erotic subjectivity. How could the therapy be authentic to the integrity of her psyche without speaking about her erotic unconscious? Not to address it would be to collude with the sexual inhibition and her demure demeanour. To begin to speak about it might take it over in a way that felt humiliating to her.

Searles ([1959] 1965) implies it is the parent's or the therapist's love that allows both the acknowledgement of the erotic and its non-hostile, non-abusive expression and this creates the language which articulates the erotic unconscious. In this way, the erotic transference dilemma that Jane presented was going to be resolved only by working it through in the erotic countertransference. My assumption is that, if the patient is creating an atmosphere, *especially* if this is unconsciously done, then the patient is bringing this aspect of the unconscious into the session the only way he or she knows how, precisely for the therapist to register and, it is hoped, find a way of speaking about. If there is not a communicative aspect in the unconscious then the material would not be in the room. Because the erotic bond draws people into relationships I would suggest that the purpose of the difficult erotic unconscious expression is to find a way in which the erotic subjectivity can be discussed and made more conscious. If there is something in the room it is there to be discovered and described.

The ethical question here is whether therapists are ready to accept and discuss those aspects of themselves that they (or part of them) did not accept. It seemed to me that the dislocations between Jane's demure presentation brought her and me into conflict with her erotic subjectivity. To be true to the integrity of her psyche required that this dislocation be discussed. It would have been more unethical to ignore her erotic subjectivity, thereby showing intolerance towards an aspect of Jane's psyche.

The moral maze

I would like now to bring the strands of this chapter together to consider the serious ethical problems in psychotherapy. The question is: what to do with the patient's erotic subjectivity in the therapeutic process. A related question, and just as important, is what to do with the therapist's erotic subjectivity in the therapeutic process.

In the two previous sections I have elaborated two seemingly incompatible processes. On the one hand, is the universality of erotic processes which permeate and infuse all relationships, especially in the intimate setting of one-to-one relationships, the therapeutic couple thus being ripe and prime candidates for the full intensity of the erotic bond. On the other hand, as I have demonstrated, there is the consistent attempt within the development of psychoanalytic theory and practice to find ways which circumvent, defuse, short-circuit and stall the erotic unconscious in the analytic couple.

Quite simply: how are we as therapists going to be true to the erotic subjectivity of the transference and countertransference while at the same time not falling into its seductions, either blatant sexual acting out (ranging from flirting, indirect gratification to penetrative sex) or flight from the erotic (causing anxiety, de-eroticization, inhibition and other defensive manoeuvres that keep therapy away from dealing with the erotic unconscious)?

Two interesting patterns emerge. Virtually every therapist, analyst and counsellor reports experiences of the erotic transference and countertransference in therapeutic practice. It is true that many are uncertain about what to do or how to approach the erotic unconscious in clinical practice, but mention of it is frequent enough to suggest its universal presence. The other interesting point is the frequency with which these same therapists, analysts and counsellors report that they did not really discuss erotic issues in their personal therapy. I have heard on several occasions: 'I couldn't possibly talk about sex with my therapist!' There is usually an interactive loop at work here: the patient's own inhibitions register what are presumably the therapist's own anxieties about erotic material. This makes the patient more anxious about erotic material which in turn makes the therapist more anxious – and so the cycle builds up, is self-perpetuating and becomes entrenched. My impression (and it is only an impression) is that a confluence of several factors are at work. Most people seeking psychotherapy, including therapists and trainees, do so because they experience some problem in their love relationships. The erotic for most therapists, therefore, already comes with question mark attached. During training, therapists discover in their personal therapy, usually unconsciously, that the erotic components of the therapy have a disreputable quality, a negative therapeutic reaction, they signify resistance to therapy. Until very recently, the erotic transference has been considered problematic in the psychoanalytic literature. These issues taken together have made it very difficult to think and work creatively with the erotic transference with one's own patients.

Anything to do with the erotic immediately takes us into areas of morality and values. I would suspect that it is probably impossible to take a neutral stance to the erotic unconscious, and this piece of writing is no exception. There are pitfalls in all directions that would inhibit flexible, creative and good enough original thinking in the therapist. There is a tyranny from both the orthodox puritans and the new puritans of political correctness: both would castigate the opposing view, thereby showing remarkable intolerance to difference and otherness. Browsing through the psychoanalytic literature the reader can find his or her own examples of both forms of fundamentalism.

It seems to me that the erotic unconscious poses *the* central ethical problems in psychotherapy: how to acknowledge and remain respectful and true to the erotic integrity of the psyche while avoiding the extremes of either sexual misconduct or de-eroticization, both of which in their own way are a degradation and impingement on the therapeutic couple, especially the patient.

The labyrinth beneath the moral maze

The therapeutic process would be difficult enough if it were just a case of finding a way to talk about the erotic unconscious. There are additional factors which make this conversation more problematic. The contemporary understanding of the transference and countertransference is much more complex than Freud originally envisaged. What I am referring to is how the patient draws the therapist into his or her world and, likewise, how the therapist draws the patient into the therapist's world. The former has received increasing attention among analytic writers (see Gabbard 1995 for an excellent summary). This is usually thought of in terms of 'object usage' (Bollas 1987), 'enactments' (Chused 1991) or 'role responsiveness' (Sandler 1976), whereby the patient induces or causes the therapist to act out unconsciously. Therapists find themselves caught in the patient's transference, unconsciously reproducing either internal objects or actual figures from the patient's past. What is enacted is usually something negative rather than positive, for example, unconsciously behaving like the strict father or an indifferent mother. Because this is an unconscious process therapists do not know they are doing it until afterwards. That is to say, you can be aware of an unconscious occurrence only after the event. Some writers consider that foreknowledge of enactments should reduce either the frequence of their occurrence or their severity. In my opinion, this is a piece of self-deception. Foreknowledge is no defence against the unconscious. The best foreknowledge can do is keep the therapist alert to the fact that they *will* unconsciously be caught in the patient's transference, and that a need to analyse the countertransference is the only way the enactment will be discovered.

To the best of my knowledge, very little has been written about what I would term 'counter object usage' or 'counter enactments' or 'counter role responsiveness'. As the countertransference parallels the patient's transference so counter enactments parallel the therapist's enactments. A counter enactment can be considered, as when patients find themselves acting part of the therapist's internal script, or, for want of a better phrase, the patient enacts on the therapist's transference. It is very hard to find evidence of counter enactments. The patient is unlikely to spot how they are acting out something of the therapist's internal and external objects. The therapist may also find it difficult to see what is happening precisely because it is unconscious and draws significance from blind-spots in the therapist's self-awareness. The best way I can describe this is by reference to the well-known phenomenon that patients with Jungian therapists tend to have very 'Jungian type' dreams, those with Freudian therapists tend to have very 'Freudian type' dreams, while those with Kleinian therapists tend to have very 'Kleinian type' dreams, and so on. What I think is going on here is that patients understand their therapists very well – only they do not know it. There is an element of compliance with the therapist's wishes in all psychotherapy: the patient agrees to follow the therapist's procedures: free associations, the use of couch, and so forth. Patients quickly learn what the therapist likes or is interested in and will either dutifully provide this or rebel, according to individual pathologies. Most patients provide what the therapist wants because most of them wish to be loved by the therapist.

In the therapeutic session the patient and therapist find themselves involved to varying degrees in the unconscious process of the other. This involvement is of course itself unconscious. Because the unconscious is so often erotic in character this involvement is in the deepest layers of the erotic unconscious.

I think of this as a deeper layer or stratum in the relationship between the therapeutic couple, a maze within a maze or, as my subtitle would have it: the labyrinth beneath (unconscious) the moral maze (erotic) confronting the patient and therapist. Since the unconscious is highly porous and permeable, the analytic encounter, which in itself encourages maximum unconscious activity, will lead both participants to 'get inside' each other in ways outside conscious recognition of either party. This creates the opportunities or the circumstances for enactments and counter enactments to occur.

If the patient's presenting problem is concerned with sexual abuse, it is clear that the unconscious erotic communication can become very difficult for both the patient and therapist. I have described elsewhere (Mann 1995) how therapists may find themselves adopting any of the abusive characters in the Oedipal triangle, that of father, mother or child. Gardner (1999) has described how various positions adopted can run counter to the therapist's expressed ethical standards. For example, the therapist may enact a sense of betrayal, powerlessness, guilt and the mind of the abuser. In a certain way this runs counter to the aims of psychotherapy. The ethical standards of the ego ideal of most therapists requires them to do the best job possible in helping patients with their problems. The positive side of this is to analyse such enactments which might then lead to psychological change once understood. At this unconscious level, the ethical issues surrounding the erotic transference and countertransference make the task of psychoanalytic work very complicated.

In summary, the picture may be described as follows: the unconscious is essentially erotic in nature and psychoanalytic therapy has sought ways in theory and technique to short-circuit, stall or circumvent this erotic process. This poses a dilemma for the therapist regarding respect for the integrity of the patient's psyche, especially their erotic subjectivity, and the ethical standard of wishing to work with the whole person without judgement. Already the therapist has a conflict within the ego ideals of psychotherapy but the nature of the unconscious process is such that the therapist and patient begin to manipulate the other into enactments, usually turning the other into what is dreaded. When the therapist enacts what the patient dreads at the level of the erotic unconscious we could describe this as an affront to the ethical standards of the ego ideal of both patient and therapist.

Put like that it makes the therapeutic process seem like an impossible profession. As Freud knew, to an extent it is. How can we ethically work with the erotic subjectivity in a way that acknowledges the erotic unconscious without abusing it? What prevents this from being an entirely stalled and short-circuited process is the fact that within the erotic unconscious is the desire for transformation; the individual develops, grows and matures through erotic experience. The analytic couple produces the desire for a new experience that takes both the patient and the therapist into a new place: what Winnicott (1971) might call a transitional space, the third area, where something different from the past might occur. This is an area of psychological overlap between individuals which creates the possibility of what we might think of as *erotic play*. I do not mean foreplay, flirting or direct sexual or erotic expression. I mean play here as Winnicott (1971) intended the term: an expression of a spontaneous gesture that comes from the authentic relationship of the erotic bond between patient and therapist. Perhaps this could also be described as intimacy through love, which accepts the erotic integrity of the other without denying desire, difference or erotic subjectivity of the other.

I think of this in terms of the analytic process as characterized by the concept of the *transformational couple* (Mann 1997a). This is not an original idea. Jung (1946) had seen that therapy affects either both participants or neither, in which latter case nothing happens. What I am emphasizing is the erotic nature of this transformational process. The erotic unconscious draws the individual into relationship with the other. Both patient and therapist seek to have less unconscious dread of each other based on a withdrawal of mutual projection and introjection. In that sense, the transference and countertransference can be thought of as a mutative process. In my terms, in the process of intimately coming to experience the other in a more authentic and realistic manner, both the therapist and the patient work towards a sense of a *good enough incestuous desire* (Mann 1999) whereby desire is acknowledged and understood, but not acted out.

The ethics of the 'good enough' erotic transference and countertransference

I think we see the power of the erotic bond throughout the development of psychoanalysis. Yet despite all the attempts to foreclose, stall and short-circuit the erotic it still will not go away: as a profession we have not been able to get away from sex. The erotic will not just disappear. It has always shadowed psychoanalytic thinking and therapeutic practice. The erotic always finds a form of expression and 'good enough' ethical practice at least requires us to try to think and talk about the subject with an open mind, even when we know that we cannot be free from morality and subjective discourse.

If the therapist cannot address this erotic subjectivity, the patient registers the belief that the therapist cannot face the integrity of the psyche, that the psychic truth of the erotic unconscious is, indeed, intolerable and must not be known. The conversation necessarily takes the therapy into the heart of anxiety in analytic practice: the dangers, real or imagined, of the erotic transference and countertransference. In my view, an ethical stance would be compromised and it would be insincere to shy away from the erotic, hiding either behind blindness or the posture of therapeutic resistances creating the 'negative therapeutic reaction'. If I can nail my code of ethics to the mast and take a moral stance, I would say it is unethical for the therapist not to respect the patient's erotic subjectivity. To foreclose, short-circuit or stall the erotic transference and countertransference is to 'close off' the heart of the patient's (and therapist's) unconscious. The core of the unconscious becomes a 'no-go-area' and confirms the worst unconscious phantasies about the erotic as a source of anxiety, rather than as a source of transformation.

What I am saying here brings me into direct opposition with some psychoanalysts. For example, Cesio (1993), who describes only once encountering an erotic transference while training and it was viewed as a problem. He concludes:

> my experience, its [transference love] direct emergence in a reasonably well conducted analysis is exceptional, so much so that I have observed it in only one case, at the beginning of my work, when I was not sufficiently experienced . . . Our observations lead us to conclude that the emergence of transference love is the consequence of the analyst's failure to perceive it while it is incipient and to resolve it by means of interpretation.
>
> (Cesio 1993: 132)

To my mind, this is an extraordinary statement. If the erotic is at the heart of unconscious experience, and I believe it is, I can see no possibility that it will not have a part in the transference and countertransference. It is possible, however, to imagine all sorts of resistances and defences against its recognition. There is clearly a variety of ways of understanding this.

I do not believe it is possible to adopt a rigid, consistent view about the erotic transference. In some therapies it is hardly an issue or only slightly important; in others the erotic may be an issue during only part but not all of the process. However, it is difficult to imagine that a reasonably well-managed transference and countertransference will not at some stage contain an erotic component.

If, as therapists, we are going to respect the integrity of the patient's psyche we must find a way to address the erotic unconscious without abusing the patient by either sexual exploitation or denial of his or her erotic subjectivity. This may be thought of in terms of 'good enough' incestuous desire which avoids the pitfalls of the Oedipal passions of acting out or of turning a blind eye. The ethics of the 'good enough' erotic transference and countertransference require the erotic needs of both patient and therapist to find a place in the work in the room and to be thought about by the therapeutic couple.

References

Bollas, C. (1987) *The Shadow of the Object: Psychoanalysis of the Unthought Known*. New York: Columbia University Press.

Cesio, F. (1993) The Oedipal tragedy in the psychoanalytic process: transference love, in E. Spector-Person (ed.) *On Freud's 'Obervations on Transference Love'*. New Haven, CT: Yale University Press.

Chused, J.F. (1991) The evocative power of enactments, *Journal of the American Psychoanalytic Association*, 39: 615–39.

Dupont, J. (1995) The story of a transgression, *Journal of the American Psychoanalytic Association*, 43: 823–34.

Fairbairn, W.R.D. ([1941] 1986) A revised psychopathology of the psychoses and psychoneuroses, *Psychoanalytic Studies of the Personality*. London: Routledge.

Freud, S. (1915) Observations on transference love, *Standard Edition*, vol. 12. London: Hogarth Press.

Gabbard, G.O. (1995) Countertransference: the emerging common ground, *International Journal of Psychoanalysis*, 76: 475–85.

Gardner, F. (1999) A sense of all conditions, in D. Mann (ed.) *Erotic Transference and Countertransference: Clinical Practice in Psychotherapy*. London: Routledge.

Jung, C.G. (1946) The psychology of the transference, *Collected Works*, vol. 16. London: Routledge & Kegan Paul.

Kumin, I. (1985) Erotic horror: desire and resistance in the psychoanalytic setting, *International Journal of Psychoanalytic Psychotherapy*, 11: 3–20.

Mann, D. (1989) Incest: the father and the male therapist, *British Journal of Psychotherapy*, 6: 143–53.

Mann, D. (1994) The psychotherapist's erotic subjectivity, *British Journal of Psychotherapy*, 10(3): 344–54.

Mann, D. (1995) Transference and countertransference issues with sexually abused patients, *Psychodynamic Counselling*, 1(4): 542–59.

Mann, D. (1997a) *Psychotherapy: An Erotic Relationship – Transference and Countertransference Passions*. London: Routledge.

Mann, D. (1997b) Masturbation and painting, in K. Killick and J. Schaverien (eds) *Art, Psychotherapy and Psychosis*. London: Routledge.

Mann, D. (ed.) (1999) *Erotic Transference and Countertransference: Clinical Practice in Psychotherapy*. London: Routledge.

Raphael-Leff, J. (1984) Myths and modes of motherhood, *British Journal of Psychotherapy*, 1(1): 6–30.

Sandler, J. (1976) Countertransference and role-responsiveness, *International Review of Psychoanalysis*, 3: 43–7.

Schaverien, J. (1995) *Desire and the Female Therapist: Engendered Gazes in Psychotherapy and Art Therapy*. London: Routledge.

Searles, H. ([1959] 1965) Oedipal love in the countertransference, *Collected Papers on Schizophrenia and Related Subjects*. London: Hogarth Press.

Spector-Person, E. (1985) The erotic transference in women and men: differences and consequences, *Journal of the American Academy of Psychoanalysis*, 13: 159–80.

Stanton, M. (1999) Primal absence and loss in erotic transference, in D. Mann (ed.) *Erotic Transference and Countertransference: Clinical Practice in Psychotherapy*. London: Routledge.

Winnicott, D.W. (1971) Transitional objects and transitional phenomena, *Playing and Reality*. London: Tavistock.

Wrye, H.K. and Welles, J.K. (1994) *The Narration of Desire: Erotic Transferences and Countertransferences*. Hillsdale, NJ: Analytic Press.

6 Ethics and values in our practice: impasse in psychotherapy and organizations

Fiona Palmer Barnes

Introduction

Practitioners in their work with patients face ethical challenges more frequently than is acknowledged. We no longer live in an age when there is the social, cultural or spiritual consensus as there was for the founders of psychotherapeutic thinking in the early twentieth century. Since the 1970s our multicultural society and political leaders have challenged and changed earlier assumptions and the consensus ethos following the Second World War has given way to a diversity of individual views and values systems. As a result, issues once thought of as shared between practitioner and patient may now be found to reflect either a shared or a differing ethical or value base. Unfortunately the practitioner may perceive these matters of value as representing an aspect of the patient's psychopathology and not resulting from differing values sincerely held by each of them. In these circumstances the practitioner looks for an answer from psychoanalytic theory or practice, and deals with the situation defensively.

I first consider the effect on patients of the practitioner's own character and personal belief system; how the practitioner's and patient's desires, perceptions and needs may affect what happens in the work and the way the work is done between them. Next, I look at the particular challenges that the practitioner faces when the work reaches an impasse and becomes stuck. Can such a situation be seen as being entirely of a technical nature or does it also raise ethical challenges? Finally, I examine the pressures from professional institutions and how they may affect the work of psychotherapy and psychotherapists. Inevitably I raise more questions than I can provide answers.

The patient and the practitioner

There is a presumption among many practitioners that those who present themselves for psychotherapy will benefit from the therapy, and share with the practitioner sufficient of their value system, their ethos, for the work to be done. This may not be so.

Consider first, for example, the conscious principles and values of both the practitioner and patient, values that may in their turn lead us to think about ethical questions. Practitioners are the product of their experience of life and of their analytic practice and training. Patients' experiences may have been very different and their value base may have little in common with their therapist's. Does this matter? Practitioners may believe that they have sufficient knowledge of their ethos and that they understand the values that underlie their work. For example the practitioner may have had an experience of the police that leads him or her to perceive them as friendly and value them as helpful, while the patient may have had a completely different experience, and perceive the police as frightening and persecutory and value them negatively. Thus one task of the therapy is to explore the patient's own ethos, values and desires and understand what they mean to the patient. Only in this way may we have an understanding of how consciously or unconsciously they may affect his expectations within the therapy.

Does the practitioner's value base matter? Many practitioners would say with Bion (1967: 18) that since the psychotherapist should be 'without memory . . . or desire' there is no difficulty, because the value base of the psychotherapist is suspended and does not enter the work at all. However, even if I were to agree with Bion's view and the implications drawn from it, I still might believe there are areas where the practitioner reflects their own values and therefore has an ethical responsibility in the work with the patient. Is there not a point where the practitioner needs to have an opinion and set of values, for example when an individual is having repeated unprotected sex, or when a woman is becoming repeatedly pregnant and having abortions? At some point might we not say: 'I am wondering why you are putting yourself at risk', thus reflecting our own values? An example of this kind of ethical responsibility can also be seen in 'the match' between the psychotherapist and patient, which may or may not affect the potential of the therapeutic work. It is important that there is a 'good enough' therapeutic fit between patient and analyst. This is in itself an ethical issue.

Values enter the work from its inception. When patients present for psychotherapy or analysis they may or may not know something of what therapists do. Patients may not have any significant sense or understanding of what to expect from the psychotherapist, but they still come requesting therapy, bringing their confusion and pain so that these can be relieved.

Patients will, of course, have a variety of preconceptions and transferences as a result of pre-knowledge and the first contact. They may assume that on the one hand the psychotherapist is likely to share their values and will be someone who has a philosophical basis that they are sympathetic with. Patients might consider the psychotherapist to be a life-saver, which can be problematic in itself. Patients may on the other hand even be sympathetic to a view, frequently expressed in the media, that psychotherapists are inclined to trap patients into long-term, three or five times a week, expensive therapy and that this must be avoided at all costs. More and more patients presenting for psychotherapy seem to fear dependency. Thus patients may fear that the psychotherapist may not share their values, particularly in terms of their own commitment to the process.

Commitment to therapy involves all kinds of resources from both psychotherapist and patient. These include the inner resources in terms of desire and purpose and the motivation of both parties. There are also the patient's resources in terms of money and time. These particular resources come under various pressures and may be challenged by the patient's obligations and commitments to relationships, family and to work. Confusion between the ethos of the practitioner and their method or practice and the needs of the patient in terms of their own resources and values need attending to and struggling with in the therapeutic work so that it can develop. In practice this may lead to further difficulties for both parties: for the practitioner, for example, where the ethos of training is long term, and for the patient who requests and may even need only short-term treatment to obtain the outcome they desire.

Consider, second, those aspects of the therapeutic frame or alliance which have ethical implications for the practitioner. There are many levels of conscious and unconscious challenges for both psychotherapist and patient at assessment and in the ongoing work.

The patient's values, whether we agree with them or not, need to remain present in the practitioner's mind and may challenge the psychotherapist's view of difference and change his or her perceptions and values. We learn from our patients and they learn from us, but only if there is a flexibility and willingness to learn.

One example of this kind of ethical responsibility for the practitioner may be seen in 'the match' between the 'type', personality or character of psychotherapist and patient, and whether it affects the potential of the therapeutic work. This is a Jungian concept but may help to give all of us an idea to work with. (This subject is approached from a different perspective in Chapters 4 and 7.) I am addressing the matter here because I argue that there is an ethical dimension to the need for a 'good enough' therapeutic fit between patient and therapist.

The personality match between practitioner and patient can be seen symbolically or actually as a matter of type. For Jungians there is a theoretical description of personality difference, namely typology. Beebe (1984) suggests that the particular typologies of the patient and analyst are significant. He posits that if the orientation (introversion or extraversion) and type (thinking, feeling, intuitive, or sensate) of the psychotherapist and patient are complementary the patient will experience the psychotherapist as empathetic. When the psychotherapist's type profile is markedly opposed, then the two individuals concerned will be drawn into misunderstanding, collusion or conflict. Should the inferior function of the psychotherapist or patient be the dominant function of the other, Beebe (1984) suggests that little useful work can be done.

More recently, in his work on 'character', Beebe (1998) has suggested that the purpose of individuation is the development of integrity. Integrity is the paradoxical combination of vulnerability and confidence that makes work on character possible. We cannot find our integrity, however, until we know our character. If we recognize that it is our integrity that individuates, and not our basic character itself, then we shall see that long work in analysis, however interminable, has something to show for self-examination and the questioning of impulses that seem to stem from the self (Beebe 1998: 61). Beebe sees integrity as being part of 'character' and is accountable for the impact of the self upon others.

Whatever we may each feel about Beebe's ideas, he raises important questions about the match of the therapeutic couple. He holds with the view taken in differing ways by other authors that psychotherapists have a responsibility to be aware of their own type or character and how it could affect the potential for the work with a patient. Practitioners from other therapeutic orientations may challenge this point of view. If so, they might think about the symbolic nature of Beebe's thesis and they may question whether there is an ethical responsibility for the psychotherapist to be aware of the practitioner–patient match, and consider the value basis on which they accept patients for therapy.

As well as the conscious pressures such as therapeutic match, various levels of unconscious processes may affect the therapeutic alliance and may influence the work itself. Clark (1995) writes of the complex nature of the struggle for patients seeking psychotherapy and thus change:

By 'change' I mean the desire to change impotent, stuck, defensive and/or repetitive patterns. Under this there is a desire not to change – even to have one's neurotic defences affirmed and strengthened. By 'understanding' I mean the desire to have another person to see into and know one at depth. Under this, as Winnicott says, there is a desire not to be seen, to be unknown and hidden, to maintain a precious secret core. By 'self-preservation' I mean the desire not to fall to bits, not to lose control or go mad. To preserve a sense of self and self-esteem. Under this there is a need to collapse, to lose control and to break down. The fourth motivating aim for seeking psychotherapy is the (fantastic) desire for an absolute and eternal loving relationship, to be loved and to love absolutely and for ever. Hopefully, this omnipotent, infantile illusion will be challenged and transformed by the disillusioning realities and necessities of human nature and relations.

(Clark 1995: 345)

Clark thus exposes the challenge to the therapeutic work from the unconscious of the patient. There are just as many levels of conscious and unconscious ambivalence on the psychotherapist's side.

If we pursue Clark's (1995) argument a little further, clearly these many levels of conscious and unconscious fantasy persist in the ongoing therapeutic work. As therapists we face the challenge of how to address these and work towards a good enough feeling between practitioner and patient.

When commencing the ongoing therapeutic work with a patient, considerable difficulties may arise in forming a therapeutic alliance. If we look at the situation from the patient's point of view, the patient comes to us, at a location we have determined, to take part in a therapy of which we, the practitioners, know the rules. There is nothing unusual with this: it is the same way that doctors, dentists and other professional people carry out their work. As with other professionals, there is an imbalance of power in this situation and the assumption is that the patient conforms to our professional rules. However, it is also true that people normally visit other professionals only occasionally. Our patients, however, come for psychotherapy once, twice, three or more times weekly on a regular basis. They may feel that they have less understanding of the nature of our work than they have of the other professionals they deal with because we do less concrete things with them and need their participation and response. These differences of expectations and values may cause the form of the therapeutic relationship to start as, or become, one of resistance to the process and thus conflict or collusion and, possibly, impasse.

The difficulties that lead to conflict in psychotherapy are various. Bion (1961) writes about how human beings try to relate to one another in managing a joint task. He describes a human being as a group animal, and as such the person cannot get on without other human beings. However, the person cannot get on very well with them either, and must establish effective cooperation in life's tasks. This Bion sees as the human dilemma. Bion's (1961) emphasis on how hard it is for individuals to work together reflects how difficult the task of analysis may be. Is it about gratitude or resentment in practitioner or patient? Or helplessness in the predicament presented in the work? Or struggles with feelings of failure in the practitioner or in the patient?

Conscious and/or unconscious envies and jealousies between the practitioner and patient may cause conflict. Difficulties may arise in relation to the client's fantasies about power of the psychotherapist, perhaps in terms of the practitioner's knowledge or persistence with the rules of therapy. The patient may feel as though they are in an impossible situation and a conflict may ensue.

Consider, for example, the patient who feels that social class, gender or ethnicity divide them from the psychotherapist. Normally these tensions can be worked with, and indeed they occur in most analyses. However, situations arise where the patient feels that the work is impossible. This may be because the patient cannot work with the situation or because the practitioner really has not sufficiently understood the problems of difference, particularly where they relate to feeling disadvantaged. In this case let us assume the psychotherapist is male, white and a medical practitioner. He may know about difference and oppression or he may not. Let us say that the patient is female. The psychotherapist may have little sense of women's experience of 'life under a patriarchy' and in Austin's terms what 'women can do with these experiences to turn them into something which serves their own interests' (Austin 1999: 8), rather than the interests of society or men. Austin argues that only by understanding a woman's aggressive fantasies can the male analyst help his female patient examine the construction of her own femininity and thus her own identity.

In another example, let us suppose that a male patient wishes to be in a relationship and have children. He may know or fantasize that his psychotherapist has children. During sessions, children are heard playing in the garden. Is there an obligation on the practitioner to silence the children, for them not to play in the garden? What if they are not the practitioner's children at all but a neighbour's? Clearly what needs to be dealt with is the perception of the situation by the patient through interpretation, and the ethical issue if there is one, is whether the practitioner is being confronting or taunting the patient with their own situation.

Another psychotherapist may have a patient whom she experiences as being socially or academically her superior, or a patient who comes from a cultural background she does not understand. She may be unwilling to see the feelings she experiences in the countertransference as oppressive or bigoted. Thus she colludes with the patient and with her own conscious and unconscious prejudices, and preserves her own values, preferring to leave those of the patient unanalysed thereby raising questions about the quality of her own training therapy as well as raising issues for her supervision.

Absence of apparent difference between patient and practitioner may also cause difficulties and another form of collusion may take place. The practitioner, through their own outer need for the patient or while working with the transference, may give more power to the patient than is appropriate and a perverse alliance may form. Atwood *et al.* (1989) noted the problems of collusion, particularly where the psychotherapist assumes a shared ethos with the patient. Descriptions of the patient's life that are in agreement with the therapist's personal vision of the world will accordingly tend to be regarded as reflections of objective reality rather than as manifestations of the patient's personality. Commonly, the specific region of inter-subjective correspondence that escapes analytic inquiry reflects a defensive solution shared by both patient and therapist. The conjunction can result in a mutual strengthening of resistance and counter-resistance and, hence, in a prolongation of the treatment (Atwood *et al.* 1989: 556).

These brief examples of conflict and collusion illustrate the significance of fantasies of presumed and projected power in therapeutic practice and the ethical issues that might arise from it.

It is possible that conflict may be caused by the practitioner's perceived power and collusion may take place in reaction to this. Or the patient may perceive themselves in a grandiose way as having the power and be involved in a fantasy where the practitioner is to be used. The countertransference symbol for the therapist might be that of the prostitute. For either situation to persist without interpretation may be abusive and lead to feelings of helplessness. Bringing the experience of the situation into consciousness through interpretation provides impetus for further work.

The very nature of the relationship between practitioner and patient holds at its core the ethical and value foundation of the practitioner's analytic attitude: that the work is for the patient's benefit. When considering issues of power, the question arises as to whether the increased use of the transference in all psychoanalytically and psychodynamically oriented analytic and psychotherapeutic work since the 1960s has an ethical dimension in itself. The importance of the ethical attitude of the practitioner is particularly significant in working transferentially with patients. Working in the transference assumes that practitioners understand their own part in the therapeutic dialogue with their patients and do not become caught up in their own unconscious processes.

Furthermore, there may be issues of power of an ethical nature to be thought about at a time when psychotherapists are having difficulties finding patients who wish to commit themselves to an intensive therapy. Psychotherapists who wish to qualify as supervisors or training analysts and trainees who need training patients are more than grateful for patients who are willing to work three or more times a week. The needs of practitioners may be at variance with those of patients.

In the therapeutic alliance, it is vital that there is a 'good enough' therapeutic match between patient and psychotherapist. Coltart (1987) understands the implications of this: 'If you are prescribing psychotherapy on a long-term basis you are making a powerful statement: and your respect for the patient should entail that you give him your own insight into his need and his character' (Coltart 1987: 134). In other words the practitioner uses their value base to address the value base of the patient. If there is not the possibility of providing a 'good enough' match, or if the practitioner feels that the work will stretch them beyond their competence, or that the psychopathy of the patient indicates that the patient is borderline or psychotic and, thus, possibly not suitable for the variety of psychotherapy on offer, then the therapy should not be attempted. Should the therapy begin and it then transpires that the work is experienced by the practitioner as particularly difficult, the therapist will face a complex dilemma, and will need to rely on colleagues for additional supervision and support or may need to refer the patient to someone more experienced.

One of the tasks of therapy is to explore the tensions within the working alliance. Redfearn (1992) refers to the bomb-like nature of the self, and its creative and destructive aspects. He says: 'The building up of strength and capacity to the point where the union of the relevant opposites can be creatively contained may take a great deal of work' (Redfearn 1992: 113). Both patient and practitioner can then feel that their positive and ambivalent feelings have a place. The creative tension between practitioner and patient helps the patient to explore their own views and values; they can be challenged appropriately but not to the extent that the patient feels coerced into an ethos of work which is discordant with their own principles.

As I have made clear, it is necessary to keep in mind the patient's own values. It is for these reasons that professional concern is felt about practitioners who are involved in working alliances with patients where there seems to be a desire to seek power over the patient, or where there seems to be a need in the psychotherapist to heal their own narcissistic wounds, such that each reference to the psychotherapist rewards their own inner world. These are instances where supervision needs to address aspects of the supervisee's own pathology.

In terms of personality, psychopathology and therapeutic alliance, it is therefore necessary to have a good enough therapeutic fit if a good working alliance is to be formed. It is also essential for the psychotherapist to be well enough analysed in order to detect the conscious and unconscious processes which come into play between them and their patients.

Ethical issues raised in working with impasse, autism and negative therapeutic reaction

In working with patients in psychotherapy, often the most difficult circumstances, in terms of ethics in practice, arise when the work becomes stuck in some way. This may be as a result of impasse or an autistic state or negative therapeutic reaction into which the patient enters.

Such cases bring to mind considerations about the quality of the therapeutic alliance and the competence of the practitioner; they often become either the central cases for discussion with colleagues or those cases that are never discussed in the supervision or consultation process. These may be situations that are capable of being worked with if they are understood by the psychotherapist, or they may become 'failures in analysis or failures of analysis' (Hillman 1975: 100). They raise ethical questions for the practitioner about whether the therapy should be concluded when the patient is in a state that might be considered as impasse or an unresolved autistic state or a negative therapeutic reaction and whether anything can be done to change or resolve the situation. (Issues around stopping and ending are addressed in Chapter 7.)

Bateman and Holmes (1995) have described impasse in analysis as 'a state in which the analysis neither progresses nor retreats'. They remark that 'the setting itself is not noticeably changed, the patient continues to talk, apparently free-associating, the analyst interprets, but nothing changes or develops'. They say that it is tempting to see impasse 'either as arising out of a technical fault on the part of the practitioner or from the patient's resistance'. They do not see it as a technical problem but, like Clark (1995), see it as 'a tangled knot created by the patient's psychopathology and the analyst's countertransference' (Bateman and Holmes 1995: 188). Thus Bateman and Holmes develop a discussion which can also be seen as an ethical argument about responsibility in therapeutic work.

> Impasse can be seen in a case where a patient, who had already had a lengthy analysis, entered training. As a result she was required to change to another psychotherapist. In the new therapy she became very regressed and silent: she felt unable to communicate with her psychotherapist. The psychotherapist continued to interpret and felt that the work was progressing adequately. The patient said later that she recognized that she experienced paranoid anxieties, particularly about what her analyst thought of her. Her negative feelings were not picked up and eighteen months later she left her analysis and her training. In this case the patient had moved into an autistic space in this analysis.

Tustin (1991: 585) writes of autism as 'an early developmental deviation in the service of dealing with unmitigated terror'. Her recognition of one of the adult manifestations of autism as trauma is important to our example, where the result of a catastrophic move in therapy was a re-enacted experience of early loss and associated terror. This understanding helps to remind us of the primitiveness of the patient's reaction in a case like this. The case raises ethical issues because the practitioner was unaware of the patient's difficulty and therefore her understanding was not alerted.

Winnicott (1958: 195) sees the difficulty that the practitioner is in with this patient as being one of unresolved inner conflict. He believes that the analysis of the practitioner should deal with all unresolved inner conflicts in the practitioner, and while practising, the analyst will deal with any unresolved material from their own analysis through further analysis. Rosenfeld

(1987) and Bateman and Holmes (1995) agree that this is a problem of countertransference, a pathological difficulty in the practitioner and feel that they should look to their own consultation or analysis for a solution. The problem again is that the practitioner may not be aware of the difficulty, emphasizing the importance of regular supervision.

In psychoanalytic literature an autistic state is largely seen as an indicator of the presence of primitive defences and is an indicator of severe pathology. However, a different understanding and attitude is represented by Kalsched (1996), an analytical psychologist, who sees autism as an expression of a life-saving defence of the self, functioning as 'part of the psyche's archetypal self-care system' (Kalsched 1996: 4). He views the psyche of the candidate, in our example, as protecting itself in a healthy way, he values her defences as a protection from an intolerable trauma experienced at the change of psychotherapist. However, there is also an ethical issue here since the patient in this scenario loses not only her original psychotherapist but also her training.

While considering how analysis can break down we must include the concept of negative therapeutic reaction. This concept was formulated by analysts who felt that their interpretations were sound, but became aware that their interpretations were making their patients worse rather than better. Freud (1923, 1937) saw it as a matter of primal masochism, Abraham (1919) as narcissistic character resistance, Klein (1975) and Kernberg (1975) as unconscious envy resulting in a compulsion to spoil the analytic work. They all interpreted the situation as resulting from intrapsychic mechanisms located within the patient.

However, more recently, it has increasingly been understood and reflected in the work of Stolorow *et al.* (1983) that these situations may result from 'prolonged, unrecognised inter-subjective disjunctions wherein the patient's emotional needs are consistently misunderstood and thereby relentlessly rejected by the therapist' (Atwood *et al.* 1989: 557–8). Again such a misunderstanding could well have been the experience of the candidate in training in our example resulting in interpretations which made no sense to the candidate and thus increased her frustration.

Certainly impasse, autism and negative therapeutic reaction have been considered in depth in the literature, by the authors already mentioned and others such as Schafer (1973) and Tustin (1972, 1991). Concerns which touch on values arising in clinical practice or in supervision have been addressed by these authors and others such as London (1989) and Levy (1995). Yet none of them has considered these clinical difficulties other than from the standpoint of good practice. Here I consider them as potentially presenting an ethical issue to the practitioner.

When an impasse is recognized by either the analyst or the patient it can be worked on within the sessions in whatever way the analyst and patient find helpful. As we have seen above, the difficulties arise when it is not. In these circumstances where the feelings are unspoken or unconscious or they are not expressed or interpreted, conflict or collusion may be occurring.

We also need to think about the factors within psychotherapists' practice which make the therapeutic alliance or practice vulnerable to an autistic encapsualization (more likely with a psychotic or borderline patient) or to a negative therapeutic reaction (more likely with a neurotic patient). These are situations where the analyst's attitudes may be a source of concern in terms of ethics and values. It is also necessary to look at the part played in these states of conflict or collusion between analyst and patient.

The practitioner and the patient need to be able to function together in such a way that the therapeutic work can take place and the patient can feel sufficiently understood. This functioning may form through a respect for each other's values or perhaps, more constructively, through working on and with these values so that a shared ethos is formed within the therapy itself. (See also Chapter 9 on the need for a convergence in values.) I am concerned here with both the patient's and the practitioner's conscious and unconscious needs and beliefs and whether they conflict or collude with one another so resulting in the analytic sessions not benefiting the patient.

> Consider the case of patient A who entered analysis and almost immediately felt an intolerable tension because, while experiencing violent fantasies, he also felt he must protect his psychotherapist. He was fully aware of his ambivalent feelings, but, since the psychotherapist was old and well respected, he felt that he should be grateful and protect his therapist from the destructive part of his thoughts. The psychotherapist did not hear the various indirect communications of his ambivalence and the analysis became stuck. The patient realized that his analyst was not aware of his negative feelings; he thought he had communicated his distress and eventually he left the therapy.

Situations like this where there is ambivalence require the practitioner to realize what is going on, to listen to the covert communications and to manage the therapeutic situation. They show us that a therapeutic alliance may, in some cases, never be established.

What may have been going on for the psychotherapist and why may she not have heard what was being said to her by her patient? She may have had a particular idealization of the patient's social position or working world or she may have found aspects of her patient's history unacceptable (say the analyst was Jewish and the patient German). Either situation could have upset or perverted the transference and countertransference and caused a conflict in the work which was not acknowledged or worked with.

> In another case, patient B and his analyst repeatedly made the kinds of errors that put each other out. The patient came late, the therapist

forgot to tell the patient about an appointment she needed to cancel, and the patient turned up for an appointment during an agreed holiday time. Each felt that the other was damaging them in the therapy and while the analyst struggled to interpret, the patient felt that he did not understand the point of the analyst's interventions.

The practitioner needs to work with such situations, since the material can be grist to the mill and help to form an understanding of the negative therapeutic transference. There are aspects of both of these cases that are familiar to us all. In most cases these problems could be worked through in the therapy but in each case something has gone wrong between the psychotherapist and the patient. The situation has deteriorated, or could deteriorate and become one of impasse so that the therapeutic link is broken.

What can we do about these problems in practice? Where does the responsibility lie for the therapy? Rosenfeld (1987) ascribes most blockages in the patient–analyst interaction to the analyst's unconscious infantile anxieties. The analyst colludes with a complementary part of the patient's personality and thus avoids becoming aware of these areas. Therefore in cases of deadlock psychotherapists have to examine very carefully their own values, as expressed in beliefs, countertransferences and feelings, and look for signs of collusion with the patient. If necessary they should seek psychotherapy once again for themselves.

Rosenfeld (1987) states that it is important to distinguish an impasse from a negative therapeutic reaction which follows a period of progress. A true impasse develops slowly, almost imperceptibly, and is only recognised when the analysis remains static or the patient seems fixed in a particular frame of mind. Interpreting hostility will be incomprehensible to the patient, as well as unfair, since the analyst's reactions are involved as well. In contrast, hostility, often in the form of manic defences, or manic attacks in acting out in the external world, usually underlies a negative therapeutic reaction and may appropriately be taken up as envy of, and triumph over the analyst. Bion (1963) expresses some hope of resolution in seeing an impasse based on 'reversible perspective' which may be so subtle as to be undetected in the therapeutic work. The patient seems to come for one reason but has a covert agenda. Here we return to Clark's (1995) ideas and the complex unconscious aims that motivate people to explore therapy.

In one of the cases described above, Mr A wanted an analysis but chose someone who was vulnerable to him and to whom he was also vulnerable. Mr B's ambivalence was unconscious and acted out; it also affected the countertransference in the analyst. Both cases underline that the practitioner has a responsibility for the work in an ethical sense, and that the practitioner needs to be vigilant if the needs of the patient are to be thoroughly addressed.

Role and pressures of psychotherapy institutions

To this point I have discussed some of the ethical issues that are raised in working with individual patients. For many psychotherapists and patients there is another pressure and influence, namely the analytic or psychotherapy institution.

Analytic and psychotherapy training normally takes place in a highly formalized way which models the way of working with patients. While this therapeutic method of working has an important containing effect, much in psychotherapeutic practice may have gone unchallenged because of the personal commitment and sacrifice each practitioner will have made during their own experience of analysis. This will have reinforced their belief in its efficacy in that particular form. Therefore practitioners may feel challenged by those who question their method of working since they have been formed in it and have made such a high investment in it.

The consequences of the difficulties and states of impasse in and between our analytic and psychotherapeutic institutions are legion. We are not alone in this as all organizations suffer from time to time in these ways. However, since we do have some understanding of the conscious and unconscious processes that affect organizations we have a particular responsibility to address these difficulties. An example is where a difficulty between a patient and psychotherapist or candidate and psychotherapist may become a difficulty for the organization itself. Or an impasse within an organization may be projected on to a candidate or patient, thus releasing the organization, for a time, from dealing with its own difficulties.

These parallel processes can be particularly problematic at all times of assessment. Candidates may get involved in reflecting difficulties between their supervisor and training analyst, or the assessment committee may reflect, by a parallel process, the difficulties between the patient and the training therapist. Psychotherapists can themselves get into difficulties when qualifying as supervisors or training therapists with the organization in which they now play a political part. Thus projective mechanisms and parallel processes affect and infect the functioning of the organization as a whole. The organization's capacity to handle these situations depends on the shared understanding of collective values of its members and the establishment of an ethos that allows for these situations to be dealt with in a fair and just way.

Isabel Menzies Lyth ([1986] 1989) speaks about the importance of parallel processes in therapeutic work, particularly where the patient becomes caught in some personal wrangle of the practitioner or in an institutional struggle where past struggles are replicated between patient and psychotherapist. She points out that weakness in the organizational setting intensifies the problem because the institution cannot act as a container and a collusive or corrupt identification takes place. She argues that when the situation is too large for the container of the organization, the situation will descend into opposition (Menzies Lyth [1986] 1989). We can see that she is referring to the defences of the organization being threatened and splitting mechanisms taking over. These may include terror, previously referred to in the work of Tustin (1991). Menzies Lyth suggests that something like this may be happening:

> There is within the [job] situation a focus of deep anxiety and distress. Associated with this there is despair about being able to improve matters. The defensive system collusively set up against these feelings consists, first, in fragmentation of the core problem so that it no longer exists in an integrated and recognisable form consciously and openly among those concerned. Secondly, the fragments are projected onto aspects of the ambience of the situation which are then consciously and honestly, but mistakenly, experienced as the problem about which something needs to be done, usually by someone else. Responsibility has also been fragmented and often projected into unknown others – 'Them', the authorities ... Such defensive reactions to institutional problems often mean the institution cannot really learn.
>
> (Menzies Lyth [1986] 1989: 30)

At every level, the practitioner and those responsible within the organization need to keep the importance of these processes in mind. Because institutions have real difficulties managing outer reality they get involved in developing defences in order to deal with the anxiety-provoking content of the perceived threat or the difficulties in collaborating to accomplish a common task.

Analytic and psychotherapy institutions are particularly inclined to produce individuals, couples and groups who provoke all the complex and collusive transferences of the membership. As members of these organizations we need to develop the capacity to recognize how the unconscious mind of the collective group is reflected in terms of content and dynamics; and how these contents and dynamics affect the conscious thoughts, feelings, speech and behaviour of all the members of the organization.

When a particular group of people has formed an organization, they have shaped its outer structures (for example its constitution) to reflect themselves and their relationships. The structures will also reflect their strengths and weaknesses. Thus when they decide to retire or leave, the organization is doubly bereaved. It loses not only their founding energy but also an effective working structure, because it may not be possible for those who follow on to fit into the particular combinations of roles of the founding group. It takes time for the organization to realize its predicament and to find the courage and energy to make the necessary structural and psychological changes (Palmer Barnes 1998: 14).

In the meantime there may be practitioners who feel that as a result of their close alignment with the founders, they are silenced or that they take the brunt of angry feelings towards the 'abandoning parents'. They may take up the position of the autistic one or feel that they are the butt of a negative reaction. Often they are sacrificed in the splitting process, having become the bad objects of the organization. Therefore, when unconscious behaviour becomes defensive or aggressive there is a real need to step back and adopt an analytic stance.

Equally the organization can become subject to projective identificatory processes. For example if the organization is made to feel the distress of its members, it will develop unconscious defence systems to deal with it. For instance, if an agency deals mainly with drug patients its administrative structure can find itself behaving in very addictive ways. Moylan (1994) observes:

> By knowing about ways in which the organisation can become 'infected' by the difficulties and defences of their particular clientele, members and those in authority we are more able to deal with them.
>
> (Moylan 1994: 59)

In organizations there is also conscious and unconscious collusive inter-action. These situations need to be seen as those of 'deintegration' in Fordham's (1985) terms, allowing a 'reintegration' to take place if the problem is understood or resolved. However, the terror of the schizoid process within the organization may cause the organization to 'disintegrate' when impasse occurs (Fordham 1985).

According to Menzies Lyth ([1986] 1989) the solution lies in a knowledge of the past, of the developmental history of the organization, in other words in the creation of its values. Then, she would posit, if it is flexible it will have a capacity to grow and create a new position. This very much parallels Jung's (1997) idea of the importance for the individual having a capacity to develop a 'new attitude' if the individual is to progress. Menzies Lyth ([1986] 1989) says that within psychotherapy organizations practitioners need to recognize and honour the loss of that which was, and to acknow-ledge the possibilities for the future while creating a new 'good enough' pos-ition to function from until the next change is necessary.

The value base of an analytic and psychotherapy organization and the strength of the common ethos is reflected in its ability to deal with its external and internal difficulties. Coping with these difficulties frees those who may be patients, candidates in training, psychotherapists and analysts from being embroiled in the processes of the organizations themselves.

Psychotherapy and analytic organizations therefore need to think about the influence they have on the ethos of practitioners. The practitioners in their turn may need to think about what their own principles and values are, how they may differ from their professional institution, how in return they may shape their professional organization, and what overall effect values may be having on candidates and clients.

Conclusion

The values and attitudes of both patient and psychotherapist clearly have great importance in the work between them. Though many may see most of the issues I have raised as practice issues to be thought about in supervision, they are matters which may arise when the practitioner is working near to the limits of their competence. The thesis of this chapter is that many of these issues also concern ethical principles and should be discussed in this light. I suggest that they arise in every practice and need to be struggled with as part of the work.

I have also posited that the internal dynamics of training organizations can play a part in the analysis of trainees, analysts, candidates and psychotherapists. The workings of these organizations and their good health are ethical issues and the responsibility of all their members.

In understanding the importance of the therapeutic alliance and the complexities of the relationship that develops between analyst and patient, or analyst or psychotherapist and their organization, we can recognize many of the difficulties which arise from working with the split-off parts of patients, which in their turn evoke 'parallel process' responses from the analyst.

Difficulties arise from time to time which cause the work of psychotherapy or analysis or the organizations themselves to become stuck in one way or another. The patient may stop coming, the candidate may give up or be failed in their training, or the analyst may be attacked or give up the work of therapy. Each of these cases are worth considering from an ethical point of view because the patient, candidate or psychotherapist has changed their view about the value of the therapy, training or practice they were involved in. Similarly an organization, once factions have developed over some dogma or other type of conflict, may lose a group of therapists who will form a new association. This may be viewed positively or negatively in the long run; but it inevitably entails a real loss for both factions including loss of colleagues and friends. What is important is the way it is done. If the conscious and unconscious processes can be captured and discussed in supervision, intervision, consultation or within the organization itself too, it may be possible to contain these for the patient, psychotherapist or organization and move towards a positive outcome. Then there may be a shared understanding of collective values, a new ethos among its members and the all-important therapeutic work can progress in ethically responsible ways.

References

Abraham, K. (1919) A particular form of neurotic resistance against the psychoanalytic method, *Selected Papers on Psychoanalysis*. New York: Basic Books.

Atwood, G., Stolorow, R. and Trop, J. (1989) Impasses in psychoanalytic therapy: a royal road, *Contemporary Psychoanalysis*, 25: 154–73.

Austin, S. (1999) Women's aggressive fantasies: a post-Jungian hermeneutic, in R.K. Papadapoulos (ed.) *Harvest*. London: Analytical Psychology Club.

Bateman, A. and Holmes, J. (1995) *Introduction to Psychoanalysis*. London: Routledge.

Beebe, J. (1984) Psychological types in transference, countertransference, and the therapeutic interaction, in N. Schwartz-Salant and M. Stein (eds) *Transference/Countertransference*. Wilmette, IL: Chiron.

Beebe, J. (1998) Towards a Jungian analysis of character, in A. Casement (ed.) *Post-Jungians Today*. London: Routledge.

Bion, W. (1961) A theory of thinking, *International Journal of Psychoanalysis*, 43.

Bion, W. (1963) *Elements of Psychoanalysis*. London: Heinemann.

Bion, W.R. ([1967]1988) Notes on memory and desire, in E. Bott Spillius (ed.) *Melanie Klein Today: Developments in Theory and Practice*, vol. 2. London: Tavistock/Routledge.

Clark, G. (1995) How much Jungian theory is there in my practice?, *Journal of Analytical Psychology*. 40(3): 345.

Coltart, N. (1987) Diagnosis and assessment for suitability for psycho-analytical psychotherapy, *British Journal of Psychotherapy*, 4(2): 127–34.

Fordham, M. (1985) *Explorations into the Self*. London: Academic Press.

Freud, S. (1923) The Ego and the Id, *Standard Edition* 19. London: Hogarth Press.

Freud, S. (1937) Analysis terminable and interminable, *Standard Edition* 23. London: Hogarth Press.

Hillman, J. (1975) *Loose Ends*. Zurich: Spring.

Jung, C.G. (1971) *Collected Works: Psychological Types*, vol. 6. London: Routledge & Kegan Paul.

Jung, C.G. (1977) *Collected Works*, vol. 7. London: Routledge & Kegan Paul.

Kalsched, D. (1996) *The Inner World of Trauma*. London: Routledge.

Kernberg, O. (1975) *Borderline Conditions and Pathological Narcissism*. New York: Jason Aronson.

Klien, M. (1975) Envy and Gratitude, in *Envy and Gratitude and Other Works 1946–1963*. London: Hogarth Press.

Levy, J. (1995) Analytic stalemate and supervision, *Psychoanalytic Inquiry*, 15(2): 169–89.

London, A. (1989) Unconscious hatred of the analyst and its displacement to a patient and supervisor, *Modern Psychoanalysis*, 14(2): 197–220.

Menzies Lyth, I. ([1986] 1989) The dynamics of the social: a psychoanalytic perspective on social institutions, Freud Memorial Lecture, *Selected Essays*. London: Free Association.

Moylan, D. (1994) The dangers of contagion: projective identification processes in institutions, in A. Obholzer and V.Z. Roberts (eds) *The Unconscious at Work*. London: Routledge.

Palmer Barnes, F. (1998) *Complaints and Grievances in Psychotherapy*. London: Routledge.

Redfearn, J. (1992) *The Exploding Self*. Wilmette, IL: Chiron.

Rosenfeld, H. (1987) *Impasse and Interpretation*. London: Tavistock.

Schaffer, R. (1973) The idea of resistance, *International Journal of Psychoanalysis*, 54: 259.

Stolorow, R.D., Brandschaft, B. and Atwood, G.E. (1983) Intersubjectivity in psychoanalytic treatment, *Bulletin of the Menninger Clinic*, 47: 117–28.

Tustin, F. (1972) *Autism and Child Psychosis*. New York: Arnson.

Tustin, F. (1991) Revised understandings of psychogenic autism, *International Journal of Psychoanalysis*, 72: 585–91.

Winnicott, D.W. (1958) Hate in the countertransference, *Through Paediatrics to Psycho-Analysis*. London: Hogarth Press.

7 Success and failure

Lesley Murdin

Lady Macbeth: Nought's had, all's spent
Where our desire is got without content;
'Tis safer to be that which we destroy
Than by destruction dwell in doubtful joy.

(*Macbeth* 3.2)

Introduction

Western capitalism invites us to contemplate images of success. We can accept or reject particular kinds of success, but we are oriented to think of change in terms of progress or regress and movement in terms of forwards or backwards. Psychoanalysis has its own forms of success and failure that need to be recognized because they will pervade any therapy. Absolute success is impossible in psychoanalysis. Where two people come together, there are likely to be two different agendas at least in the beginning. Sometimes the client will be seeking something which the therapist considers to be undesirable or harmful or simply irrelevant to the project of psychoanalysis or analytic psychotherapy. Of course we have no universally agreed agenda except perhaps in very broad terms. In any given case, therapist and client must find out what each values and how a degree of success might be possible.

In this chapter I consider some elements of the image of success in psychotherapy for therapist and client and I propose that these images need to converge during the process of therapy if the outcome is to be satisfactory to both. The agenda for the activity of psychotherapy depends to some extent on the theoretical training of the therapist and on the formation of the individual's personal value system. One of the purposes of psychotherapy might be to turn the client into an ethicist, as Tjeltveit (1999) argues. Clients need to be able to assess their own value system and weigh their own actions against it. The touchstone must be the client's own morality but it will have mutated through contact with the therapist. Value systems must become as conscious as possible and this will be necessary both for success in the search for the truth for each person and also for discovering how and when an ending to the work might be possible.

The analytic model implies that absolute success must be avoided. Adam Phillips (1997) argues that we all fear having too much of what we want. Mental processes are based on a body image, and the physiological template of success for all the strivings of the instincts could be seen as survival. Survival itself is a perpetual struggle, never complete, and if it were the only goal of the libidinal instincts, it would lead to inevitable failure in death. Perhaps Freud's death instinct is a satisfactory concept inasmuch as it makes death itself a goal. We all 'achieve' death. Freud, however, was more inclined to take satisfactory sexuality as the goal of the libidinal instincts and therefore a potential achievement for successful psychotherapy. Orgasm might be taken as a model of success in bodily terms. It can be enjoyed but it must not extinguish desire.

Success, therefore, can be only partial and must leave room for the regaining of a state of desire. In the same way, psychotherapy is expected to achieve some partial success in the client's terms but must leave much to be still achieved. Most dangerous is to have too much of what you want so that you lack desire.

These are goals as they might be conceptualized by psychotherapists. Many clients in psychotherapy, however, come with the hope of achieving the *ordinary* goals of human life, or maximizing their chances of achieving them. A baby is both the symbol for the new beginning and, in many cases, is the literal object of longing. External successes such as a new job or a new partner may be sought. Some people come to therapy because they are isolated and they seek a relationship, but therapy is a dead end if it becomes the end in itself.

Shakespeare's Macbeth has a value system in which his ideals are loyalty, kinship, hospitality, life itself. He runs into serious difficulties because his wife has different values. She places ambition, status, courage and ruthlessness above any of Macbeth's values. She cannot be content with the obvious compromises: waiting for King Duncan to die naturally or enjoying the honours that Macbeth already had. Success for Lady Macbeth implies the achievement of status as valued in her society and culture. Her ideal is an image of a certain sort of power. She makes the mistake of assuming that she will be satisfied with gaining what she thought she wanted. She neglects the inevitable truth that the person who gets something in the future is not the same as the person who wants it now. In the first part of the play, Macbeth is persuaded by his own darker wishes to go along with Lady Macbeth. They are not able to achieve a negotiated convergence of values based on their better selves and the result is their own destruction, bringing many others with them.

Very often the course of therapy involves a change either in values themselves or in the way that they are applied, but that must not imply one person submitting to the force of will of the other. The values that underlie the two different concepts of success and failure must be modified and achieve genuine convergence if the outcome is to be satisfactory. Each new client comes to a therapist with values that are different from the therapist's own and may be not only different, but also alien. These values, like the therapist's, are partly conscious and partly concealed as unarticulated imperatives. The client may arrive with a clear idea of what success and failure both in the therapy itself and outside in the world might mean. The value attached to a certain kind of success might well constitute a problem in the eyes of the therapist. It might form the nexus of a whole set of painful and counterproductive ideas, images and strivings. On the other hand, some people arrive with only a vague notion of what is the matter or what they would like to achieve in therapy: 'I just want to feel better'. Others have more grand designs: 'I would like to be happy'; 'I would like a good relationship'. For these people, the therapist might try to find specific goals especially if the therapy is time limited.

Because of the various ways in which goals can be set or unconsciously pursued in therapy, each therapist has several possible ways of perceiving the desirable outcomes of the therapy process. The psychoanalytic therapist may prefer to have no view at all of what is desirable for a given client, but sets out only to analyse what the client brings. If this stance can be maintained, this kind of therapist is likely to move the client towards a less goal-oriented approach to outcomes. In fact the outcome of such a therapy might be to decline to accept the need for goals, and to suggest instead living more on the basis of seeing what happens from day to day. A reason must then be found to end therapy. It may be ostensibly for external reasons such as a move or a new job. In fact, the reason for ending will be that the client has become sufficiently like the therapist for both to know that the newly acquired attitude is in itself a sufficiently successful outcome.

If therapist and client can agree a set of goals this may help towards a satisfactory outcome but each partner will have unconscious agendas and resistances which will hinder or altogether sabotage the work. To avoid the conflict inherent in depth work, clients may limit themselves by setting goals that both they and the therapist think are achievable. A variation of this approach is to take the agreement of goals to be in itself the successful outcome of therapy. Thus the client arrives with one sort of desire, such as to get on better with a partner. A successful outcome might be achieved in discovering that the relationship is unlikely to improve and the client sets a new goal of fulfilling their creative potential. Both client and therapist might then consider that therapy is complete when the goal is established, but not yet achieved.

When the desire of the client is for something specific to be achieved within the therapy, the therapist may well accept the client's goal, but the fact that the goals are mutual does not mean that the technique to be used is mutually agreed. Usually techniques are not agreed because they are not known to the client. For example, both may agree with such goals as: 'I would like to be cured of my obsessional thinking or my bulimia'. Very often in such cases, achieving the goal depends on an indirect approach, not meeting the symptoms head on, which merely strengthens the unconscious resistance of the client. An indirect approach might involve delving into other conflicts or deficits first, and ignoring the symptom. Some clients respond well to such a slow but thorough method whereas others might not be able or willing to wait. Successful therapy may imply therapy in which the client becomes willing to allow the process to take place in its own way and at its own speed.

Patience and trust are desirable qualities in the client. Therapists on the other hand must decide to what extent they are going to function as an ethicist in the relationship with the client. Tjeltveit (1999) usefully examines the concept of therapist neutrality and comes to the conclusion that therapists should be neutral in some ways but not others. The usual view is that if therapists do not communicate their ethical views, but remain ethically anonymous, their clients are more easily able to make their own choices. This, in practice, is not possible. Therapists are bound to show their value system to some degree, even if mainly in relation to the therapeutic process itself, for example honesty, flexibility. Tjeltveit himself is in favour of minimizing the ethical influence of the therapist. That is, the therapist does not imply for example that a person who is a teacher is 'really' trying to remedy the difficulties in their own family by vicariously helping other children, thus devaluing the teaching. Tjeltveit believes that ethical questions should be addressed in therapy. But he does not go as far as, for example, Doherty (1995) who refers to helping individuals 'to discover and apply for themselves the moral rules they already as social beings possess' (Tjeltveit 1999: 182). This intuitionist view of ethics implies that everyone has a moral sense which needs only to be discovered and drawn out. If this were accepted, the psychotherapist's problem would be less severe than if dealing with an empty slate on which anything can be written, where the temptation to write the therapist's words is greater.

Everyone has some sort of value system but it may be distorted in its application by experience, which may have given rise to envy, guilt and any of the emotions which lead to impasse, such as those described by Palmer Barnes in Chapter 6. If we could distinguish distortion in the client's own ability to evaluate, from the client simply holding values that are different from our own, we might be some way towards an attitude to goals in therapy which takes account of values but does not seek to make everyone-like the therapist. Seeing the client's view of life as a distortion does of course imply a value judgement from the therapist and carries a risk of attempting to exert too much influence. Given that the client arrives with some difficulty in judgement or in ability to perceive self and the world, the therapist should presumably be in a better position to judge than the client, given that the therapist not only has been in personal therapy but also is expected to have a greater ability to perceive what the client is like and what the client is doing. Hinshelwood (1997) discusses the difficulty in taking autonomy as an aim of psychotherapy. Clients arrive with neurotic distortions in their thinking. No one guarantees that the process of therapy will enable anyone to think so clearly that such distortions can be avoided, but the hope is that they will be less prominent. The therapist also has distortions but has presumably tried to become more aware of what they are, and therefore better at recognizing them in others.

Hinshelwood (1997) characterizes recent psychoanalytic theory as being concerned with vertical splits rather than the horizontal splits that preoccupied Freud. Both the horizontal Freudian split between what is repressed and what is conscious and the Kleinian vertical split between good and bad, between what is acknowledged to be *me* and what I prefer to think of as *someone else*, are attempts to conceptualize the difference between what is known at any given time to consciousness and what is potentially available for the future. This implies that at the beginning of therapy, large areas of potential functioning are unavailable to consciousness. The logical conclusion is that *clients are* not in the best state to make judgements about what they need or whether they have achieved all that is possible. Part of the problem is that they might well think that they can make that judgement. Clients are often concerned only with pain versus happiness. For them the only criterion of success is that the pain should hurt less.

Achieving a greater degree of consciousness for the client may be the goal of the therapist, but may not be high on the client's list of priorities. It may involve greater suffering on the way. Clients may therefore consider that they will suffer less if they leave therapy. The therapist is in a position to recognise splitting and other forms of pathology and therefore may disagree and encourage the client to wait. In many cases clients exert their power to make a decision to leave and do so whether or not the therapist agrees. On the other hand, there are occasions when clients ask the therapist to make the decision or at least allow the therapist to influence it. In this situation therapists vary greatly in their practice. At such a point, the therapist may value increasing consciousness to the point of keeping the client if at all possible; or may value autonomy and self-determination to the extent of letting the client go even if more therapy is needed and could be valuably used.

Take the following situation:

Mr A has come to a woman therapist to seek help because he finds himself unable to have an erection when he is with his girl friend, whom he loves. He finds out with the therapist's help that he is projecting some aspects of his mother on to his girl friend. When he sees this, he begins an affair with a woman at work. He says that this is purely sexual and he does not intend to continue with it. He is hiding the affair from his girl friend. He is now cured of his impotence and decides to leave therapy. The therapist is very distressed at this decision and believes that he is now splitting his mother into the sexual projection on to the new woman and the admired loved part of his mother who is still projected on to his girl friend. She tells Mr A that she is glad that he has found the sexual side of himself but she thinks he should stay in therapy with her until he discovers how to bring the sexual and loving attitudes to a woman together with one woman. He gives her a rather meaningful look and says that perhaps he will stay a bit longer after all.

The therapist appears to have influenced his decision and perhaps also done this in a way which he could interpret as seductive. The therapist is aware of this but considers that she can deal with any erotic transference that emerges and in any case, it is better for him to stay and experience it with her than to go out and ruin other women's lives. Mr A is willing to stay because he has now changed his idea of what success in therapy might mean. He no longer considers his girl friend as essential to him and would rather try to seduce the therapist, who already has all the qualities of the ideal woman in his eyes.

Therapists who have no hesitation in saying that the client should stay longer are effectively saying that the end justifies the means. Is it ethical to try to keep someone in therapy by the power of being the therapist even when one knows that in the present there is a good deal of suffering and no guarantee of a better outcome? The therapist who does so no doubt believes that continuing therapy gives more chance of a satisfactory outcome than would arise from allowing it to end precipitously.

Mr A may force the therapist to change her view of him and although the value of therapy may not change in her eyes, the value of her work for this particular client may need to be seen differently. The client displays the difficulty that he has in forming appropriate sexual relationships and the therapist has to work out her response to this situation. She can do this by imputing all difficulty and probable failure to the client, or she can see the task as a puzzle for both to work upon to find the way out of the impasse. Resistance to change is the daily bread of any therapist's practice, which shades into the difficulties of the negative therapeutic reaction. Mr A's behaviour can be seen as the client's refusal to get better; it can also be seen as the client demonstrating what still needs to be analysed.

Therapists' own criteria for success and failure are based on their thera-peutic model combined with the residual transference to their own therapist and supervisors. These values are relatively stable. The therapist of course also has personal values that are conscious and unconscious, which may need to be applied differently according to the process of a particular therapy. The therapist nevertheless has certain parameters which may not change although they may allow for different degrees of achievement. Therapists cluster mainly in schools of thought which put emphasis on:

- development and deficits of security or affection that have led to diffi-culties in relating or in self-image
- conflict and the dynamic struggle between the instincts and the forces that control and defend against their excesses
- subjectivity and the construction of the subject by the context and the dis-course in which the subject is situated.

For example, one therapist is likely to value a client's achievement of aware-ness of the context in which he or she is formed and the extent to which he or she is constructed by the wishes and desires of others. Another may value the self-assurance that comes from reliable attention from the therapist, making up for what parents could not do. These different emphases might not be problematic in that clients might be able to benefit from whatever model the therapist is following. On the other hand, there is an ethical prob-lem in that clients usually have no idea what they are likely to get from a therapist and therefore are not choosing their treatment in any meaningful sense. However much therapists wish to convey their intentions, they are not able to do so because each therapy is unique and each therapist's own nature and character also enters the picture. These are variables that are of vital importance but are impossible to measure. Jeremy Holmes (1997) has shown that the attachment styles of clients and therapists affect the process and outcome of therapy.

To understand the interaction of the concepts of success and failure with psychoanalytic goals it is necessary to consider how the ego ideal is formed since it is a conceptualization of the capacity to form positive valuations. In 1914 Freud wrote of the ego ideal as the relic of the first disillusionment. Infants begin with no concept of another. They feel the whole world to be themselves and therefore are completely self-sufficient. Frustration and dis-appointment lead to recognition that there is another person: usually the mother who feeds them and the ideal that was themselves is then projected on to her.

From then on the ego ideal is located outside the self and is the remnant of primary narcissism. It is the prototype and pattern of the unobtainable and implies always that more is sought than can be found. In writing about sexuality, Freud (1912: 180) interpreted the need for something not to be achieved: 'we must reckon with the possibility that something in the sexual instinct itself is unfavourable to the realisation of complete satisfaction'. And 'there is always something lacking for complete satisfaction – *en attendant toujours quelque chose qui ne venait point*' (Freud 1938: 300).

In this view, the ideal is the breast when it was felt to be part of oneself, always accessible, never under the control of another. It is therefore always beyond reach once it has been lost to the recognition that it is owned by another. For this reason, the ideal may be projected on to another person or thing or a state to be achieved, but it means that whatever is achieved will be disappointing because it will not be the restoration of the original state of bliss. Descriptions of heaven usually convey the desire to return to paradise and to achieve happiness which can never again be lost.

The process of therapy goes through vicissitudes which can be charted in terms of the search for the ego ideal and the attempt to accept the impossibility of finding it. The therapist may play a part as the ideal for a time and may carry the ideal of the self-image that the client wishes to achieve. This is gradually dispelled by the natural process in which the therapist is able to show weakness and vulnerability and make mistakes without either the client or the therapist being destroyed. If this can be achieved, the ego ideal is taken back and can be understood and perhaps in future projected on to other achievements that will give satisfaction and not do too much harm:

> Making money (or despising it), owning a luxurious house (or vaunting a bohemian life style), dressing in an amusing or original way, raising handsome children, practising a religion, taking to drink, adopting a particular ideology, loving or being loved, writing an intelligent book, creating a work of art etc. – each of these may represent different ways of attempting to reduce the gap between the ego and its ideal.
>
> (Chasseguet Smirgel 1985: 8)

Clearly there might be scope for differences of opinion between therapist and client about the desirability of some of the criteria of success mentioned by Chasseguet Smirgel, but if they are seen as ways in which the client comes to terms with the unobtainable, then a degree of success can be seen in whatever the client is able to find satisfying as long as it does not conflict with the therapist's own personal morals or professional ethics. The important criterion would be that the client can recognize that whatever is being sought is not the ideal but is a temporary, more or less satisfying substitute for it.

A difficulty over focusing on an ideal that represents another hidden desire is often brought to therapists. It is exemplified in the misery of the woman in her thirties or forties who does not have a partner. The same problem arises with men but seems to acquire more urgency for women because they want to have children. Maybe for some, the partner is secondary to the need to have a child. The biological imperative is strong and the knowledge that time is limited leads to a very particular kind of emphasis on success and possible failure. No amount of rational understanding that having a child will not solve all problems is able to help or console the woman who is in this state. For her the only success worth having is in bearing a child. This is a case where the therapist's view is most likely to be different from that of the client even though that divergence may include a great deal of understanding of the difficulty and empathy with the bereavement or potential bereavement of childlessness.

> This is the presenting problem for Ms B. She has had several relationships with men that have ended for one reason or another and she is now almost 40. She has no current relationship and no immediate prospect of finding one. She tells me that there are no eligible men who are also available. All men in her age group are either with someone or completely hopeless. Yet all she wants is to find a man with whom she can have an 'ordinary life with a house and a mortgage and children'. She comes to therapy with the conscious knowledge that therapy cannot produce the desired man but also with the hope that it can somehow enable her to find one. She knows that I do not have the proverbial magic wand and yet she also hopes that I can turn sows' ears into silk purses, or rather, hopeless men into satisfactory partners. On enquiry I discover that there are men around who are not attached currently, but they all have something wrong with them.
>
> Therapy begins with Ms B having a much narrower and more specific idea of what success might be than I have. She does acknowledge that maybe changes in her will help her to face her future whatever that is, but her conscious hope is that she will be happier, and being happier means having a relationship. I understand that seeking a partner is a vital quest and that human beings must strive for it. I say that I understand it and yet my view of the purpose of psychotherapy is broader. I expect that the process will lead to a greater ability to tolerate pain and to enjoy pleasure. I expect that it will make the person who stays in therapy for a while into a better companion.
>
> In this latter respect my aim and the client's already converge, but my aim is broader. I do not know whether the work of psychotherapy will need to concentrate on coming to terms with living alone or in compromising in choosing a partner who is less than ideal. My idea of the purpose of the therapy is thus much more open ended and flexible than that of Ms B. At the moment her view is that the therapy will be a success if she finishes with a partner and a failure if she does not. My view is that even a small amount of improvement will be worth having.

Failure is not often acknowledged by therapists. We become expert at consoling ourselves for therapy which seems to achieve very little. Even when a client ends suddenly with or without explanation, we can say that maybe the reason was that the therapy was too successful in the sense that it opened new areas to consciousness and this was so painful that the client could not stand any more. Perhaps we would acknowledge a failure if the client actually made a complaint or left, demonstrating some sort of incontrovertible damage. Even in such cases, we are quick to find a possibility that what we are seeing is a demonstration of new-found strength or independence. Because success is relative and marked by a point on a continuum, we are able to put failure more or less off the scale and very rarely find that work has reached that point.

> The day-to-day process of therapy with Ms B takes account of some of the principles of psychoanalytic work in the hope that they will lead to a different view of what is important. I can see and point out the ways in which her need and her disappointment tend to alienate me and make me angry or frustrated with her. She alternates between finding the time with me useful and her own thoughts to be of interest, and a state in which nothing is any use and there is no point in making the effort to come to see me. When the latter state prevails, all I can usually do is point out that she is not always like that and that some part of her retains hope or she would not have come at all. These sorts of remarks are usually greeted with scorn.

When I am tired or depressed by the seeming hopelessness of the situation, I could console myself by holding forth about the nature of immortality, for example, saying that human immortality in the long run will be only in the elements that return to the Earth and eventually to the Universe because any line of descendants may die out. The Earth itself of course will die as will the solar system and the Galaxy and so on. None of this is the slightest consolation because the reason for wanting a baby is to hold in your arms someone who loves you totally and needs you totally. I know this and I also know that Ms B has reason to think that I have a partner and no doubt imagines that I have children. Envy enters the picture. In agreement with modern Kleinians, I can see that envy can be constructive. It can lead to emulation and identification with the envied object as well as to destruction. Macbeth and Lady Macbeth in a different universe might have admired and imitated the gracious King Duncan and not have murdered him.

> I try pointing out that there are ways in which Ms B can emulate her mother and ways in which she is bound to feel, as she did as a child, that she can never achieve what her mother has. She sees the solution of her envy of her mother as encapsulated in becoming a mother herself. In the bad state, she will certainly not allow me to have more

success as a mother than I already have. My efforts to change her values merely lead to 'What good is that? There is nothing I want if I cannot have a baby.'

In this situation there is a wide divergence between my idea of what might be a good outcome and that of Ms B. She has little hope, but has not given up completely. My hope is that the small remaining gleam of hope has to do with the life of Ms B in its own right and not only with the possibility of giving birth to another. Freud's symbolic equation, baby = penis = faeces, is useful in making me think of the whole issue of potency for a woman. A baby is not just a baby although I know that I cannot ignore what a baby actually is. It is also potency. In phantasy it will make up for all the helplessness and vulnerability in Ms B's past. If she can give birth to a new person, that will be rebirth for her at a symbolic level and it will also be the most immensely powerful act which will far outdo what any man could achieve. I therefore remember the father as the template of all men who are imperfect and fail you when you count on them. Having a baby gives a symbolic independence which means that the man might no longer be needed.

I struggle to say this in a way that might enable Ms B to step back from the raw pain of deprivation. She might be able to see that there are other ways of feeling powerful and self-activating. Having a baby is not the only kind of fulfilment. She is able to evade any value that this interpretative line might have for her. I shall not be able to move her as long as she sees me as trying to persuade her of something. This is particularly true if I am seen to be trying to persuade her to accept less than I have.

One of the most difficult feats for the therapist in this situation is to remain neutral without a fixed view of what should happen. The change that needs to take place in me is in some ways as difficult to achieve as the client's needed change. I have to reach a point where I can truthfully say to myself that I do not know what outcome this person needs and I cannot turn her into a wise sage who gives up her longing for a baby. If I can say this, I am giving up my own omnipotence and at least modelling the ability to wait and see what happens. In other words, I have to give up the idea of success and failure for Ms B.

I am able to make use of my own struggle because Ms B continues to come to see me and continues to express her desire for a man and a baby. And I continue to feel useless. I say that I suppose that, just like her father, I have to stand back and endure not being able to give her the one thing that she longs for more than anything else: a baby. I have to recognize that she is constantly saying to me that the one thing she wants from me is the one thing that I can never give. On the other hand I do not agree that my inability to be a lover or to give her a baby makes me completely useless. I say that I think there is perhaps some merit in waiting with her to see what will happen, which was all that her father could do.

This has the effect of calming the sessions and making the relationship more enjoyable from my point of view, and therefore, I think, from hers. I have perhaps shown her that it is possible to feel worth something even without having the particular kind of potency that is desired. Just as I can do without success with her, she may be able to find good substitutes, if she does not have a baby. I cannot give her enough of what she needs and I have to give up my own longing to be a successful therapist in order to help Ms B to find courage for what must be the ongoing struggle to survive and to be fruitful. Macbeth and Lady Macbeth would still not have had an easy time if Macbeth had won the argument and they had not murdered Duncan. But their success in making do with a more ordinary life would have been very different from the image of success that they chose to follow.

References

Chasseguet Smirgel, J. (1985) *The Ego Ideal*. London: Free Association.

Doherty, W.J. (1995) *Soul Searching: Why Psychotherapy Must Promote Moral Responsibility*. New York: Basic Books.

Freud, S. (1912) On the universal tendency to debasement in the sphere of love, *Standard Edition*, vol. 11. London: Hogarth Press.

Freud, S. (1914) On the history of the psychoanalytic movement, *Standard Edition*, vol. 14. London: Hogarth Press.

Freud, S. (1938) An outline of psychoanalysis, *Standard Edition*, vol. 23. London: Hogarth Press.

Hinshelwood, R. (1997) *Therapy or Co-ercion*. London: Free Association.

Holmes, J. (1997) Too early, too late: endings in psychotherapy – an attachment perspective, *British Journal of Psychotherapy*, 14(2): 159–71.

Phillips, A. (1997) *On Flirtation*. London: Faber & Faber.

Tjeltveit, A. (1999) *Ethics and Values in Psychotherapy*. London: Routledge.

8   Values and ethics in researching psychotherapy

Georgia Lepper

Introduction

Research will play a critical role in the ways in which psychotherapy will develop in the coming years. The 1970s, 1980s and 1990s witnessed the very rapid growth and professionalization of psychotherapy. This growth has occurred in the context of changing social attitudes from one in which the professions as a whole were revered, to one in which they are seen as services and, as such, subject to the expectations of consumers of any service for their worth and accountability. One implication of this change is that the value of the professional service may be scrutinized for its effectiveness, in terms both of the quality of the service delivered, and its cost. Does the service justify the resources, both personal and financial, expended on it? These are questions increasingly being asked by service providers and by consumers, and the answers are frequently being sought from research.

In the case of psychotherapy, these kinds of questions pose particularly acute problems. On the one hand, much psychotherapy is conducted in circumstances of complete privacy, with clients who may be in particularly vulnerable states of mind. The need to know about the potential benefits and possible ill effects of treatment in order to protect the client is therefore acute. On the other, for many practitioners the impingement of observation on the treatment for the purposes of research and critical study is unacceptable in view of the nature of the psychotherapeutic contract – its engagement with that which is most personal. How can these two competing needs be reconciled?

The subject of this book is values and ethics in psychotherapy. There is a distinction commonly made between ethics – adherence to a set of rules governing correct actions – and values – the worth of a thing. The notion of worth carries an additional distinction: intrinsic value and contributory value. A thing which may not have intrinsic value to an individual in that it is neither pleasure giving, nor immediately beneficial, may nevertheless have contributory value to the overall good. It may be that benefit is not directly experienced by the subject. Much research in social and behavioural science relies on this distinction, and on an appeal to individuals to contribute their, researcher-observed, experience in a way which may well not have intrinsic value to them, but which will contribute to the common good. What are the implications of such an appeal?

Issues raised by these questions have engaged moral philosophers who, since the early Greek thinkers, have debated the basis upon which the nature of human values can be judged. An important aspect of the consideration of what constitutes value is based upon the opposing positions of objectivism, according to which intrinsic moral principles of right and wrong are not contingent on individual judgement, or relativism, in which moral principles of right and wrong are historical and contingent on human action and judgement. There are many variants. (See Chapter 1 for a full discussion.) This basic dilemma also presents itself in the form of debates in the philosophy of science about the relationship of the scientist, as observer, to the observed, or data. Some hold that the material world exists independently of our knowledge of it, and that research into its nature, conducted according to the principles of scientific method, is 'value free'. The activities of research are agent neutral; they are guided solely by the procedures of scientific method. Others hold that science is constrained by the nature of knowledge, and that its methods are constituted, and constrained by, human judgement and values no less than any other human activity. Science is agent relative. Its practitioners are responsible for the consequences of their actions.

In the context of such debates, psychotherapy struggles to find its place as a discipline which can make its contribution to the understanding and relief of psychological suffering. The familiar range of these debates characterize the core understandings of what psychotherapy is, and what it can do. Is it a science, the correct practice of whose method will inevitably lead to an ultimately materialist understanding of the nature of human psychology? Freud, no less than the behavioural psychologists and contemporary cognitive scientists, sought to establish the materialist basis for the understanding of human psychology, and the scientific nature of his 'project': the investigation of the unconscious. Those psychotherapists who reacted to this materialist assumption (and they were not alone – similar shifts of theory and method were also occurring elsewhere in the social sciences), built and occupied an opposing camp. Psychotherapy, they held, was not a science, and could make no claims to objectivity. It is a subjective process, rooted in the experiences of the individual subject, whose rights and privacy are inviolable. It is therefore not agent neutral, but agent relative, and any research which is undertaken is consequently constrained and governed by the same considerations. Carl Rogers was an important figure in the growth of this perspective. He was also one of psychotherapy's early systematic researchers.

No full consideration of psychotherapy research can escape addressing these contentious issues, which have moral, social and political aspects, in addition to implications for research method and the interpretation of findings. In the early days of the development of the social and behavioural sciences, little consideration was given by most researchers to the implications of their activities for the subjects of their inquiry. Considerations of method, and the impact of the research process on the subjects, are in an active state of development in all of the social sciences. I shall, therefore, use a discussion of these problems as they arise in the research method itself as the means of attempting to address some of the dilemmas and opportunities generated by the growing demand for, and practice of, research in the field of psychotherapy. It is intended as a starting-point of inquiry for those who are thinking of engaging in research, as well as for those who want to read and understand reports of all kinds of research inquiry with critical understanding of the implications of the findings.

Contemporary psychotherapy research is characterized by three distinct strands of activity. Perhaps the most common, and better funded, is outcome research: *What Works for Whom*, to borrow from the title of the most recent review of psychotherapy research into the effectiveness of psychotherapy (Roth and Fonagy 1996). Most psychotherapy research can be described under these two headings:

- *Evaluation*: how effective was the treatment; what were the outcomes in terms of patient improvement, on the basis of either (or both) standard measures of observable behaviours, or patient reports of their experience of themselves and their treatment; what were the treatment factors related to successful or unsuccessful outcomes? Through outcome research, it is hoped that we can ensure that limited resources are expended on therapies which will benefit clients; conversely, providers seeking cheaper treatments may and do use outcome studies to restrict access to treatment and/or limit what is offered.
- *Process research*: research into the therapy process itself, including validation of theoretical constructs; identification of the factors active in the therapeutic process; the understanding of the functioning of psychological health and illness.

In addition, many services also undertake audits asking such questions as who used this service, what treatment did they receive, how long did it last, were they satisfied/dissatisfied, how much did it cost? An audit is not strictly speaking research, but it does have implications for funding of services. In the discussion which follows, I consider the methods employed in all these models of research, and the ethical implications of those methods in terms of their impact on the individuals who are studied. Studies often address more than one kind of question, and similar methods may be used in both evaluative and process research.

Evaluating psychotherapy as a treatment for psychological distress

Much psychotherapy research which falls into the category of evaluation employs methods and the kind of logic which is employed in the evaluation of medical treatments. The objective of the research is to generate knowledge about the effects of treatment interventions on populations, and to compare treatments. An important method employed in medical research which is also used in psychotherapy research is the 'randomized trial'.

In this kind of research, patients are allocated randomly to one of two groups, a treatment group or a non-treatment group. This method, used in outcome studies in the case of psychotherapy, normally involves allocating some patients on a waiting list to one form of treatment, or to different treatments, and comparing the group or groups thus created with those left, untreated on a waiting list. In some cases, a psychotherapy treatment group may be compared to a group given ordinary primary care. Where a large enough trial can be mounted, patients are 'selected' for individual factors, such as age, gender, diagnosis, case history factors, which are comparable across all the groups being studied. In non-randomized studies, a treatment group or method is evaluated in the absence of a 'control' or non-treatment group. In these cases, the aim of the research is often to evaluate the outcomes of a particular model of therapy, or to compare it with other models, without asking the question, 'is this or that therapy better (or worse than) than no therapy?'

In many studies of these types, the therapy may be conducted according to 'manualized' procedures. The issue at question in this kind of study is whether the differences in outcome within one treatment mode may be affected by the individual differences of the therapists themselves in the application of the method. The use of treatment manuals seeks to reduce the differences between therapists in order to evaluate the active effect of the treatment method itself. In such treatments, a set of procedures, based on the theoretical model being studied, is built prior to the study, and therapists are trained to work within that set of procedures. Sessions included in the research study are then sampled by the researchers to establish that the procedures being followed conform with the manual.

These methods derive from the 'agent neutral' model of scientific practice. They make two important assumptions:

- that carefully controlled groups such as these can be used to generate results which will demonstrate convincingly that the treatment is or is not effective, and with which groups
- that the therapy process itself can be rendered 'agent-neutral' through the use of manualized procedures.

Effectiveness studies are important. They are enabling the slow accumulation of knowledge about which therapies are effective, giving practitioners the opportunity to offer treatments which have been shown to be effective. They begin to provide indicators of preferred treatments for certain kinds of problems. Recent development of a technique called 'meta-analysis' has enabled researchers to make stronger generalizations on the basis of larger samples, by aggregating data from smaller studies. Such meta-analyses, conducted in the 1990s, have begun to show a picture of contemporary psychotherapy treatments available, and the kinds of benefits which may be derived from them. We already know from the meta-analysis of the accumulating evidence of 30 years of psychotherapy outcome research that of those who receive psychotherapy, 'the average client who is treated is better off at the end of therapy than 76 percent of the persons who did not receive therapy' (Bergin and Garfield 1994: 32). By 'better off', Bergin and Garfield mean that on a standard measure of social and/or psychological health, these patients can be said to have improved. Such evidence supports the demands of consumers for more psychotherapy services, a voice in the complex social dialogue involved in the political and social decisions which have to be made about the distribution of money, training, and space for health services.

However, as with medical treatments, ethical issues arise in the administration of research which offers treatment to some but not to others, or which standardizes procedures. Consider the implications of these methods. To be in a 'randomized controlled trial' means that those patients who are 'randomized' to a waiting list (no treatment) group, do not receive the benefit of treatment, and according to the evidence, lose a proven potential to benefit. The research has demonstrated the benefit of treatment, and had an influence on the growth of the funding and provision of psychotherapy, but what would be the judgement of a client, 'randomized' on the waiting list? Such patients are not, of course, informed of the fact that they have been assigned to a 'no treatment' group. Patients who are allocated to a treatment may be randomized as much for demographic and other criteria, as for diagnostic criteria. When is it no longer appropriate to use this method? These are questions which researchers can, and must, consider. How are such judgements to be made?

Or consider the implications for the patient of being treated according to a treatment manual. In the case of medical treatments, the use of treatment manuals guards against 'wild' treatment unsupported by the evidence of experience. As patients we would rather have a proven surgical procedure, than one that surgeons would like to try to advance their career. However, this logic does not strictly apply to psychotherapy, where there is convincing evidence that it is the therapist–patient alliance which is the main factor in good therapeutic outcomes. What are the implications for the therapeutic alliance if the therapist is constrained by the procedures prescribed by a manual, regardless of the situation they may find in the consulting room? Is the difference between 'wild' and 'evidence-based' treatment the same for processes which depend on communication?

These considerations lead to the problems also encountered in medical research which come under the general heading of 'informed consent'.

Informed consent

It will be clear already that the methods applied to psychotherapy research raise issues which also apply to medical treatment and research. Foremost among these considerations is informed consent, a term which is now familiar to everyone who has been a hospital patient. All medical procedures, including research, are governed by the principle that the recipient of those procedures should be informed of the implications of the treatment, and give consent to that treatment with full knowledge of those implications. Informed consent means that an individual grants to someone the permission to do something they would not have the right to do without such permission. Need for consent arises from the recognition of the individual's right to autonomy and self-determination. Though these values have long been enshrined in theory, in practice they have not been applied in the application of treatments and research. The notion of eugenics, and the wide tolerance of the sterilization of those deemed mentally incompetent, persisted long after the horrors generated by the Nazi pursuit of racial purity; medical experiments on individuals continued in other western countries long after the experiments on concentration camp victims were revealed and condemned.

However, the story of the potential for abuse of power in the pursuit of 'knowledge' does not stop with the arrival of formal policies on consent, and ethics committees which oversee the activities of researchers and practitioners. Certainty that consent has been given is not self-evident, and attention to the context in which consent is given inevitably must inform judgement about the validity of the consent. How, therefore, do we define ethical considerations, the appropriate application of procedures, to the values which should underpin the pursuit of knowledge? How do we set the dignity and right to autonomy, and privacy, of subjects against the need to protect individuals individually and collectively against poor methods, or poor practice, in the treatments offered to them in the name of health and well-being?

In clinical practice, the word 'consent' often involves another set of considerations which can be described by the adjectives 'implied', 'informed', 'voluntary', 'competent', 'valid'. Similar considerations apply to the obtaining of consent for research.

Let us take the case of the patient who has been asked to give consent to participation in a treatment which involves the completion of forms, before, during and after treatment, which will measure aspects of his or her emotional and social functioning. Many such instruments exist. They involve multiple choice answers to questions about the patient's thoughts about and experiences of themselves, others and the world. They are used as baseline measures of psychological functioning and change in outcome studies. Suppose that the patient is informed that the information gathered will be used in research within the unit offering the treatment. The information is anonymous, but it is personal. It reveals things about a person. Now suppose that the information given, aggregated as part of a larger dataset, becomes part of study which is not directly conducted by the unit which collected it? Can implied consent to this wider use of the information be presumed, or should the patient be contacted once more?

Does informed consent imply full knowledge of all that could possibly be done with the knowledge/information, or a general consent to the use of such materials as and where appropriate, within the constraints of professionally regulated practice? How much knowledge should an individual subject be presumed to have. Details of the processes and uses of research instruments will probably not be available to the subject who gives consent. These kinds of judgements are the responsibility of individual researchers. They are also the responsibility of professional ethics committees. Practitioner probity relies on the application of judgement about when informed consent to a process may justifiably be considered to include implied consent for which decisions about the correctness or not of the use of materials becomes the responsibility of the researcher both to the subject and to the principle of professional standards.

A second and important issue is the application of voluntary consent. When is consent voluntary? Suppose the patient is told that all those attending a clinic are asked to give consent to participating in research, which will involve the application of a variety of research instruments over the period of treatment, and later, during a follow-up. The patient has been waiting for a long time for free or low-cost treatment. Is consent given in this context unquestionably voluntary, even if the patient is fully informed and fully competent? Might not the patient feel that giving consent is necessary in order to get treatment? How can those conducting the research be certain that patients are not giving consent because they think they will be denied treatment without it?

This question leads to a further question: is the consent thus given competent consent? Those seeking treatment for psychological disturbance may not be in a clear enough state of mind to consider the implications of the consent they are giving. They may be in an emotional crisis, and desperate for help whatever the conditions it is given in; or their thinking and judgement may be disordered because of severe mental illness. What are our responsibilities to individuals in these cases? We want to know more about what their disturbance is about, and what interventions are likely to alleviate suffering and distress; at the same time, they are uniquely vulnerable. All of these considerations lead to the principle of valid consent.

- How much information should the patient be given in order to be able to give informed consent? And at what point in the process of assessment for, or discussion of treatment should consent be sought?
- How comprehensible is the information given?
- Has it been fully understood?
- How can the researcher be sure that consent is given voluntarily? Is there an achievable code of practice which could guarantee that all consent is given voluntarily in the widest sense, that every subject gives consent freely and fully in the interests of knowledge? The likely reply would be, 'Probably not'.

If that is the case, how then do we make judgements about the balance between fully informed, voluntary consent, competence, and the need for knowledge when circumstances are such that unequivocally informed, voluntary consent cannot be a certainty? If we take a strict legal view – that only fully informed consent should be taken as valid – urgently needed research into severe mental illness would be impossible. If we take the position that the strict legal view is required to protect the researcher, then urgently needed research into severe mental illness might be severely restricted by the reluctance of researchers to risk entering into uncertain territory. This is the kind of dilemma faced by doctors in offering treatments whose outcome is uncertain, but where successful intervention might save lives or improve health and well-being.

A further consideration is that of unintended consequences. These may affect subject and researcher alike. Suppose, for example, that the results of a clinically validated trial were to show that 'six-session' therapies of a particular kind have had good results, according to criteria of symptom reduction, set by a researcher in order to measure the presence of a real, if limited, benefit to the client. With its basis in medical research methods, effectiveness is primarily a measure of symptom reduction, and of the relationship of costs to benefits. The consequence of such an approach to mental healthcare may be to favour management over treatment, and symptom reduction over structural change when funding decisions are made. The consequence may be to support managed care models which emphasize relief and control, and see therapy as a series of short-ranged problem-solving activities, and assign little meaning to the therapeutic relationship. The patient is managed not treated, and the therapist's role is one of a manager rather than a 'treater' (Barron and Sands 1996: 149). Sometimes that is appropriate. Is it invariably so? Consider this effect against that of the Consumer's Report (Seligman 1994) survey of psychotherapy conducted by the American Consumers' Association. This showed that longer term psychotherapies, with psychotherapists who were chosen by the patient, as measured by the consumer's evaluation, were significantly more successful than those provided through the 'managed care' system operated by US insurance companies. The Consumer's Report was consistent with general findings, assembled through meta-analysis, that no one method of therapy is demonstrably superior to any other, except in very particular cases. It would appear that elements of process, as much as of outcome, are important indicators for the evaluation of psychotherapy treatments (Seligman 1994).

What role do researchers have in these debates? The responsibilities of the researcher cannot be shirked: the researcher must take into account, and take responsibility for, the implications of the process on the individuals and the communities they work in; and of the impact of the outcomes of the project. Research is not a neutral process; it also includes values, the worth of a thing, which may not be expressed in terms of effectiveness. To research efficacy, the worth of a therapy independent of the relationship between costs and benefits, involves other research methods, which also present dilemmas of ethics and method.

Researching psychotherapy as process

Outcome research is based on the classical rules of scientific method which are used in the natural sciences. It attempts to control the generation of data within a framework set by the researcher; to generate observations in a form which is analysable in terms of quantities, using the standard research tools of statistics. Its logic is to see what goes into the therapeutic process, and to evaluate what comes out, without attending to the process itself any further than attempting to ensure as much as possible that the process is uniform, so that real comparisons can be made. These constraints give it great power in generating convincing results. However, they also limit its powers of discovery. To find, as outcome research seems to have done, that the therapeutic alliance is an important factor in good outcomes, does not say much about what the 'therapeutic alliance' is, or how to develop it in good practice. Because of the complexity of such a question, researching the therapeutic process is not so easily designed, and only slowly are systematic approaches to its study being devised.

The traditional framework for the study of psychotherapy – for educational as well as for the purposes of research and development – has been the case study, developed originally by Freud out of the case history form of the medical interview. Many critiques of the case study have been made (Strenger 1991; Grunbaum 1984; Ward 1997) and will not be discussed in this chapter. What may be important to note, however, is that this most prevalent of methods of inquiry is often accepted without question in terms of the implications it has both for and the ethics and values of research inquiry. The issue of informed consent also arises in relation to the therapeutic contract: how many practitioners inform their clients that their sessions may be subjected to a case study which will be read by others? These matters are seldom raised in relation to case studies presented for training or scientific meetings. The caveat about 'confidentiality' is deemed to cover all possible issues. If a case study is considered for publication, full concealment of the identity of the client is expected. But what about the effects on the client of having another's understanding of his or her character, personality structure, behaviours, objectified in such a way? For the client will recognize the person in the case study. What implications does this have for the privacy, dignity and freedom from harmful effects which the client has a right to expect? What is the meaning of informed consent, when someone who may have been in therapy for many years, is suddenly confronted with a request to be used as the subject of a report being written in the interests of scientific inquiry? Further, most case studies are based on the process notes of the therapist. The words and experiences of the client are reported second-hand, through the lens of memory. Research has demonstrated without doubt the inaccuracy of recall; later events inevitably colour recall of earlier events. The process recording is the recording of the experienced session from the perspective of one of the participants. What is the scientific or ethical status of that report?

Contemporary research has attempted to go beyond the limitations of process recording, and the case study form based on them, to study the psychotherapy process from the perspective of communication. One of the great problems for research of analytic psychotherapy, as indeed for all psychotherapies which rely on the therapeutic relationship, is the nature of the process itself, and the difficulty of 'operationalizing' its theoretical constructs in ways amenable to classical research methods. Though at the time, the case study was the only resource available for the creation of a science of psychoanalysis, Freud's hope for a 'scientific project' for psychoanalysis akin to that of the natural sciences has been all but destroyed by the critiques of philosophers of science, and particularly by the critique of the case study as an instrument of inquiry. However, in the 1980s and 1990s, several promising research projects have come to fruition. All rely on the use of empirical tools derived from the analysis of language. Spence (1988) has focused on the evolution and development of the psychotherapeutic narrative. Bucci (1996) has developed a model of psychoanalytic process built on the basis of findings in cognitive science which offers the potential for a scientifically testable and replicable analysis of what she has termed 'referential activity'– the process of free association. Mergenthaler (1996), who works closely with Bucci, has devised a method of analysing the content of analytic sessions which can show the movement between abstraction (moments of reflection) and emotion (moments of expression) in the analytic exchange. Attachment theory, and its empirical tool, the Adult Attachment Interview (see Goldberg *et al.* 1995) are being used extensively by researchers to build a model of the development and vicissitudes of psychodynamic mechanisms in the individual. All of these methods aim to provide an objectivist – agent neutral – research account of the intersubjective therapeutic process, and the possibility of building a generalizable model of the basic concepts used in practice by clinicians.

The development of these research methods depends upon the use of tape-recording, in combination with computer analysis, to analyse the detail of the psychotherapeutic process. Many in the field of psychotherapy consider tape-recording to be an invasion of privacy, which will inevitably distort the therapeutic interaction by inserting an 'observer' into the process. It is certainly the case that the careless use of tape-recording can constitute a violation of an individual's rights to privacy and dignity. In practice, the use of tape-recorded data, subject to its being obtained by informed consent before the beginning of a treatment, used in studies such as these is as anonymous as the data obtained by questionnaire and generalized in statistical studies of outcome. Unlike the case study, for the most part, the patient is unrecognizable as an individual.

For those who conceptualize the psychotherapy process in terms of inter-subjective processes, and wish to develop a means of studying the experiences of the partners to the therapeutic interaction, new research tools are in the process of development. In addition to self-report measures of individual functioning employed in outcome studies, an instrument called 'Interpersonal Process Recall' (Elliott 1986) has been developed since the 1980s in an attempt to alter the status of both client and therapist to review the tape-recorded session, soon after the completion of the session, to identify the important, or 'key', moments which they experienced in the course of the therapeutic session. The client's experience then becomes equal in importance to the therapist's in the understanding of the therapeutic interaction and its meanings. Such research is based on an understanding of the therapeutic process which makes the assumption that it is agent relative, and unreplicable, and can only be researched as such. Though the method depends on tape-recording, this tape-recording is much more within the client's control. A question which arises, however, is: what is the impact on the patient of the request to move from a setting in which his or her concerns were paramount, to one in which the research interests, which may well not be of interest to the client, will be attended to? Those whose tape-recorded sessions are treated as data, separate from their persons and identities, are free to use their therapy entirely for their own purposes. The values embedded in the therapeutic process inevitably impact upon the research process and the decisions the researcher makes in terms of method and analysis. Privacy and confidentiality are not absolute conditions but are achieved through the application of codes, judgements and considerations of value, and the uncertainty of any human action and its consequences.

Conclusion

The divide between the rationalist and inter-subjective perspectives colours not only psychotherapy practices, but also the research practices which have grown up round them. The debate has been part of the gradual evolution of the Research Principles for American Behavioural Scientists (American Psychological Association) (APA 1992), whose Code of Ethics governs the practice of all members of the American Psychological Association. This was the earliest such attempt at regulating the conduct of psychological research on human subjects. This most recent form of the document was the product of a 40-year developmental process, which began in 1950, in response to the Nuremberg Code of Ethics, the immediate response to the Nazi 'scientific' experiments in the concentration camps. The APA developed its first code through an empirical method in which researchers were first consulted about the kinds of dilemmas they experienced in the field. Slowly over the period of its development, the document has evolved, partly under the influence of criticism that it biases 'cost and benefit' concerns (the pragmatic concerns of the researcher) more heavily than the value concerns (the individual right to dignity, privacy and protection from unwarranted distress). The consequence of this slow evolution and development resulted in the following preamble, which summarizes responsibilities of the psychological researcher:

> The decision to undertake research, then, rests upon a considered judgement by the individual psychologist about how best to contribute to psychological science and human welfare. Having made the decision to conduct research, the psychologist considers alternative directions in which research energies and resources might be invested. On the basis of this consideration, the psychologist carries out the investigation with respect and concern for the dignity and welfare of the people who participate and with cognizance of federal and state regulations and professional standards governing the conduct of research with human participants.
>
> (APA 1992, quoted in Kimmel 1996: 26)

The Code of Ethics of the British Psychological Society, developed somewhat later, includes the recognition that 'psychologists owe a debt to those who participate in research and that in return those participants should expect 'to be treated with the highest standards of respect and consideration' (BPS 1995, quoted in Kimmel 1996: 336).

These are serious standards to be set and to be aimed for. Still, however, they involve making judgements. *Research is not a neutral activity.* It involves:

- The protection of clients and subjects through awareness of risks, and the balance of dangers to benevolence, both individual and social.
- The avoidance of fraud or duress through the application of self-audit by professionals – motives need to be scrutinized.
- The requirement of professionals to explain and justify their methods.
- The promotion of public and social values; education of the public attitudes and concerning the public role in decision making.

It will have become evident that the conduct of ethical research cannot rest solely on a set of rules, however carefully they are constituted. The responsibility of the psychotherapy clinician to the client is one which rests on the human values of right to autonomy, dignity and such well-being as is achievable. One factor frequently left out of this equation is the question of value in relation to the responsibility of the researcher to the client. How is it possible for the researcher to give back something of value to the client, who agrees to be scrutinized, over and above the considerable scrutiny already inherent in the psychotherapy process?

We have seen how the measure of outcomes can work both for and against clients. In the hands of a well-informed assessor, with adequate resources at their disposal, outcomes findings could be used to improve the accuracy of referral and the chances of improvement for the client; outcome findings could help providers of services make informed and competent decisions about the deployment of resources. In practice, outcome findings remain a very incomplete map. Behavioural and cognitive psychotherapies are structured in such a way, and rest on basic assumptions about the nature of the studied, which coincide with popular outcome measures. The consequence is that there is a great deal of outcome evidence for these therapies, which is not so of the more difficult therapies to research. Psychoanalytic psychotherapy is certainly the most important of those therapies which have been seriously under-researched. This is not only due to the difficulty of designing good studies with which to measure results. It also has to do with the slowness of the psychoanalytic world to see the need for, and begin to design, research which is relevant to its methods and values.

One of the consequences of this is that outcome findings can also be used by assessors to promote their own methods, and by service providers to resource with the cheapest methods, usually brief therapies with clear treatment plans and goals. These therapies have enormous value. However, they are not adequate to every problem. The risk of evidence based medicine or 'Managed Care' (as treatment management is known within the insurance system of US healthcare) is that resourcing prerogatives take precedence over human values, in the form of 'proven' treatments whose outcomes are little understood in relation to the, as yet, very incomplete and inconclusive map of psychotherapy effectiveness (Henry 1998). The risk of lack of evidence is that inadequate, or frankly damaging practices continue in the name of treatment.

Researchers and clinicians have responsibilities to clients to take the possible uses of their findings and claims into account when writing up and presenting/publishing their work. There is a potential conflict of interest at every stage: researchers want their projects to generate important findings (these may be 'positive' or 'negative' indicators, but either case could count as an 'important' result). We cannot expect researchers to be without such motives; research is, after all, a slow, painstaking and often unrewarding process. Clinicians feel allegiance to the form of treatment to which they have devoted their own resources of time, energy, and often, money, in the process of training. To accept contrary findings can be a blow to self-esteem and the sense of purpose.

The consequence of this conflict of motive and interest is that the community of researchers meets in workshops and conferences, debates the meanings of hard-won findings, speaking to each other in a specialist language. Clinicians, uninstructed in how to understand the research process and its results, largely ignore the activity of research, and feel vaguely threatened by its potential to destabilize accepted practice. The political and social implications of evidence based medicine for clinicians and their clients are likewise poorly understood.

How then is the interest of the client best served in this tension between the need for a greater understanding of the process and outcomes of treatment, and respect for the privacy and autonomy of the individual? Both professionals and their clients have to grapple with the paradox that safe treatment, that is, treatment whose value has been demonstrated, requires the participation of researchers, clients and practitioners in a constructive collaboration. Thus knowledge evolves and has the potential to add to the real value of the therapeutic process.

I believe we need two changes to ensure the sound and ethical development of an evidence based treatment provision for psychotherapy. First, researchers have an obligation to their subjects, to return to them the benefit of the gift they make when they agree to participate in research. The most important conduit for meeting that obligation is to contribute to the development of clinical practice. This means that it is incumbent upon researchers to make their findings available to practitioners in a usable and relevant form. I would recommend for your attention, as examples of good practice, the article on outcome by Guthrie *et al.* (1998) in the *British*

Journal of Psychotherapy for its clarity, relevance and accessibility to practitioners, and the article on the psychotherapy process by Stern *et al.* (1998)
in the *International Journal of Psychoanalysis*. Such a dialogue between
research and practice has the potential to empower both client and clinician
in the inevitable battles over the funding of services.

Second, much of the work which has gone on in the development of ethical codes of practice for the behavioural sciences has emerged from the
work of psychologists working within the constraints of experimental
method. Much of the work of outcome research in psychotherapy has been
conducted, in the context of these codes, by psychologists working in the
USA, in the UK and in mainland Europe. These codes have evolved, over
time, into a powerful statement of the responsibilities of psychological
researchers in the conduct of their work. However, as I hope I have indicated, codes of ethics provide a frame for the process of decision making
only in the design and progress of research. Of concern is the fact that a
similar code has not been developed for the conduct of psychotherapy
research. A set of guidelines being developed by the United Kingdom Council for Psychotherapy goes some way to meeting this shortfall, but it is based
on existing codes of ethics and practice for clinicians. As we have seen, the
boundaries between clinical practice and research may not always coincide,
and as in the example of case studies, the erosion of the boundary between
observer and observed may cause problems particular to the researching of
psychotherapy which are not covered by the constraints of experimental
research.

My proposal would be that the method initiated by the American Psychological Association in the 1950s would be timely for the further development
of a Code of Ethics and Guidelines for Practice for psychotherapy research.
What is required is a developmental approach which sets out to balance the
costs and benefits of each kind of methodological approach to inquiry
against the fundamental human values which must underpin the judgements
which will inevitably accompany the process of research.

References

American Psychological Association (1992) Ethical principles of psychologists and
code of conduct, *American Psychologist*, 47, 1597-611.
Barron, J. and Sands, H. (1996) *Impact of Managed Care on Psychodynamic Treat-
ment*. Madison, CT: International Universities Press.
Bergin, A. and Garfield, S. (1994) *A Handbook of Psychotherapy and Behaviour
Change*. New York: John Wiley.
British Psychological Association (BPA) (1995) *Code of Conduct, Ethical Principles
and Guidelines*. Leicester: BPA.
Bucci, W. (1996) *Psychoanalysis and Cognitive Science*. New York: Guilford Press.
Elliott, R. (1986) Interpersonal process recall as a process research method, in L.

Greenberg and W. Pinhoff (eds) *The Psychotherapeutic Process: A Research Handbook*. New York: Guilford Press.

Goldberg, S., Muir, R. and Kerr, J. (eds) (1995) *Attachment Theory: Social, Critical and Developmental Perspectives*. Hillsdale, NJ: Analytic Press.

Grunbaum, A. (1984) *The Foundations of Psychoanalysis*. Berkeley, CA: University of California Press.

Guthrie, E., Moorey, J., Barker, H., Margison, F. and McGrath, G. (1998) Brief psychodynamic-interpersonal therapy for patients with severe psychiatric illness which is unresponsive to treatment, *British Journal of Psychotherapy*, 15(2): 155–66.

Henry, W.P. (1998) Science, politics and the politics of science: the use and misuse of empirically validated treatment, *Psychotherapy Research*, 8(2): 126–41.

Kimmel, A.J. (1996) *Ethical Issues in Behavioural Research*. Oxford: Blackwell.

Mergenthaler, E. (1996) Emotion-abstraction patterns in verbatim protocols: a new way of describing psychotherapeutic processes, *Journal of Clinical and Consulting Psychology*, 64(6): 1306–15.

Roth, A. and Fonagy, P. (1996) *What Works for Whom? A Critical Review of Psychotherapy Research*. New York: Guilford Press.

Seligman, M. (1994) The effectiveness of psychotherapy: the Consumer's Report, *American Psychologist*, 50(12): 965–74.

Spence, D. (1998) Rain forest or mud field?, *International Journal of Psychoanalysis*, 79: 642.

Stern, D. *et al.* (1998) Non interpretative mechanisms in psychoanalytic psychotherapy, *International Journal of Psychoanalysis*, 79: 903–18.

Strenger, C. (1991) *Between Hermeneutics and Science*. Madison, CT: International Universities Press.

Ward, I. (ed.) (1997) *The Presentation of Case Material in Clinical Discourse*. Northampton: Freud Museum Publications.

9 Complexities of practice: psychotherapy in the real world

Mark Aveline

Introduction

The archetypal psychotherapy or counselling relationship is a series of one-to-one meetings between patient and therapist, hermetically sealed from the outside world and freely entered into by personal contract – one with the other. The obligation of the therapist is to the patient or client alone; the requirement of confidentiality is often seen as absolute. This arrangement is not of the everyday world and this is its strength and its weakness. The other worldliness suggests an illusion of timelessness and absence of judgement. For the most part, the illusion is liberating. However, therapists embracing the archetype as an ideal ignore their relatedness to the world beyond the consulting room door, where families, communities of place and work, and, especially relevant to this chapter, collaborating healthcare workers, link interdependently. This real world, more complex than the simplified one within the consulting room, has to be recognized even by therapists who aspire to the archetype.

In this chapter, I consider the complex dilemmas that face therapists in the real world. The challenge for the therapist is to find principled ways of serving the patient well. Such ways are not easy to find as each way may involve choosing between competing professional, moral, legal and employment imperatives when the consequential ends are unclear. Particularly difficult choices may have to be made when either the patient or another is at risk of harm. Working in the National Health Service brings with it practices of team working and extended confidentiality which are often of benefit to the patient but which may conflict with the isolationist ideal typified in the preceding paragraph.

In this chapter, I use two terms in special ways. By 'therapist', I mean the practitioners of psychotherapy, psychological therapy and counselling, and 'patient' to identify the person who suffers and is seeking help. Other therapists might prefer the term 'client' or, even, 'customer'. To my mind, neither of these does justice to the twin requirements of therapy that is professionally done: passionate commitment and cool judgement.

The consulting room with the closed door: ideal or idealized situation?

While Freud at times conducted analysis when walking with his patients on the streets of Vienna – therapy *en plein air* – the setting within his home on the Berggasse is the one that set the tradition of the consulting room with the closed door. Few therapists go to Freud's extreme of a consulting room with separate entrance and exit, an arrangement designed to guard against the potential embarrassment of two patients meeting. Many therapists, however, are powerfully influenced by the image of private discourse between patient and therapist, hidden from the gaze of the outside world by the closed door, and regulated by the metronome of the fifty-minute hour, once, twice or five times per week, regardless of external events.

The closed door symbolizes the inward focus of many therapies. In psychoanalysis, the duty of the patient is to free associate, to say whatever is in mind. The duty of the analyst is to analyse, to be neutral and hold a position of 'evenly suspended attention' (Freud 1912). These imperatives form two important rules that direct conduct within this world behind the closed door and lead on to another feature. While the physical boundaries of therapy – length and frequency of sessions – are clear and definite, time within sessions is more fluid, flowing from one session to the next and creating an illusion of timelessness as the therapy marches to its own drumbeat, measured and constant. In timelessness and exclusivity, it is not of the everyday world.

The character of this space has many advantages for the patient. It facilitates exploration by offering a guarded arena, free from interruptions and reserved for that person. The therapist self-abnegates; the patient is put first. While the patient, transferentially, may put the therapist in the role of critic or judge, the first duty of the therapist is to be neutral and serve the patient well. The encouragement to explore, to confront the dark recesses of the soul, to reveal shameful secrets and desires, to be afraid (and have achievements recognized) and to take psychological risks, both within and without the consulting room, is enhanced by the aura of confidentiality that enshrouds therapy and is given physical form by the closed door.

Privacy and confidentiality are clearly very important elements in practice and have beneficial effects in building trust. The British Association for Counselling in its Code of Ethics (A3) states: 'Counsellors offer the highest possible level of confidentiality in order to respect the client's privacy and create the trust necessary for counselling' (Palmer Barnes 1998: 118). The

United Kingdom Council for Psychotherapy has a similar statement on confidentiality in its Code of Ethics (2.3). It begins: 'Psychotherapists are required to preserve confidentiality' and then interestingly continues 'and to disclose, if requested, the limits of confidentiality and circumstances under which it might be broken to specific third parties' (Palmer Barnes 1998: 138). A comparable modifier in the BAC Code is to be found in code item B3.2: 'The counselling contract will include an agreement about the level and limits of confidentiality offered. This agreement can be reviewed and changed by negotiation between counsellor and client' (Palmer Barnes 1998: 123). Note the use of the word contract.

Some therapists, however, see absolute confidentiality as the bedrock of practice (Langs 1973). On the level of law and the concept of duty of care to others, either as a therapist or a citizen, absolute confidentiality is a nonsense. Yet it remains a seductive fiction, buttressed by the idea of the analytic attitude. The implicit message to the patient – sometimes unwisely promised explicitly – is: you can speak of everything and I will not reveal what you say to another without your permission. This supposedly frees both parties, patient and therapist, to make best use of the therapy opportunity. If the undertaking is taken literally and not qualified by reference to potentially overriding duties, there may be times when the result is unhelpful, unwise and unsustainable. By overriding duties, I mean duties of care in situations of risk of self-harm or harm to others, and certain aspects of team working with its practice of extended confidentiality.

Fundamental to much therapy is the concept of personal contract between patient and therapist, freely entered into, one with the other. The primary obligation of the therapist is to the patient: to respect their autonomy and promote self-determination (BAC) and to alleviate suffering and promote well-being (UKCP). The job of the therapist is not to make decisions for the patient but to help the other arrive at a position where they can make their own decisions. Though it may be a contradiction in terms, neutrality can be a powerful force in achieving that aim. In this particular world of therapy, the therapist has served the patient well if the frame that gives pride of place to exploration and self-observation is held. Some would argue that this is a priceless advantage.

Bollas and Sundelson (1995), respectively psychoanalyst and lawyer, passionately argue in their book *The New Informants* against the intrusion of third parties into the therapy space. They see it as a bad thing, which harms the proper practice of analysis; nay more, makes it impossible. Specifically, adding in concerns about external persons and authorities interferes with the reflective process about the patient's communications. The analytical quiet which allows the analyst to imagine silently all the possible meanings of the patient's comments is shattered by the call to evaluate and possibly step outside the analytic role to take action in the external world. For the analyst, the inductive question about how can we understand what passes between and around us is superseded by the question of what do I have to tell others. This distraction erodes psychoanalytic therapy in another, even more fundamental way. It strikes at the need of the patient not to be taken literally. The discovery and expression of fantasies, and unconscious and unwelcome aspects of self depends on uncensored free expression, free from the fear of confidences being betrayed and not restricted by premature closure on meaning or the social opprobrium of the everyday world.

Often having the consulting room door closed is a matter of principle for the therapist, conveniently buttressed by the hallowed ground rules of the world of analysis and its therapy derivatives. However, there are two further practical points that impel therapists in the direction of caution about the validity of conclusions that they may draw about the patient's world. The world that the patient presents is always a partial one; it is partial in perspective, incomplete in account, and depicts, only at second-hand, the significance and influence of other, relevant social worlds that the patient inhabits. Psychotherapists know a great deal about their patients but a great deal is a long way from knowing the full picture. Much as they might like to be prescient, therapists are simply not that good at predicting the future (Holmes and Lindley 1989).

Confidentiality, privacy, neutrality, exclusivity and timelessness make a powerful foundation for therapy practice. The structure encourages the development of trust. The message to the patient that the time is there for them to use as they wish conveys respect for their autonomy and helps promote self-determination. But there are significant limitations, which are examined in the next section.

The real world

In therapy, two people meet, the patient and the therapist, with the 'intention and hope that one may learn to live more fruitfully' (Lomas 1981). The simplest practice is for both parties to focus on the patient alone, the person in therapy. Yet to do so ignores the worlds beyond the consulting room. The patient does not exist in isolation, but as a member of many intersecting and overlapping social worlds, sometimes as participant, sometimes as instigator, nearly always as a person with rights and responsibilities. What happens in one world influences the others, oft times profoundly. The same is true for the therapist.

The therapist participates in this therapy world as a professional whose duty is to serve the patient well and as a citizen with legal and moral responsibilities. Let us examine these duties in turn.

As a professional, the therapist has responsibility to prepare him or herself adequately for the service that is to be rendered to the patient. Periods of formal training, continued clinical supervision, good assessment of the nature of the patient's problems and realistic self-appraisal combine to help answer the professional question: do I have the requisite skills and time to treat this patient (Aveline 1997)? The responsibility extends to providing the frame, a sufficiently quiet, constant and private space in which to meet and work. But what is the work? To strive to understand the other and convey that understanding in such a way – timing and content – that the added meaning can be assimilated and found to be helpful by the patient for sure. The attentive reader will notice that the activity is not truth at any cost. But there is more in the list of therapeutic intent: to help the patient change and live more fruitfully. Therapy is not onanistic. At its best, it is generative; generative of new solutions to old conflicts, and the achievement of less self-restrictive ways of living through being brave and taking risks. The acid test of therapy is change in the real world. Therapy cannot be without external purpose. Reflection alone is not enough to justify the enterprise. Therapy is not a substitute for life.

The therapist hears of the problems in living that the patient hopes to remedy and has an insight into these worlds at second hand. Additionally, the therapist may experience key aspects of the problems directly, enacted in the transference. The therapist has to keep an eye on the personal social systems of family and society as it is change there, rather than change within the consulting room, that counts. This perspective is explicit in cognitive-behavioural therapy where experiment and reporting back **are** central to the endeavour. The therapist does not have primary responsibility for the inter-acting people in the outside worlds – that rests with the patient – but does have a varying degree of responsibility for what happens, in particular for ill-considered or incompetent (in the legal sense), deleterious acts that the patient might make to their loss or the loss of others.

Therapist neutrality is a useful starting-point but it is not an absolute. Of course, the patient's life is theirs and it is for them to make their own decisions. Furthermore, the therapist not taking sides aids existential choice. But in practice, therapists are selective in their attention. The selectivity is driven partly by theory but more influentially by personal attitude and principles. The resultant focus shapes what therapists are told, and they have – or should have – a view about the implications of what they learn. I recall one extreme example.

A man sought therapy for escalating sado-masochistic practice. He would have his wife dress in tight-fitting rubber and place over her head an all-in-one mask. It was difficult for her to breathe. What scared them both was his practice of choking off the air supply, more and more. He could not trust himself to stop and she felt unable to resist his demand. He was offered therapy to help him change, subject to an essential requirement. He was to leave home until such time that we all felt it was safe for him to return. The offer was accepted with relief.

Nowadays, similar executive situations arise in childhood sexual or physical abuse when the abuser is in contact with the children and cannot be trusted by themselves or the therapist not to abuse.

The therapist has to take a view on what they are asked to do or, more commonly, what they are asked to become involved in by agreeing to work with a particular patient. No therapist, I imagine, would agree to help a sadist to become a better sadist or an abuser to abuse more. Therapists recognize this when they speak of working with the healthy part of the person. When patients reveal perverse or dangerous aspects of themselves, they are sometimes asking the therapist to help them take healthy action. Telling a secret is not a mandate for the therapist to act, but is usually an invitation to explore and can be a prelude to action by either party.

If therapy is effective, there will be change in the external world. Partly because of the therapist's selective attention but more because of the change-promoting nature of therapy, the therapist has some responsibility for what happens there. At the simplest level, this might be to caution a patient about the potentially disruptive effects of deep self-exploration at times in that person's life when stability is the high priority. One example of such a time might be during pregnancy when the women's central preoccupation is with her unborn child and bringing psychological conflicts to the surface would just make a complex process more complex; another, the run-up to a crucial examination when the life-task is to pass and the patient can ill afford the distraction of new insights. Clearly different therapists might come to other conclusions about the import of these examples but the point remains that the therapist has some foresight about what may happen through therapy and needs to think with the patient about possible consequences of therapy and, hence, about its timing. In addition, the therapist has moral responsibilities as a citizen and legal responsibility as a professional and, possibly, as an employee.

By convention, what happens within therapy is confidential. Yet the communications have no legal privilege. Only the conversations of lawyers and their clients are privileged. Records, including therapy process notes, can be subpoenaed. Therapists who refuse to answer when directed to do so during a legal trial risk being found to be in contempt of court. A principled defence may be accepted by the court though therapists should not rely on this being the outcome (Bond 1993). Thus, therapists wanting to keep the consulting door firmly closed must look to reasons other than legal ones to buttress their position.

Considering the worlds beyond the consulting room

Therapy takes place within contexts, a created world within existing worlds, some discrete, most intersecting and overlapping. As therapists lift their eyes from the immediate task of exploring the meaning of the communications within the consulting room, difficult therapy dilemmas may come into view. Three key areas are risk of self-harm and harm to others, and extended confidentiality.

Risk of self-harm

Many people's lives are desperate; they reel under the weight of external burdens in the form of poverty, unemployment, and family and personal illness or trauma. Internally, they may be equally buffeted by a psychological legacy from life experience of fear, mistrust and bleakness in outlook. They may be acutely aware of personal failure to achieve satisfying relationships and work; to their sadness, their capacity in Freud's words 'to love and to work' is limited. Suicide may be seen as an attractive solution.

Suicide, itself, can be a considered, competent act, arrived at after careful consideration of all the circumstances. However, it is also often the product of mental disorder, particularly recurrent depressive disorder, bipolar affective disorder and, occasionally, delusional disorder. In these three groups of disorder, categorized in the International Classification of Mental and Behavioural Disorders (version 10) (World Health Organization (WHO) 1992), there is temporary or persistent severe distortion of reality through delusions or hallucinations. In these circumstances, the suicidal wish may be a symptom, not a reaction. To end one's life on the basis of delusional misperception is tragic, especially if the misperception is treatable.

Sorting out what is what for the patient is not easy for the therapist. Is the patient's life depressing, how entrenched is the patient's contribution to their difficulties, and is the way they are viewing their life the product of mental disorder? The answers to these questions are not mutually exclusive. Someone may have a rotten life, selectively attend to the negatives in it, and feel ten times worse when clinically depressed, or any combination of the three.

Therapists may sidestep the issue by taking a narrow view of their responsibility. They construe their role as helping the patient reflect on themselves and, only in the most desperate circumstance, evaluating mental state and taking action. That position, intellectually consistent though it is with the closed-door mentality, does not seem to me to be properly responsible. It elevates the principle of respect for personal autonomy over that of taking care. The cost of maintaining the reflective position in clinical practice is much anxiety for the therapist. My more evaluative alternative is not anxiety free either. It presents the therapist with the dilemma of steering a course between the rocks of intrusive over-protection and neglect.

Jane is a senior nurse. She rules her clinical area with a rod of iron, demanding the highest standards of practice. Patient care comes first, way ahead of staff convenience and sensitivities. The ward works well, though woe betide anyone whose practice is not exemplary. For Jane, the way the ward works is more than the means of providing good service. It constitutes her family, somewhere in which she has an assured place and where her own standards will be beyond reproach. Her childhood was brutal. She was humiliated and beaten. She tried to avoid trouble by hiding her inner thoughts from her parents and appearing to conform. She defied her father by attempting not to cry during the beatings. At the earliest opportunity, she escaped by leaving home to train as a nurse. She took with her, however, a legacy of mistrust and a compulsion to be above reproach and to be secretive.

The price for Jane of being safe is distance in her relationships and, as we join this story, a desperate, growing sense of loneliness. Her social world beyond the ward is barren. Her obsessionality, once an asset, starts to become a liability. She finds it hard to adapt to new regimes; she over-reacts to failings by her juniors and is savage in her verbal chastisement, a sad repeat of her father's behaviour. Staff complain and refuse to work with her. Management raises the question of a transfer, even early retirement. She becomes depressed and is unable to work. The clinical picture strongly suggests a biological component for which she is prescribed an anti-depressive. This makes a useful improvement. The Director of Nursing understands the plight of this valued colleague and fears for her future; she refers her for psychotherapy.

As we talk, profound schizoid fears surface. Her attempts to form intimate relationships have all ended badly. She does not want to be hurt again and is acutely sensitive to any hint of rejection. At times, she is consumed with the sense that her life is futile and empty. Then, she wants to kill herself. I believe her, and fear that I will not see her again from one week to the next. I also believe that, if she can find the courage to risk greater engagement with others, her life can be turned round. We lurch from one stance to the other, from encouragement to take the risk of moving towards others and being more open in interaction to scaling down therapeutic ambitions to that of simple survival as set-backs occur and her nihilism surges to the fore. In this *pas de deux*, I am mindful that therapeutic hope can be burdensome. We negotiate again and again what are our shared aims, and how hard to press them.

In this desperate situation, what desperate measures may one as therapist have to take? My basic principle is to try to avoid the endgame. Once someone is dead, there are no more ways to try in this life. I have already mentioned renegotiating goals and backing off as ways to safeguard the other. At various times, I offered Jane extra sessions, made pacts that she would not kill herself before the next week's meeting, and, even, gave her my home telephone number. I rarely do the last and, when I have done it, I have never found the access misused. As many patients do, she kept a secret store of pills to take if life got too much for her to bear. Paradoxically, having a way out of life often helps people stay in. Though it worried me, I accepted this as one of the realities of our work together. One time she did not come to a session and I had a presentiment that she was at great risk. I went to her flat, got access through the caretaker, and found her unconscious having taken a massive overdose. She was admitted. She did not thank me at the time for rescuing her.

Fast-forwarding to now, some fifteen years later, Jane is still alive. She left nursing, formed an intimate relationship, was badly hurt by its ending, had a dog, and resumed nursing, albeit in a junior capacity. Her inner conflicts continue in the same form but at lesser force.

Another patient, again with schizoid and paranoid fears and with too clear a vision of how he destroyed any potential good in his life, did kill himself. We had both worked hard to improve his situation without avail. One day, he came to say goodbye. Sad though it was, the message was not unexpected. Over many months I had thought about his mental state and had satisfied myself that he was in the position to make a considered, competent decision. When he came to say goodbye, I was sure that his intent was not the symptom of delusional depressive disorder. This is an unusual conclusion, not to be lightly reached and needing to be based on extensive knowledge of the patient.

Much more common is the ambiguous situation when the balance between the depressing nature of the patient's life, and negative view from personality and/or mental disorder is unclear. Seeking a psychiatric opinion then can be very useful and is a responsible act. Sometimes, there will be little time for considered reflection. Except in circumstances as I have described above, a patient who declares in front of you that they are going away to kill themselves has to be taken very seriously. In extremis, you may need to use every means at your disposal to persuade someone to accept referral for immediate psychiatric assessment. A useful guide to risk assessment can be found in the Sainsbury Centre for Mental Health guide (Morgan 1998). Remember that someone can refuse treatment unless they are not legally competent to make an adequate decision. The graver the decision, the more rigorous the standard of competence has to be but, for the most part, people have the right to decide their future and whether or not they are going to accept health advice (Hassan *et al.* 1999; Hewson 1999).

Risk of harm to others

Some patients have much in their lives to be angry about. Others have poor impulse control. Yet others are ill-prepared for the demands of intimate relationships and parenthood. Situations now that in their meaning echo past problematic interactions can trigger overwhelming feelings of hate, anger and fear, sometimes of psychotic intensity, which may put third parties at risk of harm. Those at risk may be other adults, commonly the patient's partner, and, not infrequently, the patient's own children. There is a further category of potential risk that therapists may become aware of during their work, that of harm by a third party, for example the sexual abuser of children who is still at large, possibly within the patient's family, and in contact with children.

Sarah just survived a childhood of great poverty and violence. She has chilling memories of hearing the front door open and slam shut as her father returned home after a bout of heavy drinking. She knew what was coming next. The children would be lined up and beaten, seemingly for the fact of existing rather than any misdemeanour. Crying only served to worsen the assault. Satiation marked its end. There was little food. The children sexually abused each other and were abused by their father and, later, by other men. Their mother had schizophrenia and contributed little to the stability of the home.

Now in her mid-thirties, she has three children. Her relationship with them and with their father is deeply ambivalent. She has married and divorced the same man twice; they are currently living apart. Their relationship is volatile to say the least. Most of the time, she was able to make a separation in her mind between the man she married and the abusive representatives of the male gender that she had known in the past. However, it is during sex that her husband was most at risk. Sometimes in her mind's eye, his face would be transformed in a sinister way and the distinction between past and present blurred, almost fatally for him. She would be seized by a terrible, frightened rage and lash out. Once she stabbed him with a knife. He was lucky to survive.

Sarah's husband tries hard to make a go of the relationship. Not surprisingly, he contributes to the volatility. He is possessive and has a temper of his own. Sarah is deeply mistrustful of men and knows it. She feels that she is better off living alone. Sarah hovers on the line between hate-filled, sex-loathing avoidance of men and a difficult, unstable accommodation with them. She has distanced herself from her husband and that is probably the safest position but what if they were living together? The risk would need to be openly addressed in therapy. Is there anything Sarah could do to recognize and minimize the sinister transformation before it is too late? Can her husband approach her in a way that does not echo the past horrors? Should they avoid sex until she has resolved her conflicts (an unlikely outcome) and what are the consequences for their relationship? These are difficult questions with no clear answers.

There is yet more complexity in Sarah's case. She has daughters aged 7 and 5 and a son, Jason, aged 11. She does not love her son like her daughters. She ignores him, treats him roughly, and favours the girls. She knows what she is doing, can see the source in her own bad relationships with men, but cannot desist. She works on this in therapy and makes slow progress. The son is suffering but Sarah is moving towards being a better mother. For the therapist, the balance of concern between mother and child suggests continuing as we are. But what if she tells of locking the boy in a cupboard in the dark. That is bad but it is done to protect him from worse. He is big for his age. His cockiness and size triggers in Sarah hateful memories of her childhood abuse. She wants to beat him. Like many people who have been abused, she worries with some justification about her own potential to abuse. There may be steps that Sarah can take to safeguard her son. Her sister lives nearby and the boy can seek refuge there. Both Sarah and therapist foresee the situation worsening as Jason reaches puberty and becomes sexually active and stronger. Even now, the balance of concern is shifting, the urgency of risk is escalating, and we are close to the point where social services need to be notified of the risk of harm.

I have chosen a more difficult example of potential harm to others than the common one of contemporary sexual abuse of a child by an adult third party. Section 47 of the Children Act 1989 places upon local authorities a duty to investigate situations where they believe that a child is suffering, or likely to suffer significant harm. This they do through social services. The Act creates a qualified duty on specified organizations to assist the local authority in their enquiries by providing relevant information and advice. These organizations include local social, education and health services. The duty is tempered by the exemption that no one is obliged to assist the local authority 'where doing so would be unreasonable in all the circumstances of the case (S.47(10))' (Bond 1993: 136). By terms of their employment, social workers have little discretion in this matter.

While no one could condone child abuse, there is a danger of the therapist acting in a moral ferment and notifying the authorities precipitately and without exercising professional judgement. Writing as a clinician and not a lawyer, I favour corrective action by patients themselves if at all possible. This means a degree of risk taking and living with the inherent uncertainty of risk assessment as inevitable parts of the therapy endeavour. I do not mean being foolish or ignoring evidence of risk. The situation has to be addressed openly. The limits of what can be said without the therapist having to take action needs to be made explicit. A dangerous situation cannot be left to unfold without challenge.

Extended confidentiality within healthcare teams in the NHS

In discussing healthcare, much is made of holistic practice, seeing the person as a whole and making interventions that go beyond part systems to address the interconnected whole. Clinical practice at its best, especially in the NHS, does just this. Groups of professionals collaborate together, each contributing their special expertise to the full care of the patient; in most situations, one healthcare worker cannot meet all the patient's needs. In primary healthcare, complex clinical problems may need input from the general practitioner, nurse, health visitor, physiotherapist, social worker and practice counsellor or psychotherapist to name but a few. Similar networks are brought to bear in hospital care. To varying degrees, each needs to know what the other is doing in order that their input is relevant and coordinated. Sometimes this is given visible form by having a common health record, accessed by and entered into by all the collaborators. From its wartime usage, the term collaborator has acquired unfortunate overtones, implying treachery and betrayal. It is exactly that gut-reaction that may be triggered in the therapist who, used to operating with a closed door, is faced with everyday expectations to share their contribution with the other members of the team.

Healthcare teams operate with extended confidentiality. This may be an explicit part of the employment contract, sometimes as a requirement to bring criminal acts to the attention of authority, sometimes embodied in the requirement to use a common record. Often, extended confidentiality is essential for safe practice. As a routine, doctors may substitute for one another. In crisis, the emergency service needs to know the clinical background. Colleagues may appropriately want to know more than the simple fact that a contribution is being made. This is not to say that everything has to be shared. The guiding principle for therapy is a 'need to know' basis. This means saying enough to be helpful in the total care but not needlessly or thoughtlessly disclosing sensitive confidences. Without being pretentious, therapists can be advocates for good practice in this area.

In the NHS psychotherapy department in Nottingham, we keep two sets of notes, one a psychotherapy file, the other a psychiatric record. The former contains process notes, psychotherapy questionnaires and other sensitive documents, and can be accessed only by staff within the department. The latter contains psychotherapy assessment, progress and discharge letters, may be accessed by other clinical services in the mental health trust, and is their record for concurrent or sequential clinical care.

In recent years, there have been many sad instances in health and social services where children have been suspected to be at risk of harm but the information has not been put together, comprehensive judgements have not been made, and effective action not taken. The poor performance of certain heart surgeons at the Bristol Royal Infirmary in the early 1990s was known by some but not acted upon. The government's concern about these and similar cases is encapsulated in the publication *Clinical Governance: Quality in the New NHS* (Department of Health 1998). High quality service is built on high standards. It is not enough for a clinician to be responsible for his or her work alone. In an interdependent world, we share responsibility for our colleagues' work. We are our brother's keeper. We cannot and should not be bystanders (Clarkson 1996). This is at the heart of the drive to clinical governance, a process which requires transparency of standards and actions, not just in the public sector but in any organization that provides or is responsible for clinical service. Clinical governance certainly applies to the NHS but is highly relevant for the solo private therapist and that person's professional network. Excellence of practice transcends the individual and is a shared responsibility.

Good practice

Does therapy have to be hermetically closed off from the outside world to be effective? My answer is clearly 'no', although, for reasons put forward in this chapter, a degree of closing off is beneficial. The question, then, splits into two: first, when is keeping the door closed not beneficial and, second, to what extent should the door open? I am not making an absolutist argument: door open, disclose, inform, restrict, regardless of circumstance, more one in favour of thoughtful judgement that recognizes the context of the therapy and takes note of what may happen after the patient exits the consulting room. I am challenging the position where useful therapeutic principles, such as confidentiality and respect for self-determination, are elevated to the position of rules.

In therapy, the therapist has a dual responsibility, a primary one to the patient and, in varying degrees of urgency, a secondary one to others. In our reworking of the Hippocratic Oath for Psychotherapy and Counselling, Petruska Clarkson and I wrote that the therapist undertakes to 'enter every therapy primarily for the good of my patient/client, keeping myself from all intentional ill-doing'.

> My primary duty of care is to those with whom I work professionally. At times, I may also owe a duty of care to others, either because of legal or contractual requirement or ethical or moral duty. I will keep the secrets entrusted to me and explain where and when it may be necessary to share them with others.

> (Aveline and Clarkson 1997: 11)

What is good practice in this area?

1 As a therapist, be informed about legal and employment requirements that set overriding limits on confidentiality for the particular context.
2 Make these limits clear to potential patients.
3 Consider supplementing verbal description of limits with a written contract.
4 When practising with extended confidentiality, share on a 'need to know' basis.
5 Being trustworthy is vital to the therapy endeavour. This is earned by safeguarding the exposed vulnerability of the patient, by not ducking issues, and by being open and honest about dual responsibility dilemmas.
6 Breaking confidentiality should never be an unheralded imposition by the therapist. It should be part of an ongoing discussion between patient and therapist.
7 Helping the patient to take healthy action is much better than the therapist having to act.
8 There are few absolute rights and wrongs in this area. Action in a particular circumstance should be informed by professional judgement and not by arbitrary fixed points.
9 Accept that life and therapy involves taking risks.
10 Do not rush to act. Most patients come to therapy to learn to live more healthy and mature lives. Entering therapy can be a step on the way to greater health. Fantasies of violence or perverse taboo breaking sexuality are not the same as acts. Someone struggling to control their impulse needs the therapist's support and encouragement. However, rarely, the risk of self-harm or harm to others is so great that therapist action is imperative. A rule of thumb is: is tangible progress being made and is the balance of risk in favour of continuing to have the door kept closed?
11 Ask yourself again and again: what would be helpful for this patient and to whom do I owe duty of care?
12 Discussing the case with a supervisor or manager helps contain worry or, conversely, overcome ill-conceived therapist reticence.
13 Beware promising what you cannot deliver. Do not fall into the professional trap of acceding to the patient's wish when expressed as 'If I tell you this secret, you won't tell anyone else, will you?'
14 In circumstances where there is a specific legal requirement for disclosure to a third party, be prepared to warn the patient during sessions that if they tell you more, you will be under an obligation to act.
15 Aim to serve the patient well.

Conclusion

Ideally, Bion (1967) advised the psychoanalyst to enter therapy sessions without memory or desire and to be in a state of reverie. For the analyst, the technical objective of this difficult position is to be as selfless as possible. For the patient, at its best, it offers an unique experience of a free space, there for the patient to use as they will, with no preconditions, no prejudgements, a platform for exploration and self-observation, a world in which the deeper recesses of their psychic reality can be discovered.

The obverse to this clarion call to analytic principle is neglect of what may happen to the patient or to others in the world beyond the consulting room. Beyond the closed door, which supportively and conveniently insulates therapist and patient from life in the real world, lie more complex, less known worlds. These are the worlds in which the patient wants to live more fruitfully, an aim which I assume most therapists share. They are worlds for which the patient has primary responsibility. But partly because of the therapist's selective attention but more because of the change-promoting nature of therapy, the therapist has some responsibility for what happens there.

In lifting their gaze from the narrow perspective of the world within the consulting room, the therapist complicates the work; the twin elements of evaluation and purpose enter the room, though not to dominate the proceedings. In my view, there is no valid alternative to so doing. I would argue this, even if there were not as there are legal and employment imperatives in place which dictate action in cases of child protection, terrorism and competency to hold a driving licence. To serve the patient well means thinking about the context of the patient's life and the context within which the therapy conversations take place, the related social worlds that some therapists might wish to ignore but which have to be faced. It means exercising professional clinical judgement.

References

Aveline, M. (1997) Assessing for optimal therapeutic intervention, in S. Palmer and G. McMahon (eds) *Client Assessment*. London: Sage.

Aveline, M. and Clarkson, P. (1997) The psychotherapy and counselling oath, *Counselling*, 8(1): 11–12.

Bion, W.R. ([1967]1988) Notes on memory and desire, in E. Bott Spillius (ed.) *Melanie Klein Today: Developments in Theory and Practice*, vol. 2. London: Tavistock/Routledge.

Bollas, C. and Sundelson, D. (1995) *The New Informants*. London: Karnac.

Bond, T. (1993) *Standards and Ethics for Counselling in Action*. London: Sage.

Clarkson, P. (1996) *The Bystander*. London: Whurr.

Department of Health (1998) *Clinical Governance: Quality in the New NHS*. London: Department of Health.

Freud, S. (1912) *Recommendatons to Physicians Practising Psychoanalysis*. London: Hogarth Press.

Hassan, T.B., MacNamarra, A.F., Davy, A., Bing, A. and Bodiwala, G.G. (1999) Lesson of the week: managing patients with deliberate self-harm who refuse treatment in the accident and emergency department, *British Medical Journal*, 319(7202): 107–9.

Hewson, B. (1999) The law on managing patients who deliberately harm themselves and refuse treatment, *British Medical Journal*, 319(7214): 905–7.

Holmes, J. and Lindley, R. (1989) *The Values of Psychotherapy*. Oxford: Oxford University Press.

Langs, R. (1973) *The Technique of Psychoanalytic Psychotherapy*. New York: Jason Aronson.

Lomas, P. (1981) *The Case for a Personal Psychotherapy*. Oxford: Oxford University Press.

Morgan, S. (1998) *Assessing and Managing Risk: Practitioner's Handbook*. Brighton: Sainsbury Centre for Mental Health and Pavilion Publishing.

Palmer Barnes, F. (1998) *Complaints and Grievances in Psychotherapy*. London: Routledge.

Symington, N. (1986) *The Analytic Experience*. London: Free Association.

World Health Organization (WHO) (1992) *ICD-10 Classification of Mental and Behavioural Disorders*. Geneva: WHO.

10　The sanctum, the citadel and the souk: confidentiality and paradox

Jan Wiener

Sir Robert Morton: *I wept today because right had been done*
Catherine Winslow: *Not justice?*
Sir Robert Morton: *No. Not justice. Right.*
It is easy to do justice – very hard to do right.
(*The Winslow Boy* by Terence Rattigan: 95)

Introduction

Psychotherapists in private practice are only rarely faced with situations in their clinical work that lead to moral or legal decisions to break professional confidentiality. For this reason, it is perhaps easy to ignore these issues. In this chapter, I put forward the view that we do indeed have a responsibility to consider our personal, moral and ethical views about confidentiality. For psychotherapists and analysts working psychodynamically, a unique feature of our method is that we work with fantasies, which make definitions of objective truth difficult. Because of this, the issues are likely to pose particular problems and paradoxes which are by no means easy to resolve. Using a psychodynamic frame of reference and with specific reference to analytical psychology, I reflect on the psychotherapist's psychological state of mind when faced with moral dilemmas in different work settings, about whether to break the boundaries of confidentiality.

The nature of confidentiality

Matters of confidentiality come under the rubric of ethics. Jung himself was more interested in ethics, with what are 'right concerns' and what is good, than he was with morality. As Higgs (1999: 139) puts it, 'ethics are concerned particularly with issues of conduct or character, with values and veracity, with rights and respect'. As members of the psychotherapy profession, we have a commitment to provide high standards of service to our patients within self-regulating organizations that control entry and provide codes of ethics to guide working practice. Ethics inform codes of practice which place great stress on the moral importance of respecting our patients' rights to confidentiality, emphasizing its link to the relationship of trust, so crucial for creating a space for unconscious exploration. Ethical dilemmas are most likely to occur when conflicts of values are experienced, not least when these are conflicts concerning confidentiality.

In the field of medical ethics, we find a sophisticated and fertile literature to contemplate. Confidentiality is important for doctors for two main reasons (McHale 1999: 62). First, if it is not respected, patients may not agree to be treated and second, so that patients are assured of their rights to privacy in clinical consultations. McHale quotes two eminent American academic commentators, Warren and Brandise (1890), who spoke of the right 'to be left alone'. From the first Hippocratic Oath to present-day ethical codes developed by the General Medical Council, doctors have been exhorted to preserve the confidentiality of their patient information. The Hippocratic Oath states that 'all that may come to my knowledge in the exercise of my profession . . . which ought not to be spread abroad I will keep secret and never reveal'. For analysts and psychoanalytic psychotherapists, two thought-provoking questions arise from this oath: first, the reasons why knowledge 'ought not to be spread abroad' and second, our capacity to put our hands on our hearts and promise that we will always 'keep secret and never reveal'?

The medical principles of autonomy, beneficence, non-maleficence and justice (Gillon 1985: Beauchamp and Childress 1994) provide a structure for our ethical thinking about confidentiality and are helpful as a means by which to focus the mind. But they are in themselves insufficient, especially for psychodynamic psychotherapists caught in the subtle matrix of conflicting conscious and unconscious pressures as to whether 'to reveal' something that emerges during therapy. Ethical principles are often divorced from the everyday realities of our work and method and can even undermine our own feelings of worth and moral integrity. The four principles require special explanation in the field of analytical psychotherapy where good practice (beneficence) is difficult to define unless we interpret the 'action' involved as a responsibility to *make meaning together*. The principle of non-maleficence probably comes closest to the tone of many of our codes of ethics.

Conflicting issues about confidentiality for psychotherapists lie in three main areas:

- problems in defining confidentiality
- different kinds of disclosures
- revealing or reporting?

Problems in defining confidentiality

A consideration of the reasons why it is important for psychotherapists to guard carefully the material of their patients takes us into a twilight area where conceptual overlaps and subtle distinctions between privacy, secrecy and confidentiality become relevant.

Privacy is a universal professional principle:

> a fundamental right that allows individuals to decide the manner and extent to which information about themselves is shared with others. Self-determination in this respect is also central to preservation of the safety and dignity and the integrity of the individual.
>
> (Wiener and Sher 1998: 129)

Secrecy frequently imbues the events, thoughts, feelings or fantasies which patients choose to tell us and are often associated with guilt or shame. There are what I think of as 'ordinary' secrets and 'extra-ordinary' secrets. Ordinary secrets are part of the fabric and texture of our day-to-day work to be listened to sensitively and non-judgementally. Jung (1929: 153), highlighting the stages of psychotherapy, emphasized how final each stage, including confession, can seem: 'catharsis, with its heart-felt outpourings, makes one feel: now we are there, everything has come out, everything is known, the last terror lived through and the last tear shed; now everything will be all right'. Secrets are likely to include personal and intimate revelations from our patients' inner and outer world including sexual experiences and fantasies, betrayals, secret longings and events or thoughts which may generate strong feelings in both patient and therapist. There is no reason to break confidentiality. However, if a patient is becoming psychotic, threatening to harm themselves or someone else, telling us they are abusing a child, imagines raping or torturing someone, or tells us they are infected with the HIV virus and infecting lovers, then we are in the area of extra-ordinary secrets. The boundaries between fantasy and reality become blurred for both patient and therapist and therapists may well ask themselves the questions; should I be *doing* anything about this? Why is the patient telling me this now? Should I be encouraging the patient to report this to the authorities?

Confidentiality is about the commitment to maintain boundaries, to take no action. For therapists, the temptation to take actions to break the boundaries of the analytic container is dependent on personal or moral principles, codes of ethics, clinical judgement and, not least, the role of the law. But, and this is central to the argument, if patients do not implicitly or explicitly believe that the thoughts, fantasies and feelings they bring to therapy will be confidential, they will not come. A shadow is cast over our profession as a whole.

Different kinds of disclosures

Distinctions between different kinds of revelations made by psycho-therapists are essential if we are to be able to unpack some of the psychological factors involved. Relevant questions are to do with 'what' is revealed, 'to whom' and 'where'. What is the nature of the action we are taking, to whom will we convey information from the consulting room and in what kind of setting are we working? I believe that what we do is likely to vary according to the setting in which we work, the kind of therapy we practise, our background profession, the code of ethics we adhere to and how we interpret our code of ethics.

The structure of our profession and the culture of contemporary practice mean that there is, in my view, no such thing as absolute confidentiality. We all speak about our patients sometimes, we hope without damaging the therapeutic relationship and more likely in the interests of furthering its growth. More relevant considerations are the distinctions between *revealing* and *reporting*, between a *choice to reveal* and an *obligation to report* and finally, between those revelations which could be seen as *benign* and those likely to be considered more *malign*, probably constituting acting out by the therapist. It is in the sifting of these distinctions that the seeds of disquiet and paradox may stir for the therapist.

Revealing or reporting?

Revealing

We reveal personal information about our patients when we seek supervision for our work, when we consult with colleagues, give talks or publish articles and books which contain case examples from clinical work. We can, I think, make a distinction between these kinds of revelations and what I shall later define as 'reporting', but the question as to whether they are ethically justifiable must nevertheless be addressed.

Wharton (1998: 217) thinks that it is 'ethically justifiable' to reveal information from the consulting room as it is useful to share clinical material as a means of learning our craft, to relieve the loneliness of the work and to promote discussion of new ideas in the field. Bollas and Sundelson (1995) would also agree but only so long as we take great care to preserve the anonymity of our patients:

in this area, the psychoanalyst is not unlike a journalist . . . revealing
what a source has said to him but not revealing who the source is . . .
psychoanalytic writing falls in the domain of what we might call benign
revelation, a form of disclosure aimed to advance the understanding of
psychoanalysis, revealing something of what takes place.

(Bollas and Sundelson 1995: 187)

Budd (1997) thinks we can be too precious about the ethics of publishing:

there is always a point at which concern for confidentiality, or respect
for individuality, can become secrecy and a desire for concealment, or
the solipsistic feeling that nobody can understand us anyway . . . a
discipline whose subject-matter is private and intimate, and concerned
with secrets, is constrained in its organization. If psychoanalysis is to
have any claim to be a science, we have to find a way of communicating
case material.

(Budd 1997: 30–1)

The views of these authors certainly help to justify our revelations but may
mask any personal anxiety that revealing may bring. Spence (1997) brings us
closer to the particular role and responsibility of the therapist and his concept of 'narrative smoothing' begins to address the therapist's state of mind
when reporting or publishing clinical material. He talks of the real difficulties
we have in conveying the music of a therapeutic relationship as distinct from
its content, 'the clinical material that forms the basis of our psychoanalytic
literature speaks with more than the patient's voice . . . the analyst can
impose a story line on the patient's productions' (Spence 1997: 77–8).

It is Britton (1997) who steers us most helpfully towards the therapist's
inner conflicts and paradoxes about breaking confidentiality. He describes
the analyst's psychological conflicts associated with the act of publication.
He names the guilt about publication 'betrayal of affiliation',

what had seemed like the mental content of a private relationship has
become the raw material for other minds . . . the communications internal to one relationship have become the means of furthering the
development of another relationship.

(Britton 1997: 12)

However, he points out convincingly how it would involve a different kind
of betrayal if he did not write at all:

I would be betraying a commitment to an objectivity shared with professional colleagues past and present and with psychoanalysis itself . . .
there are circumstances where objectivity is felt to be the death of subjectivity and others where subjectivity is felt to threaten the demise of
objectivity.

(Britton 1997: 12)

This is surely the essence of the fundamental dilemma for therapists, whether they are weighing up the effects on their patients of publishing papers containing clinical material, deciding whether a patient needs psychiatric support, or reporting abuse which emerges in the consulting room. Choosing to reveal information from our work with patients, whether orally or in writing, will bring inevitable feelings of anxiety; the wish to further a search for truth on the one hand but a fear of behaving unethically on the other. In lending our support to objectivity and psychic truth we may abrogate confidentiality and betray our patients' subjective truth.

Reporting

To 'report' means to reveal the identity of a patient to another; to other healthcare professionals such as GPs and psychiatrists, to social services, to the police or, in some cases, in court. It could be said that we are under increasing pressure to 'report', given the general public's attitude to psychotherapy. Bollas and Sundelson (1995) remind us of the tendency in today's culture to create political objects of corrective vilification. We live in a society where anger is often projected on to key issues (such as a register of paedophiles, the Royal Family). There is now less faith in understanding and reflecting with the individual in mind; rather, more faith in punishment and protecting society. Psychotherapists may be mindful of this and the conscious and unconscious pressures to 'mind their backs'.

Jenkins (1997: 115) points out that 'confidentiality is one of the areas where therapy and the legal world may potentially collide'. GPs are required by statute to maintain confidentiality in the case of venereal disease and infertility treatment and to break confidentiality when it is in 'the public interest'. Whether or not something is in the public interest, however, can be the subject of strenuous debate and leaves much discretion in the hands of the doctor. The law states that public interest must come before privacy, but 'therapists may focus their attention on the idea of privilege, but without necessarily stopping to consider the over-riding principle of the public interest, which is of crucial significance in the world of law' (Jenkins 1997: 115).

Few of us would disagree that the role of affects is central in the therapeutic relationship. The countertransference, that is, our own thoughts, feelings and body responses to our patients, are crucial to the work. It could be argued therefore that if we are to practise effectively, we must be protected from intrusions and the destructive effects of the law including the requirement to report. The intrusion of the law on the analyst's frame of mind, the thought police, can lead to the practice of defensive psychotherapy:

the screen of receptive listening no longer exists . . . in turn, the capacity to receive the patient's communications from an attitude of evenly suspended attention – when the analyst drifts along in his own world of associative thought and feeling – is (also) destroyed as the clinician will bear an increasingly menacing internal object: the heavy footsteps of the state.

(Bollas and Sundelson 1995: 90–1)

Legal examples

The following legal examples are likely to make psychotherapists quake in their boots.

Tatiana Tarasoff

On 27 October 1969, Prosenjit Poddar killed Tatiana Tarasoff, on the campus at the University of California after threatening to Dr Lawrence Moore, his therapist, to kill her. Dr Moore had warned the campus police, who detained Mr Poddar briefly and then released him, satisfied that he was rational. Dr Moore did not notify Tatiana Tarasoff or her parents that their daughter was in danger. The therapist therefore predicted violence and 'in the public interest' reported it to the campus police, but did not extend his report to the threatened victim or her family. The judgment stated that protective privilege ends where the public peril begins and laws were introduced so that therapists had a duty to warn intended victims; in some cases, this was interpreted as the therapist's responsibility to assess danger and protect foreseeable victims. There was one dissenting judge (Justice Clark) who maintained the position that confidentiality was essential to treat the mentally ill effectively, and that imposing a duty on doctors to disclose patient threats to potential victims would greatly impair treatment. Such a duty would frustrate treatment, invade patient's fundamental rights and increase violence. The assurance of confidentiality was important for three reasons: not to deter patients from seeking help; to ensure full disclosure from patients and to maintain trust in the treatment. Justice Clark remained a lone voice.

Anne Hayman

Hayman (1965: 785), a British psychoanalyst, was subpoenaed to give evidence in the High Court of the UK about a former patient and struggled with two conflicting moral obligations; whether to obey the law or to abide by her personal and professional ethical beliefs. She attended court but chose to remain silent – a contempt of court – though the judge did not sentence her, saying that it was obviously a matter of conscience. Hayman states her views clearly: 'if I were to speak indiscreetly about patients, I should not only be behaving unethically, but I should also be destroying the very fabric of my therapy . . . I had to be completely reliable in all my dealings with my patients, and this included keeping their secrets under all circumstances'.

Hayman makes a stalwart attempt to justify our method of work to the point that even asking for permission from patients may mask unconscious motives encouraging them to give permission: 'patients attend us on the implicit understanding that anything they reveal is subject to a special protection . . . It would be as if a physician invited a patient to undress and then arrested him for exhibiting himself . . . Justice, as well as our ethic is likely to be served best by silence'.

The essence of psychodynamic psychotherapy

The above legal examples bring us to the question of the nature of our model of work and how to communicate its substance to the outside world. A central paradox when reflecting on our attitudes to confidentiality is that the same sharing of information can be seen on the one hand as:

1 in the interests of child (or other adult) protection; public interest in mind
2 good multidisciplinary 'working together'
3 necessary managed care
4 compliance with child abuse reporting laws, especially in the USA

versus the

1 betrayal of patients' rights to privacy
2 betrayal of the clinician's personal right to privacy
3 violation of rights to practise our profession
4 violation of the principles of privilege granted to other professionals such as the clergy, lawyers and journalists.

Of the situation in the USA, where the law has exerted more influence and impact on psychotherapists, Bollas and Sundelson (1995) launch a stringent attack on psychoanalysts and psychoanalytic psychotherapists:

> lawyers still have privileged relations with their clients, priests with their penitents, journalists with their sources, but therapists have allowed their privilege – equally, if not more important to the practice of their profession – to be destroyed . . . A schizophrenic imagines his sexuality in persecutory ways and constructs a delusion of abusing someone; his therapist may be legally obliged to report him. And then there is the child raised in a sexually oppressive environment who can

only permit herself to imagine her sexuality by conjuring up a belief that she has been ritually violated. She will suffer horrific consequences when her therapist provides an account of these quite imaginary events to the authorities.

(Bollas and Sundelson 1995: xii)

They think that to break confidentiality by reporting is to betray the central tenet of our method and therefore, by implication, it is a betrayal of our patients' rights to absolute privacy. We should never abrogate confidentiality but bear the anguish that this uncomfortable position will generate. Our method involves creating a space for fantasies to emerge from the unconscious and working with them. Truth is often subjective and provisional and when it comes to reporting, is likely to be experienced by our patients as a betrayal of what we ask of them, to talk to us openly and honestly.

Bollas and Sundelson argue in favour of the 'restoration of privilege' to analysis. Analysts, psychotherapists and counsellors working psychodynamically should not be legally bound to 'report' on patients who are abusing or being abused. We should fight our corner, they say, by explaining our methods of work to lawyers and the government. They provide a recommended statement from training institutes:

the contents of a psychoanalysis are strictly confidential and any or all disclosures, such as discussing a patient with colleagues, arranging for hospitalization, acting in the interests of a child patient must be given on the understanding that confidentiality is maintained and that in all circumstances, privilege is retained by the psychoanalyst.

(Bollas and Sundelson 1995: 156)

Confidentiality in different work settings: the sanctum, the citadel and the souk

I have made reference in previous work to the extent to which authors neglect the significant role of context in a comparison of particular psychotherapy environments (Wiener 1996) and in the assessment of patients for psychotherapy and analysis (Wiener 1998). Many of us work in different settings and while our model of work remains constant, the nature of this setting is likely to affect our attitudes and behaviour to issues of confidentiality and the subtlety of conflicting principles in these settings.

The sanctum

Private practice is the setting where we have the individual in mind. We are living and working with unconscious processes and the images and affects from the inner world. Patients are encouraged to say whatever is on their mind, psychic truth is highly valued and distinctions between fantasy and reality our building blocks for exploration. We may see our patients several times a week for several years and a secure frame is an essential precondition if the sanctum, that place where two selves, patient and therapist, have the potential to relate to each other authentically, is to be entered. Here, 'consulting' and 'supervision' and occasional 'management' actions are generally in the interests of good practice – the frame has some elasticity – but 'reporting' could be seen as a major betrayal of trust and can have implications for all other private practice patients. Some analysts and therapists would extend this to the publishing of clinical papers even though the identity of patients is disguised and permission for publication sought. In my private practice, my personal ethical attitude dictates that I do consult with a colleague if I am in difficulty and there is a special kind of thinking involved when I am writing papers or I think a patient should be consulting with their GP. My own defences, narcissism in the case of publishing clinical material and omnipotence when a patient may for a while require more help than I can provide, force a particularly strenuous inner struggle between the subjective and the objective, between unconsciousness and knowledge.

The citadel

Psychotherapy clinics require a strong-walled citadel environment to preserve therapeutic integrity and to deal with the large numbers of referrals and political pressures to modify the methods we believe in. Here again, we have the individual in mind though also sometimes the group or the couple. In the UK, dissolution of the NHS into managed trusts is part of the corporate mentality that generates 'managed care' (not teamwork) leading to pressures to dilute our methods of work. The citadel can feel inaccessible and rigid to outside referrers such as physicians, psychiatrists and practice counsellors, but its strong outside wall is the means to preserve a frame within the clinic for psychodynamic work and the space for essential reflection.

It is accepted good professional practice to consult with clinic colleagues and seek regular supervision, most particularly with difficult borderline patients who often present in the NHS. The unspoken ethic of confidentiality is rather like a moat around the citadel. Within the portals, patient files are freely consulted and cases discussed, identities disguised, but contact with neighbouring citadels is restricted. The door of the citadel opens from time to time for information on a 'need to know' basis to pass out to referrers. Assessment and end-of-treatment reports are common practice, not abrogation of confidentiality. Where departments have attached social workers, consultation about violent and abusive patients is greatly facilitated; they take over any necessary 'actions'. Our faith in transference and countertransference processes to make informed clinical judgements about when to contain and when to act, remains paramount. Reflection comes before action.

The souk

GP surgeries are chaotic places in which to work (Wiener and Sher 1998). GPs are notoriously inefficient at creating space for reflection about their clinical and organizational work. They have to cope with whomever walks through the door and must decide what is treatable, and what must be borne or managed. Most practices have teamwork in mind and use a model of confidentiality not of a patient therapist couple, but one operating within the bounds of the practice team. GP practices have a broader cohort of patients including many with physical or psychosomatic problems who require physical and psychological help. Therapists must modify two sets of cherished training beliefs if they are to adapt: first, that information is profitably shared with GPs on a 'need to know' basis; second, that a more flexible work style is essential.

In primary care we are not practising analysis but we use an analytic attitude to the work to understand the conscious and unconscious matrix of relationships within the surgery and the effects patients can have on the staff. Coltart's (1993: 18) phrase 'adventures of the spirit' accurately describes the nature of the atmosphere in the surgery. Patients' expectations are different to those in private practice. It can be containing to have two figures (GP and therapist) who talk together and as Elder (personal communication) remarked, 'what is the point of having a therapist in the practice if they don't talk to you?' There is a need to redefine our terms and models of confidentiality; working 'in' not 'with' the surgery; involvement in teamwork rather than referrals to the therapist.

There are two models of confidentiality observable in primary care. First, where exchanges between patients and therapist are absolutely confidential. Here the therapist is in danger of rigidly adhering to a private practice model and can become marginalized and isolated. Second, as a member of a multi-disciplinary team, applying shared boundaries of confidentiality to the team as a whole. Patients commonly split between GP and therapist especially if both are working in the same place. My problem about reporting on patients if I am anxious about them becomes a practice problem; after all, the GPs are responsible for my patients. This said, actions such as housing applications may be helpfully deflected on to the GP to preserve the therapeutic space and the integrity of the work. Elder (1996), a GP, delivers words of wisdom to psychodynamic therapists:

if you live in a very exposed spot (GP) it is hard not to look for shelter, but if you live in a rather sheltered spot (therapist) you may begin to forget that outside the shelter lies the wilderness. As mental health professionals move closer to the world of general practice, interesting things begin to happen in response to the new setting, and some of the boundaries and apparent distinctiveness of different approaches begin to melt away, and then reform in new ways as a response to new challenges.

(Elder 1996: 61)

The psychotherapist's state of mind: an ethical space

Jung's (1952: 219) alchemical metaphor of the *vas bene clausum*, the well-sealed vessel, is a precautionary measure very frequently mentioned in alchemy, and is 'the equivalent of the magic circle ... to protect what is within from the intrusion and admixture of what is without as well as to prevent it from escaping'. Jung (1935: 410) describes this magic circle as 'a kind of holy place or *temenos* to protect the centre of the personality'. Here he introduces the idea of a therapeutic frame or container, to use the more usual word, which creates a space inside it in which something vital, a relationship between two selves, patient and therapist may evolve. The frame may seamlessly expand or contract a bit, or vary in its permeability at different times during therapy with no adverse effects for patient or therapist or their relationship. But when the therapist feels under pressure to reveal or report, knowing that this may have an adverse effect on the therapeutic relationship, the frame becomes brittle, potentially breakable.

This brings us to the nub of the issue. How may we think about the therapist's state of mind when in the grip of a countertransference experience of anxiety leading to a wish to report or reveal what is emerging in the therapy? At these moments, rare though they may be, we struggle to make an ethical space to unpack our countertransference responses. This is normal practice. However, this is not a normal situation but rather a special form of countertransference experience constellating particular inner psychic processes. Unconscious processes continue in day-to-day work untrammelled by decisions as to whether to break the bounds of confidentiality. Then the therapist is plunged into a liminal place, in the sway of an archetypal experience where the pressure from psychic opposites can be intense. Jung (1936: 82) points out that 'the chief danger in succumbing to the fascinating influence of the archetypes is most likely to happen when the archetypal images are not made conscious'. What we know about archetypal experiences is that they provoke particular affects such as fascination, a sense of something numinous or of being possessed by something awesome – terrible or beautiful or significant. They are also marked by an all or nothing quality so that whatever is archetypal is experienced as stark and powerful and absolute – good or bad, bigger than big or smaller than small. The quality of these experiences means that codes of ethics developed by our particular societies are likely to be insufficient when faced with ethical dilemmas such as:

- Should I write now about an aspect of a patient's analysis? How will she feel about it? How will it affect the work?
- Is my patient breaking down? Do I need to consult a colleague, suggest he visits his GP?
- An anorexic patient is dangerously losing weight. Should she be in hospital?
- I am frightened for my own safety when a patient is talking about acting out his violent fantasies. What, if anything, should I do?
- A colleague seems to be unaware of the debilitating effects of a prolonged physical illness on her state of mind. Should I report her to our ethics committee?

These are uncomfortable situations and we may wish to avoid them, to defend ourselves against our beliefs and wishes. We are caught in a psychic area where distinctions between inside and outside, between what is subjective and what objective, between fantasy and reality are blurred. The guardian of our everyday beliefs fails and the therapeutic frame is under threat so that inevitably, the nature of the therapeutic space within it is changed. We may collude with a patient and do nothing or alternatively act too hastily. Generally we talk to a colleague to bring these opposing forces closer together but at these moments, therapist and patient become embedded in a larger set of values. We are citizens as well as therapists.

Roger Poole (1973), the philosopher, describes the process of finding what he calls an ethical space:

> thinking is double ethical. First it involves transforming the terms of a thinker's system into terms which can be grasped, comprehended and redeployed in one's own system. And then, in a second moment, thinking has to refuse certain terms in the original system . . . to become independent enough not only to understand the law but to change it
>
> (Poole 1973: 145)

The psychological space in which psychotherapists operate when considering breaking confidentiality can be conceptualized as an intermediate area of experience (Winnicott 1971), a transitional space, a liminal state (Wiener 1989). There is a wealth of anthropological literature on *rites de passage*. Van Gennep ([1909] 1960) recognized that various rites make possible a passage from one stage to the next. Turner (1974: 231–2; 1977: 95) uses the term 'liminality' to describe 'transition rites' which accompany every change of state or social position. He talks of three phases: separation, margin and reaggregation. This second phase, or margin comes from the word *limen* the Latin for threshold. Turner comments: 'cunicular, being in a tunnel, would describe the quality of this phase in many cases its hidden nature, its sometimes mysterious darkness'. Turner (1974) goes on to describe the character

of this liminal period as one where the ritual subject (the passenger or limi-
nar) becomes

> ambiguous, neither here not there, betwixt and between all fixed points
> of classification; he passes through a symbolic domain that has few or
> none of the attributes of his past or coming state. This is a state of 'out-
> siderhood', the condition of being either permanently and by aspiration
> set outside the structural arrangements of a given social system . . . tem-
> porarily set apart, or voluntarily setting oneself apart from the behav-
> iour of status-occupying role-playing members of that system.
>
> (Turner 1974: 232)

How may we turn a liminal place or threshold state that is uncomfortable,
into a third area where an ethical space for thinking becomes possible? It
is firstly important to clarify the precise nature of this tension; what are
the clashing opposites? Solomon (2000) makes an important distinction
between morality and ethics:

> morality is indicated by the adherence to a set of stated principles or
> rules which govern behaviour (for example the Ten Commandments,
> or a professional Code of Ethics), whereas ethics implies an attitude
> achieved through judgment, discernment and conscious struggle, often
> between conflicting rights or duties.
>
> (Solomon 2000: 1)

Therapists in a threshold state are experiencing a tension between their
moral principles and their ethical principles; a conflict between the code of
ethics they adhere to (moral principles) and their own personal, internal
ethical attitude. Jung (1958: 825) puts it well: 'conscience is a complex
phenomenon consisting on the one hand in an elementary act of the will, or
in an impulse to act for which no conscious reason can be given, and on the
other hand in a judgment grounded on rational feeling'.
Several authors helpfully conceptualize this third area in which meaning
and therefore new thinking can emerge. Winnicott's (1971) concept of cultural experience locates a potential space between the individual and the
environment where cultural experience emerges. I like to think of this as the
place where an ethical space and attitude may form:

> to describe human nature, we must not only look at interpersonal
> relationship and inner reality/the inner world but also at an inter-
> mediate area of experiencing to which inner reality and external life
> both contribute . . . it shall exist as a resting-place for the individual
> engaged in the perpetual task of keeping inner and outer reality sepa-
> rate yet interrelated . . . the intermediate area between the subjective
> and that which is objectively perceived.
>
> (Winnicott 1971: 2–3)

Gordon (1993) in a paper echoing Winnicott called 'The location of archetypal experience' illustrates how we tend to think of archetypal content as a potential source of information to trust almost blindly yet on the other hand an elemental force to leave behind if growth is to be possible, 'we should withdraw from them [archetypal contents] but if this process of identification or projection did not occur, life would be flat, without sparkle or adventure'. Gordon makes a marriage between Jung and Winnicott, finding a third psychic area where archetypal experience may be lodged appropriately and meaning, one of our primary needs, found. This third area is

> the crucible where phantasy and reality meet, fuse, defuse and re-fuse ... a process made possible by the symbolic function which has its roots in the third area and through which are linked the conscious to the unconscious, the sensuous to the abstract, the unobservable realities to observable phenomena. The phantasies that meet here with reality originate from both the personal unconscious and the archetypal, that is, the collective levels of the psyche.
>
> (Gordon 1993: 137)

Ogden (1994: 4) talks of the interdependence of analyst and analysand, but tells us that we need a third term, 'which defines the nature of psycho-analytic experience and differentiates it from all other intersubjective human events'. The 'analytic third' is experienced differently by analyst and patient, 'since each remains a separate subject in dialectical tension with the other'. The analytic third is also 'a form of experiencing I-ness (a form of subjectivity) in which (through which) analyst and analysand become other than who they had been up to that point. The analyst 'not only hears about the analysand's experience, *but experiences his own creation of it*' (Ogden 1994: 4, my italics). This process seems to me to describe accurately the formation of a space in which an ethical attitude to a particular dilemma may develop.

Decisions as to whether or not to 'act' depend on the therapist's beliefs. Britton (1998) points out that:

> the status of belief is conferred on some pre-existing phantasies, which then have emotional and behavioural consequences which otherwise they do not. Beliefs may be unconscious and yet exert effects. When belief is attached to a phantasy or idea, initially it is treated as a fact. The realisation that it is a belief is a secondary process which depends on viewing the belief from outside the system of the belief itself.
>
> (Britton 1998: 9)

Britton, like Winnicott, Gordon and Ogden, emphasizes the individual's need to find a third position from which to view their subjective beliefs in order to find internal objectivity:

once a belief is conscious it can be tested against perception, memory, known facts and other existing beliefs . . . when a belief fails the test of reality, it has to be relinquished in the same sense that an object has to be relinquished when it ceases to exist. As a lost object has to be mourned by the repeated discovery of its disappearance, so a lost belief has to be mourned by the repeated discovery of its invalidity.

(Britton 1998: 9)

Britton thinks that beliefs are essential in order to act and react but a good deal of the time we have to do so without knowledge. We can defend ourselves against our beliefs:

belief, as an act, is in the realm of knowledge what attachment is in the realm of love . . . we embrace beliefs or surrender them; we hold beliefs and we abandon them; sometimes we feel that we betray them. There are times when we are in the grip of a belief, held captive by it, feel persecuted by it or are possessed by it. We relinquish our most deeply held beliefs, as we relinquish our deepest personal relationships, only through a process of mourning.

(Britton 1998: 12)

In addressing how beliefs become knowledge, Britton puts forward the idea of 'triangular psychic space', a third position in mental space where 'the subjective self can be observed having a relationship with an idea'. This comes close to my idea of ethical space.

Symington (1996: 5) discusses traditions in modern psychodynamic psychotherapy and illustrates how 'the individual's own moral decision is considered to be an important determinant of the state of his mental life'. He also illustrates how in all therapies 'there are therapeutic and anti-therapeutic forces at work'. It is precisely when these anti-therapeutic forces are at work that we are most likely to search for shelter behind impersonal dictums as to what we 'should' do, neglecting our more personal subjective feelings which can also validly inform any decision as to whether to break confidentiality. Collusion with inertia often offers a path of least resistance. Issues of confidentiality confront us with our own ethical dilemmas and the need somehow to find a third position where conflict and paradox, structures and feelings, concern for our patients, our model of work and ourselves may helpfully interact. When beliefs come to be trusted, thinking becomes possible, meaning is found and decisions as to whether or not to 'act' facilitated.

Conclusion

In this chapter I have attempted to identify some of the psychic factors which underpin the painful conflicts involved when dilemmas about breaking confidentiality arise in clinical practice. I have provided no answers, simply raised questions, illustrated problems and paradoxes and pointed to some of the conflicts. At these moments we should practise what we advocate in our day-to-day work; to think about the issues with care and concern for the welfare of our patients. During the course of our professional careers, there will be times when we are all faced with ethical dilemmas about confidentiality and a subsequent conflict between our moral obligation to protect our patients, to protect others from our patients and in turn to protect ourselves. Our own codes of ethics and the law are not always containing. They are sometimes destructive to our method of work as psychodynamic therapists and paradoxically, we may have to ignore legal intrusions in order to do our work properly. In today's culture of increasing litigation and vilification, I wonder how easy this is to put into practice.

How we respond (or not respond) in such situations is likely to depend upon our clinical integrity, the meaning we attribute to our beliefs about what to do, the setting in which we work and our capacity to find a third position, an ethical space, from which to view the relationship between our moral principles and our personal ethical attitude so that the subjective and objective can become more companionable bedfellows. There will however always be some element of subjective choice. This process is likely to be facilitated if there are etiquettes and institutional structures to help contain us but ultimately, they will not prevent the necessary internal struggle for each one of us between the chaos arising from our archetypal shadow, narcissism and omnipotence, and the wish to behave ethically in the face of adversity.

I have used the sanctum, the citadel and the souk as metaphors to characterize three different work settings using subtly different models of confidentiality; I am tempted to stretch these metaphors to describe the psychotherapist's inner psychic drama when working with issues of confidentiality. We turn to the sanctum, that inner private place of feelings, of intuitions and of thoughts – the centre of the self – to search for subjective knowledge to foster an ethical space for reflection that facilitates ethical behaviour. Along the way, we hope for support from a strong-walled citadel to contain this intrapsychic process but we shall certainly have to struggle in the chaos of the souk, that shadow force, the source of what is most unethical within us. It is to this inner process which the barrister, Sir Robert Morton, refers, in Rattigan's *The Winslow Boy* when he stresses that it is easy to do justice but much more difficult to do the right thing.

References

Beauchamp, T.L. and Childress, J.F. (1994) *Principles of Biomedical Ethics*, 4th edn. Oxford: Oxford University Press.

Bollas, C. and Sundelson, D. (1995) *The New Informants: Betrayal of Confidentiality in Psychoanalysis and Psychotherapy*. London: Karnac.

Britton, R. (1997) Making the private public, in I. Ward (ed.) *The Presentation of Case Material in Clinical Discourse*. Northampton: Freud Museum Publications.

Britton, R. (1998) Belief and psychic reality, *Belief and Imagination: Explorations in Psychoanalysis*. London: Routledge.

Budd, S. (1997) Ask me no questions and I'll tell you no lies, in I. Ward (ed.) *The Presentation of Case Material in Clinical Discourse*. Northampton: Freud Museum Publications.

Coltart, N. (1993) *How to Survive as a Psychotherapist*. London: Free Association.

Elder, A. (1996) Primary care and psychotherapy, *Psychoanalytic Psychotherapy*, supplement, vol. 10. Conference proceedings: *Future Direction of Psychotherapy in the NHS: Adaptation or Extinction*. Huddersfield: Charlesworth Group.

Gillon, R. (1985) *Philosophical Medical Ethics*. Chichester: John Wiley.

Gordon, R. (1993) The location of archetypal experience, *Bridges: Metaphor for Psychic Processes*. London: Karnac.

Hayman, A. (1965) Psychoanalyst subpoenaed, *The Lancet*, 16 October: 785–6.

Higgs, R. (1999) Depression in general practice, in C. Dowrick and L. Frith (eds) *General Practice and Ethics: Uncertainty and Responsibility*. London: Routledge.

Jenkins, P. (1997) *Counselling, Psychotherapy and the Law*. London: Sage.

Jung, C.G. (1929) Problems of modern psychotherapy, *Collected Works*, vol. 16. London: Routledge & Kegan Paul.

Jung, C.G. (1935) The Tavistock lectures, *Collected Works*, vol. 18. London: Routledge & Kegan Paul.

Jung, C.G. (1936) Archetypes of the collective unconscious, *Collected Works*, vol. 9. London: Routledge & Kegan Paul.

Jung, C.G. (1952) The symbolism of the mandala, *Collected Works*, vol. 12. London: Routledge & Kegan Paul.

Jung, C.G. (1958) A psychological view of conscience, *Collected Works*, vol. 10. London: Routledge & Kegan Paul.

McHale, J. (1999) The general practitioner and confidentiality, in C. Dowrick and L. Frith (eds) *General Practice and Ethics: Uncertainty and Responsibility*. London: Routledge.

Ogden, T.H. (1994) *Subjects of Analysis*. London: Karnac.

Poole, R. (1973) *Towards Deep Subjectivity*. London: Allen Lane.

Rattigan, T. (1996) *The Winslow Boy*. London: Nick Hern.

Solomon, H.M. (2000) The ethical self, in E. Christopher and H.M. Solomon (eds) *Jungian Thought in the Modern World*. London: Free Association.

Spence, D.P. (1997) Case reports and the reality they represent: the many faces of Nachtraeglichkeit, in I. Ward (ed.) *The Presentation of Case Material in Clinical Discourse*. Northampton: Freud Museum Publications.

Symington, N. (1996) *The Making of a Psychotherapist*. London: Karnac.

Turner, V. (1974) *Dramas, Fields and Metaphors: Symbolic Action in Human Society*. New York: Cornell University Press.

Turner, V. (1977) *The Ritual Process: Structure and Anti-Structure*. New York: Cornell University Press.

Van Gennep, A. ([1909] 1960) *The Rites of Passage*. Chicago: University of Chicago Press.

Warren, E. and Brandise, L. (1890) The right to privacy, *Harvard Law Review*, 193.

Wharton, B. (1998) What comes out of the consulting room: the reporting of clinical material, *Journal of Analytical Psychology*, 43(2): 205–23.

Wiener, J. (1989) Threshold states in analysis, unpublished qualifying paper, Society of Analytical Psychology.

Wiener, J. (1996) Primary care and psychotherapy, *Psychoanalytic Psychotherapy*, supplement, vol. 10. Conference proceedings: *Future Direction of Psychotherapy in the NHS: Adaptation or Extinction*. Huddersfield: Charlesworth Group.

Wiener, J. (1998) Tricky beginnings: assessment in context, in I. Alister and C. Hauke (eds) *Contemporary Jungian Analysis: Post-Jungian Perspectives from the Society of Analytical Psychology*. London: Routledge.

Wiener, J. and Sher, M. (1998) *Counselling and Psychotherapy in Primary Health Care: A Psychodynamic Approach*. London: Macmillan.

Winnicott, D.W. (1971) *Playing and Reality*. London: Routledge.

11 | The private face and the public face of psychotherapy

Edward Martin

Introduction

Psychotherapists make poor dinner guests when the conversation gets round to 'What do you DO?' The answer, 'Nothing', will not, of course, satisfy the enquirer, who suspects already from reading even the more responsible papers that psychotherapists are charlatans, who charge high fees, keep patients dependent for years on end and do nothing very much to help them. Of course psychotherapists know better, but I think that few would have the ready proof to satisfy even the mildest of dinner guest critics that long-term psychotherapy was a good investment.

Even if the enquirer were sympathetic, how could we respond? Our codes of ethics forbid us to gossip about patients. Perhaps there is an additional taboo: if we feel free to gossip then our inner voice might whisper that our own therapist/analyst would gossip about us. 'I once had this funny person on my couch who thought s/he could train just like that . . .!' If we feel inhibited about gossiping how do we describe what happens in our consulting rooms in a manner that will satisfy the conversationalist? 'Do you give advice?' 'Well, no, actually we never do'. That often meets an incredulous response, 'You *never* give advice?' And as we know that is not totally true, suddenly the ice we are skating on becomes dangerously thinner. Dare we describe the intensity of the transference relationship, the dead, funny, depressed, erotic, lustful, parental, caring, sadistic feelings that evolve in the course of a long-term therapy? If we dare we might meet with, 'Well everyone knows patients fall in love with their therapists, how does that help them?' We note of course that it is always 'they', the enquirers projecting their own disabilities on to 'them', that indefinable other group, the 'others' who come to see us. The idea that these 'others' might be senior executives, directors of major companies, high-ranking police officers, athletes, consultant physicians, the people who go to their dinner parties (or the people they would like to go to their dinner parties!) cannot really bear to be thought about. Either psychotherapists deal with the real cripples in society, those whom the Nanny State has left behind (thank goodness), the nutters whom we would not want near our garden gate, or those with so much money they can spend large sums on such unnecessary indulgences as psychotherapy.

Of course psychotherapy conversations, like dinner parties, happen in a social and political context and there are a number of major issues that affect the private and public lives of psychotherapists. I would like to focus on two. First, the internal jealousy and strife that has riddled the world of psychotherapy. This is as tribal as any of the internecine wars being fought for instance in the Balkans or in Northern Ireland and it has eaten away at the profession's energy. Second, it appears that the new millennium is being accompanied by the return of repression, a remodelled form of Puritanism. Looking at or touching another is increasingly becoming taboo. If one breaks the taboo and looks at or touches another there could be terrible consequences. If lucky the result would be a charge of assault. If unlucky, death or injury could result, as touch or look are registered by the other as an attack and a counterattack unconsciously launched.

The question 'What do you do?' often has another question underlying it, which at a personal level is 'What values do you hold?' and at a collective level 'What does psychoanalytic psychotherapy stand for?' Perhaps one of the many factors that once made this profession so attractive to its practitioners was the sense of (inner) freedom it imparted. Is the sun of inner hope once enshrined in psychotherapy still shining bright or has it begun to set, leaving only long lingering shadows? What has happened to this giant and what is happening to its practitioners?

The death of psychotherapy

In 1966 Rieff, among other writers, was postulating two downfalls. The first was Christian culture. Rieff's opening sentence in *The Triumph of the Therapeutic* talks about literature and sociology being the eloquent and knowing mourners at the wake of Christian culture. Later, he talks of 'the struggles in the camp of one among these displacing centres of belief' that of psychoanalysis. Rieff (1996) makes a long and not unsympathetic examination of psychoanalysis, which he describes as 'a cultural artefact, devised primarily to protect the outer life against further encroachments by the inner and to minimise the damage caused by disorders of the parts inside'. In other words, Rieff's view of psychoanalysis was not unlike that of Iris Murdoch (1999), who once described it as 'too superficial'. Rieff reviews the parts played by Freud's powerful successor-critics namely, Jung (The Language of Faith), Reich (The Religion of Energy) and Lawrence (The True Philosophy).

He suggests that post-Freudians and post-Jungians and those influenced by them should move beyond and assimilate an analytic attitude in their world-view. Even so (in the final analysis) Rieff could postulate in the 1960s 'The Triumph of the Therapeutic'. It cannot be taken for granted that the contemporary follower of either Freud or his critical successor Jung could so readily affirm that the therapeutic has triumphed.

If therapeutic triumph can no longer be assured, the goals of therapy have to be curtailed. Hard science does not wish it well, hard business views it with distaste and hard religion links it with the Devil. The armoury of the media, smelling blood, has predictably joined in the war to fell this Goliath of philosophic thought and humanitarian treatment. Its founders, Freud and Jung, are submitted again and again to the charge of either intellectual or emotional deceit. Through these personal attacks a philosophy that has dominated western thought since the 1950s is being torn to shreds. Its intellectual basis and the methodology of its treatment are in the dock and there is apparently little defence. Has anybody really been helped, let alone cured by this treatment? Is it not true that the therapeutic brats spawned by this dinosaur are actually more effective, cost less and are better liked? Is it not true that training counts for little? Cannot everyone follow the guidance of our television soap opera's scriptwriters and become do-it-yourself therapists? Is it really necessary to spend enormous sums training for eight to ten years? While in the dugouts of the private societies which train the next generation's therapists, huddles of old hands are heard exchanging secret wishes such as 'If only they understood about the internal world, that therapy is not about external change but internal attitudes'. 'They' do not. They are demanding that psychoanalytic psychotherapy should explain itself and in a language they, the world, understands. The message is no longer that psychoanalysis is challenging the world, but the world is challenging psychoanalysis. The public that always enjoys the spectacle of watching heroes fall under constant media attack, the twentieth century's equivalent of public executions, bare-knuckle fighting and the lion pit, joins in delightedly.

The prurience reflected by the majority of press articles seems to be clearer when they are read, in concentrated form, from a researcher's files. Strangely, most of the headlines quoted below relate to book reviews, some by practising psychotherapists, others by interested writers. The qualities of reflection and insight within the actual article seem to make no difference, the headlines scream, reminding readers that it is the profession which is in the dock, accused, tried and sentenced by the media. Psychotherapists, on the other hand, rightly treat media ethics with caution. They know that the media's task is to succeed in playing the numbers game, and entertaining readers best achieves this end. One sure way is about them hearing of gods being demoted and made human. As Victoria Funk comments in her review of McLynn's biography of Jung: 'If, in the end we find it difficult to reconcile

Dr Carl Jung The Great Thinker with Dr Carl Jung The Great Creep, the problem probably lies in our own need to keep our heroes safely on a pedestal'.

Thus of Jung:

- 'Jung Lied about His Big Idea Claims Scholar' (*Sunday Telegraph* 4 June 1995)
- 'Harvard Scholar Says Jung was a Fraud' (*Daily Telegraph* 5 June 1995)
- 'Charismatic Charlatan' (*Sunday Telegraph* 9 June 1996)
- 'He Was the Man Who 'Invented Free Love'. But for his String of Mistresses his Theories Would Mean Only Cruelty' (*Daily Mail* 29 June 1996)
- 'The Crown Prince in Deep Waters' (*Independent on Sunday* 8 September 1996).

Freud fares no better:

- 'The Dirty Old Man who Seduced Us All (*Observer* 1 June 1997)
- 'The Great Intellectual Con' (*Financial Times* 21 June 1997)
- 'The Master's Mad Move' (*Guardian* 30 January 1999).

The couple fare little better with headlines like 'Truce in the Bitter War of The Couch' (*Observer* 10 September 1995) and 'Analysts in Need of a Couch' (*Financial Times* 26 February 1994).

The headlines proclaiming that Jung was 'The man who "invented free love". But for his string of mistresses his theories would mean only cruelty', was followed by a review of a new biography, *Jung* by Frank McLynn (1996). The article concentrates on describing Jung's affairs and his general misogynous attitude towards women (Kelly 1996). Jung's interest in the paranormal and his research into it (while having an affair with the medium) are described as 'odd'. That it led to Jung's breakthrough into understanding sub-personalities is set in the context of Jung's betrayal of his teenage lover.

But which of us has not betrayed someone? We care not to remember it too clearly, we have rationalized it to ourselves and the hurt one has probably moved on and away. Looking back we feel regrets, even if the raw feelings of betrayal are now less intense. So Jung joined the many and betrayed a lover, but apparently in his case the world does not allow his past to be forgotten, let alone forgiven. How do we inwardly respond to that? Are psychotherapists meant to be the new secular priesthood whose ability to maintain professional celibacy is as doubtful as that of their religious counterparts? What does this enforced celibacy do to us as human beings? Certainly we have been told during our training of the importance to us of having healthy emotionally satisfying lives to help us live celibately in the transference relationship. But the price we pay for this in our private lives is one of keeping secrets, because if we dare to share our working life with our nearest and dearest we are betraying our patients.

Psychotherapists lead private public lives and public private lives. During a long-term therapy which has worked well, our patients will have explored every minute detail about us. Once the door of our consulting room is closed what happens remains (or should remain) a secret between two people forever. Even supervision, often viewed as a measure to protect the public from suffering from poor clinical practice, interferes with this total confidentiality. Although unconsciously accepted by most patients, most therapists have occasionally used words that came from their supervisor rather than from themselves and have witnessed the patient's anxiety at hearing them. We also know only too well how tempting it is for us to want to boast about a patient, particularly if we deem that patient (in our small world) to be somehow exciting. In the somewhat shaky start to this new profession such confidences were not kept, and the identities of Freud's, Jung's and Klein's patients have been traced. Some patients self-publicize, like the composer Michael Tippett or the filmmaker Woody Allen. To do so is their privilege and concern, even if it evidences that their therapy failed to explore important aspects of the psyche that may have helped them protect their intimate selves from public gaze. That we know so little about Jacqueline Du Pré's analyst, despite the recently published envious attacks on her, gives us reason to be proud of some aspects of our profession. However, this secret public life in which the wounded healer attends to another's wound does not easily sit in a world which is governed by results and led by economics – a world in which individuals are sacrificed to the economic Kalashnikov as others are sacrificed to the reality of its cold ruthless metal. Such economic 'realities' with their emphasis on short-termism constantly challenge the philosophy underpinning long-term psychotherapy such as time limited, focused, goal-oriented counselling. In such a setting often the ideal of individuation is replaced by a counselling programme designed primarily to optimize the patient's performance as a worker and as a useful economic unit within an organization. The aim, to get them back to the madness of the workplace, is perhaps as great a perversion of the aim of psychotherapy as were the efforts of the early group therapists to ensure that soldiers returned to the madness of the trenches in the years 1914 to 1918. In such situations older and more primitive responses replace more reflective ones, one contemporary example being fundamentalist repression.

The return of the repressed

One undisputed aspect of the millennium is its link to Christianity. It provides a new platform for those who still search around for the bones of Jesus. Humans do not, as Rieff (1966) suggested, invent new religions; the old, in spiral fashion, return, sometimes in a more virulent form than before. In the course of this spiral the philosophy of Luther, the architect of

Protestantism, has returned in the form of fundamentalism. The Young Man Luther (Erickson 1958) who disarmingly allowed us to gain entry into his secret by admitting to thinking up the fundaments of the Reformation while sitting on a privy has forever linked the Protestant Reformation to anality. Fundamentalism is a section of the Christian church that is growing numerically faster than any other. It has either predominantly middle-class adherents (including in its ranks significant numbers from the medical, scientific and legal professions) or people of African or West Indian origins. In the United States it is represented in powerful repressive political pressure groups such as the often vicious, anti-abortion and the pro-capital punishment lobbies. In this it has close links with right-wing politics. Critics of Christian fundamentalism point out that it does not allow for that honest struggle of heart and mind by which truth is revealed, but it is selective in choosing only parts of the Bible which fit in with the dominant ideology.

Perhaps fundamentalism can best be likened to a certain type of computer virus – one that has found its way into the part of the memory that tells the computer it is a computer. It lurks there undetected, psychotically waiting to destroy the computer's functioning power. For fundamentalism is always 'the enemy within'. It is a secret army. Christian fundamentalists rarely identify themselves as such. They adopt pseudonyms to hide their identity and are found hidden under the guises of 'Born Again Christians', 'Evangelical Christians', 'Bible Based Christians' or 'Charismatic Christians'. Fundamentalists cannot share or compromise and therefore any form of dialogue or partnership between depth psychology and religion, which White (1952), Lee (1948), and Robinson (1963) following Tillich (1962) have, in their turn suggested, would be impossible.

Because the link between fundamentalism and right-wing capitalism is well established, it is therefore not surprising that the rise in fundamentalism has happened during a period in which the 'right' has dominated world politics. The deadly potency of the Thatcher–Reagan 'special relationship' with its emphasis on the free market spawned its religious counterpart, a religion that is individualistic and morally narrow. Its influence spreads – sound bite journalism. A televisual society in which all is revealed but nothing really seen. Popularist jingles such as 'Back to Basics', the hardening trend towards punishment and away from rehabilitation, all have the hallmarks of both right-wing and fundamentalist attitudes towards understanding people and events. There is no breadth, no depth. At the same time there is an emphasis on performance and individual success. There is the popularist debunking of the 'Nanny State'. This has led to the rise in attempts to misuse depth psychology insights. They are not used to enable the process of individuation or integration to take place, but to ensure that individuals fit into the requirements of society. In short to ensure that the moral being is replaced by the conforming being.

In *Memories, Dreams, Reflections* (Jung 1967), that edited fantasy of Jung's old age, he talks about his break with Freud. One important component of this is the memory of a conversation that took place in Vienna in 1910 when Freud said, 'My dear Jung, promise me never to abandon the sexual theory. That is the most essential thing of all. You see, we must make a dogma of it, an unshakeable bulwark'. Jung reports that this was said with great emotion, in the tone of a father saying: 'And promise me this one thing, my dear son: that you will go to church every Sunday'. Jung tells that, astonished, he asked Freud: 'A bulwark – against what?' To which Freud replied: 'Against the black tide of mud', adding after a pause 'of occultism'. Jung reports that this struck at the heart of their friendship for he knew he could never accept such an attitude.

Jung's recall of this event in the last years of his life is important because it illuminates Jung's problem with his own lurking fundamentalism that he had projected into Freud. It raises the issue first as to whether psychoanalysis could remain rooted in its scientific tradition and has led others to charge it with becoming a quasi-religious movement. It also poses the question as to whether psychoanalysis could be, and in particular whether society would allow it to be, an open or closed system. This has always been an issue of central importance to the profession. It concerns each therapist's individual ethic and how this impinges on the external codes of ethics of psychoanalytic psychotherapy. It concerns how far the ethical code of psychoanalytic psychotherapy has to conform to that which society deems to be fit. It concerns society's need to regulate the profession. This might include compulsory state registration which some may view as a very good idea. However, the sanctity of the confidentiality of the consulting room might be threatened by such state interference, a subject which has been passionately argued elsewhere (Bollas and Sundelson 1995). It concerns the manner in which the state may interfere with the way therapists understand and respond to issues that society deems are emotive, such as incest, recovered memory syndrome, and so on.

Fundamentalism is not just a religious phenomenon. It hosts itself randomly and secretly in many organizations and philosophies. It tricks the unsuspecting enquirer into thinking that something is good, creative and useful when the opposite is true. Thus religious fundamentalists probably are closer to worshipping the Devil than God. Like a computer virus it also spells disaster. Note how computer-speak uses Armageddon-type images when a virus is found, referring to it more like a revisitation of the Black Death than it being merely a technological problem. Fundamentalism is the idolatry of the word, a kind of internalized political correctness or ethnic cleansing. It tends to manifest itself wherever one group assumes moral superiority unilaterally. Like, perhaps the notion that only people who have had five times a week analysis can be charged with the training of others? However, when a dominant group can claim divine inspiration for their superiority then their potential for wielding emotional power is even more enormous and damaging. The media love fundamentalism – it always provides good sound bites!

Sound bites and psychoanalytic psychotherapy, which seeks to understand humans as the unique people, are incompatible. We return to the question, 'What do you do?' It cannot be explained in a sound bite. 'What people do you see?' 'People like you' might be a truthful, but not a very diplomatic, sound bite response to make over a glass of wine. In a world where the sound bite dominates communication, what chance is there to explain our work to others?

It seems ironic that at a time when there seems to be a counsellor available to help people over every human trauma, the key aim of psychoanalytic psychotherapy, that of integration or individuation, has been lost. Virginia Ironside's (1999) journalistic polemic centred on just that. Therapy is no good, she says, and cites Woody Allen as an example. For him thirty years' therapy apparently helped him 'that much' (said he, moving his forefinger about an inch from his thumb). For Virginia, of course, that says it all. It seems she cannot visualize that that inch could represent the difference between life and death, prison and freedom, creativity and deadness. It seems that if therapists do not join the ranks of the do-gooders, aiming to take the pain away as economically (that is painlessly) as possible they are useless. Relief is all: understanding is viewed as the icing on the cake, available only for those who can afford this luxury. The needs of budget holders and company profitability are placed before the needs of people. And yet the training courses still attract candidates. What motivates the trainee therapist?

Psychoanalytic psychotherapy as a profession

There is much about the profession which might not commend itself too readily as a way of earning a living, like unsocial hours, relatively low financial rewards, the loneliness of working in private practice, the uncertainty of referrals and therefore of income. On top of these external matters there are internal pressures which make the profession a uniquely difficult one to follow. Not the least of these is the intensity of the intimacy of the transference relationship lived *in abstentio*, not only including sexual feelings but also having to channel aggressive and other responses into a sublimated form. There is no hiding place in the transference relationship. All aspects of the therapist – disabilities, weight, age, youth, size of house, room, car, taste in furnishings – all, and more, will come under the scrutiny of the patient. If this is not happening the therapist knows that there are warning signs that the therapy may be in some sort of difficulty. The therapist also will nearly always be working with the negative transference, which, while of great importance for a good therapeutic outcome, is wearying for the therapist to stay with, especially as it may well extend over a protracted period of work.

There are, of course, great rewards. Being trusted to enter intimately into the lives of people is perhaps the greatest. To observe the gradual blossoming of a person is another. A third is that of knowing that all the words spoken are spoken in total confidence. However, therapists also need to be affirmed in the work they do. Supervision does not inevitably supply this. A famous personality, an interesting case, or financial reward may threaten to loosen therapists' tongues. The pressure to supply, for public consumption, juicy morsels of '(in)famous' patients may be too much for some therapists to bear. There is also simply a need at times to relax, to open up, to gossip, but any gossip, even to colleagues, breaks one of the major cornerstones on which this profession/vocation is built – confidentiality.

If gossip is avoided the therapist still has to deal with the other aspect of confidentiality, secrecy. Secrecy can camouflage abuse and much media pressure is brought to bear on professions that operate secretly. The press, hungry as they are to open any can particularly if it contains worms, continues to attempt to break into others' secrets. The profession has to debate what is reasonable. Behind codes of ethics lies the question of how straight, honest, a therapist should be (or needs to be?) with potential patients. Are therapists required to be any straighter than members of other professions are? Should indeed the buyer beware? Sexual seduction is not the only thing to muddy a patient's struggle to gain good mental health.

Stories of the tax-avoiding therapist may help focus this issue a little. A potential patient telephones for an initial interview. During it the question of the fee arises. The patient 'innocently' offers to pay in cash. This opens up the possibility of the therapist interpreting and exploring whether the patient believes the therapist will declare the fee for taxation purposes. However, if the therapist having made the 'correct' interpretations about the patient's unconscious motives then secretly decides not to include the fee in the tax return, does this adversely affect the therapy any more than if the therapist offers to reduce the fee if cash is paid, with the obvious inference that the fee will not then be declared. Something of this ilk happened between Jung and Sabina Speilrein. During her treatment her parents were alerted (by Jung's wife?) that there was more than a professional relationship developing between them. They wrote for some assurance about this. In Jung's now notorious reply to Sabina Speilrein's parents, Jung stated that if a fee were paid then that would guarantee that he would be sexually circumspect. Hinting though, that if no fee were paid, then anything goes. While this is not one of Jung's finest hours, its candour at least allows us to recognize that the profession's gurus have problems with ethical issues concerning money and sex.

It leaves the debate open to what difference, if any, is made to the therapeutic outcome if the transference relationship is not based on a honest foundation.

Ethnic cleansing and the Hundred Years War

Fundamentalism occurs only in patriarchal societies. One of the important aims of fundamentalist groups is to restore or establish patriarchy under a charismatic leader who draws legitimacy from God or some other transcendent referent usually but not always on the basis on a revealed text that has had magical properties projected into it. The earlier reference to Jung and Freud's conflicts over their own fundamentalist inclinations shows how such attitudes penetrated the profession from its earliest days. This is one possible reason for the enormous unconscious emotional investment in the continuation of the 'hundred years war', that is the history of the psychoanalytic psychotherapy profession. This can only deplete the emotional investment available for other tasks. If only the energy expended on the war effort were turned towards (re)constructive work then the riches the profession has might have a greater impact on society. The publication of Sabina Speilrein's diaries was revelatory in demonstrating the deadly competitiveness between Jung and Freud and the level to which both would go to undermine the work of the other. Speilrein is found to be an attractive piggy in the middle pleading with the two testosterone-loaded men to discover their mutuality and realize what they might have in common, which ironically included her, her considerable wisdom and insights. To no avail. They could not, would not, or dared not. And so the tribal war continues within the various professional bodies to which therapists subscribe and attempts at 'ethnic cleansing' still continue. Repression does not have to feel undesirable. It is infectious and deadly; it is insidious.

Ethnic cleansing no doubt feels headily good to the powerful group of cleansers even if it traumatizes its victims and horrifies the televisual world. Helen Bamber's biographer reminds us how easy the infection can spread when he documents her recalling the actions of a British staff officer, working in starving Germany at the end of the war (Belton 1998). Groups of refugees were then wandering Europe. Disorientated and traumatized they tended not to trust officialdom to go where they were directed. This resulted in an incident whereby a group of 'displaced persons' arrived in a place where officialdom had decided they 'shouldn't be', and therefore were being denied any welfare. Bamber went to act as intermediary between them and the authorities. She found that the British officer apparently dealt with such groups by telling himself that, as far as he was concerned, 'they do not exist'. Bamber struggled to understand his attitude while negotiating practical matters such as how she was going to get food allocated for a group 'who did not exist'. Suddenly the officer reluctantly agreed to feed them, but his agreement was accompanied with the extraordinary outburst of: 'My God, these people must have done something terrible to deserve this!'

The staff officer probably was not an uncaring individual. He was probably overwhelmed by the task. He represented a society in which disorder caused anxiety. His task was to civilize his patch of war-torn Europe. Probably it was an attempt at benign ethnic cleansing. The refugees refused to cooperate. Perhaps it is not too fanciful to suggest that the unconscious has a similar refugee status within contemporary society, a society in which the unconscious is at best a guest who, like a displaced person, is tolerated only for a short time. If it cannot be 'civilized' then it has to be repressed. Many of the 'displaced persons' in the Europe of 1945 were eventually found a new home a long way from Europe. They did 'disappear' but later re-emerged; some found themselves once more at war this time theologically with each other and at arms against their neighbours. Rejected by their brothers and sisters they have found it hard to live at peace.

The effect of society's fear of the unconscious has taken its toll on those who make most claim of understanding it. Providing such practitioners are on the fringes or are contained in a quasi-religious group then society allows them to mumble along. However, if they dare to claim the mainstream then society engages with them and the truth of the old adage 'united we stand, divided we fall' becomes evident again.

Living and working in a repressive culture

In his prefatory remarks to 'Dora', his first published case history, Freud ([1899] 1977) addressed an issue that is as pertinent now as it was one hundred years ago. It is the conflict over protecting the privacy of the patient versus the usefulness of heuristic single case study research that helps to establish and justify the scientific art of psychoanalysis. Specifically Freud addressed the conflict over confidentiality that arose from the publishing his patients' case histories, against the need to protect the identity of his patient. Freud recognized that he would be blamed if he gave no information but equally he would be blamed about the information he was about to give. He made his apologia both to Dora and his critics about divulging intimate details, but explained that he needed to do so in order to clarify his methodology. At the same time he intended to do all he could to protect his patients from prurient voyeurism. However, Freud made it quite clear that he intended to discuss matters in his case studies which for some might appear to be scandalous, unpleasant or inappropriate. He recognized too that because the studies dealt with unconscious material some readers would therefore find them incomprehensible. To support his intention Freud ([1905] 1977) draws on a quotation from another researcher into psycho-sexual pathology who says this:

It is deplorable to have to make room for protestations and declarations of this sort on scientific work; but let no one reproach me on this account but rather accuse the spirit of the age, owing to which we have

reached a state of things in which no serious book can any longer be
sure of survival.

(Schmidt 1902: 38)

In presenting Dora, Freud attempted to prepare his readers to encounter the
world of heuristic research which emphasizes connectedness and relationships, retaining the essence of the person in experience, rather than the
detachment of phenomenological research, distilling as it does cause and
effect relationships. But what was the aetiology of Dora or Little Hans and
of others who suffered from these 'nervous' ailments? It was the experience
of being a child in a world where sexual expression was repressed, a society
described sensitively by Kerr (1994: 479) as one where 'young ladies did not
perspire . . . where even eating might lead to thoughts of defecation and
shame'. A society in which a daughter's purity had to be protected even if
the cost was her ignorance and later exploitation. For the society which kept
some women pure was also a society in which prostitution was rampant and
a society which tolerated a father who wished to indulge his sexual fantasies
through spanking his young children. 'A world where sexual desire perme-
ated everywhere but was nowhere to be named' (Kerr 1994: 479).

It may seem a world now far removed from the politically correct, child-
protected society that we occupy at the start of the new millennium. But is
it? A read of the Sunday tabloids which mercilessly exploit what they consider to be sexual deviants, a cursory glance in inner city newsagents' win-
dows or making a phone call from a central London call box decorated as
they are by a multiplicity of prostitute advertising, invites us to consider the
possibility that sexual repression is as alive and well today as it was in
Vienna, St Petersburg or London at the turn of the twentieth century.

It is a world where people's images, monitored (for 'our security') by
CCTV cameras, are sold regularly to media companies to provide cheap
voyeuristic television. Where one's credit rating, health, tastes, choices and
priorities are sometimes better known to third parties than they are to oneself. Where one's conversations are recorded, where one's sex life can be
monitored cheaply and easily. The video or audio image thus obtained is the
equivalent of the sound bite, designed to entertain not inform, to pry and
not to protect, to repress and not to free. It is a society in which provocation
and aggression are promoted instead of negotiation and compromise. All
provide an environment that is in opposition to two of the core values of
psychoanalytic psychotherapy, respect for the individual and protection
of that individual's privacy.

Psychotherapy is an anarchic profession. The unconscious, while civiliz-
ing in itself, does not obey the rules of society. This causes society to be wary
and so warily treats the advocates who concern themselves with unconscious matters. If only the repressed self (represented by the press) could
'civilize' this profession. And what energy society is producing to attempt

this! Calls for statutory registration, tighter and tighter codes of ethics, are coupled with more and more stories of patients apparently harmed for life by dubious practices. This is a dangerous unregulated profession, we are told, and must be brought into line.

The difficulty is resisting this pressure. It was slightly easier being an anarchist in the relatively liberal society of the 1960s, but in the UK the Thatcher years produced a society that is far less liberal and, apparently content to remain so, making the task harder. For the Thatcher years were accompanied by an upsurge in fundamentalism. Sound bite religion and sound bite journalism. 'She was', some would tell us, 'just what Britain really needed': a woman who was a charismatic leader, who claimed to draw legitimacy from God and who was not ashamed to make scriptual references to point up her policy statements. Some ten years after her resignation, British society still reflects many of the values she bequeathed.

Being a psychotherapist has become harder because there is a malignant mirroring of the psychotherapist's intent by society. The profession says: 'Come to me and I will save you from relationships you have had in society which have been detrimental to you'. The press says: 'Believe in us and we will keep you in society and save you from relationships with psychotherapists which will be detrimental to you'. The psychotherapist's work is their private life and their work consists of observing and commenting on how the patient relates to this professional private life. Therefore psychotherapists need to develop and nurture another private, private life without producing conflicts or splits.

There is a myth that psychotherapists train in gratitude for their own analysis. This is easy to rationalize as sentimentality. Such rationalization is probably a defence against residual envy. Gratitude may also embrace the possibility of another form of fundamentalism, making one's own analyst into one's God. If we practise as a result of our analysis we disenfranchise ourselves from voting either for or against the efficacy of psychoanalytic psychotherapy. To practise because of gratitude is in effect to sentence ourselves to the place of not knowing. It is to sentence ourselves to an approach to life that musicians with 'perfect pitch' have towards music. For such people music, their love, becomes persecutory. For psychoanalytic psychotherapists so professionally attuned that, when asked over dinner 'What do you do?', whatever verbal response is made, the inner response automatically is 'Why is that question being asked of me now?'

What price gratitude: a ruined dinner party?

Perhaps the real gratitude is that through their own analysis psychotherapists benefited from finding a silence and in it a new kind of relationship that watered a parched but otherwise fertile soil. It is that silence in a relationship that takes place within a contract that allows verbal freedom and what probably can be no more than an illusion of confidentiality that creates a sense of gratitude. And that gives therapists the possibility of a great reward. Therapists, together with their patients, can in as full a sense as possible embrace equally Eros and Thanatos so that both, illuminating each other, become servants of the ego. Fundamentalists worship death alone while deluding themselves and others that they are really worshipping life. The psychotherapist knows this and that is the profession's anarchic secret. It has to be protected for it is a pearl of great price and society is greedily envious of it.

References

Belton, N. (1998) *The Good Listener: Helen Bamber – A Life Against Cruelty.* London: Weidenfeld & Nicolson.
Bollas, C. and Sundelson, D. (1995) *The New Informants.* London: Karnac.
Erikson, E.H. (1958) *Young Man Luther.* New York: Norton.
Freud, S. ([1899] 1977) Dora, in A. Richards (ed.) *Sigmund Freud*, Vol. 8. London: Pelican.
Freud, S. ([1905] 1977) *A Case of Hysteria*, vol. 8. Harmondsworth: Penguin.
Ironside, V. (1999) Unhappy? Why not ditch the analyst, *Independent*, 10 May.
Kelly, J. (1996) He was the man who invented free love, *Daily Mail*, 29 June.
Kerr, J. (1994) *A Most Dangerous Method.* London: Sinclair-Stevenson.
Jung, C.G. (1967) *Memories, Dreams, Reflections.* London: Collins.
Lee, R.S. (1948) *Freud and Christianity.* London: Pelican.
McLynn, F. (1996) *Carl Gustav Jung: A Biography.* London: Bantam.
Murdoch, I. (1999) A Certain Lady, BBC Bookmark Show, 15 February.
Rieff, P. (1966) *The Triumph of the Therapeutic.* London: Penguin.
Robinson, J.A.T. (1963) *Honest to God.* London: SCM Press.
Schmidt, R. ([1902]1977) *Beiträge zur Indischen Erotik.* Leipzig: Pelican Freud Harmondsworth.
Tillich, P. (1962) *The Shaking of the Foundations.* London: Pelican.
White, V. (1952) *God and the Unconscious.* London: Fontana.

12 Beyond psychotherapy – beyond ethics?

Mary Anne Coate

Introduction

This chapter seeks to look through and beyond the theory, practice, techniques – and associated codes of ethics and practice – of psychotherapy, to an exploration of the underlying principles, values and, indeed, worldviews that may currently be exercising an determinative influence in this area or which could make a contribution to future thinking.

I want, first, to examine the development of accountability in an increasingly complex professional world; why it is needed, how in fact it is developing and the ethical questions and dilemmas to which it gives rise. I shall then explore further the derivation and determinants of ethical and moral thinking and behaviour.

Finally, I wish to re-examine the purpose of ethical thinking and codes of ethics and practice, the limitations of current formulations and trends and the possibilities for change. In this I hope to offer a contribution relating to the place of the so-called 'higher' values – and, specifically, forgiveness – in this enterprise. I have identified Christianity as my starting-point for this contribution, though I do not think it is also the end-point.

The need for accountability and the complexity of the task

We live in an increasingly complex and confusing world in relation to ethics, though to say this is not also to imply that it is necessarily a bad thing. It is, rather, inescapable. Two factors seem primarily to contribute to this complexity – one relatively new and one very old. The first is that the second half of the twentieth century, in particular, saw a very considerable increase in what we can do now and perhaps even more importantly in what we are *potentially* able to do; the rate of change has been colossal. The second is human nature which, it could be argued, changes and develops, if indeed it does at all, at a rate so slow as to be imperceptible. Within the lifespan of individual human beings and between one person and another there are manifestly lesser or greater amounts of compassion, cruelty or indifference; altruism, or selfishness; wisdom or foolishness. But it is not easily possible to extrapolate from this to a positive development in humanity *per se*; history will not provide the evidence for this. The atrocities of the twentieth century serve rather to indicate the opposite.

It is the interplay between these two factors – the possibilities and the people – which, in my opinion, gives rise to the confusion. This interplay highlights the dimension of values and value systems, and gives rise to questions of morality and ethics. We can, for example, apparently genetically engineer. Do we want to? Should we do so? Medical advances have made many new treatments possible; economic issues affect accessibility, giving rise to appalling moral dilemmas in relation to a perceived and an actual 'rationing' of treatment or care in the face of individual human need. We can stay alive longer. Do we want to? Should we be able to choose? There are many such dilemmas and the fact and experience of ethical dilemma itself is not new. Issues of life and death, health and illness and how to deal with and make sense of them – in terms of, for example, primitive taboo, rational philosophy or religious faith – have been around as long as we have. What is new perhaps is that decisions in these areas may previously have been made by individuals, acting on their own responsibility, without regulation and sometimes in secret; now they have come very much more into the public domain. This is for better and for worse. Increased transparency in relation to these issues focuses positively on the need for accountability, but is also vulnerable to media and other distortions.

It is, though, not quite true to imply that past generations lacked a sense of public accountability. The perpetrators of human atrocities such as the French Revolution or the Holocaust believed themselves accountable to a cause, a worldview and a particular set of categories into which to put human beings. In one sense this scheme of things was publicly accountable – in each case to the ruling state. But such accountability was linear and one-dimensional, lacking a dialogue and necessary confrontation with other forms of accountability such as that to 'higher values', human rights and, most profoundly, with an accountability to actual individual human persons rather than 'discarnate' causes or human categories. The Inquisition is slightly different and complicates the picture; its perpetrators might well have claimed that they were accountable to God for individuals – for their eternal salvation or damnation which take precedence over this earthly life. Yet to us the chain of thinking that followed from this belief is unacceptable and the outcome barbaric.

Accountability in psychotherapy

Accountability in the service of psychotherapy is no stranger to these sorts of private and public issues. In one sense psychotherapy is a very private and hard-to-hold-accountable activity. In the case of individual psychotherapy the enterprise takes place between two people without witnesses, though this scenario is somewhat modified for group and family therapy. Human recall and record keeping cannot provide an entirely accurate record of a session or an objective analysis of how each party is experiencing and interpreting the process or content of the exchange. Even though psychotherapy tries to fill in the gaps, making the unconscious conscious and the 'unsaid but thought' verbal, it inevitably partakes of the inexactness and vulnerability of all human communication. This would be true along the spectrum of psychotherapeutic orientation, regardless of whether the overt model is cognitive/behavioural or one whose essence is the expression and analysis of words and feelings. It would also be true along the 'time and intensity' spectrum whose range is from brief interactive therapy to psychoanalysis. Furthermore, the art of psychotherapeutic assessment is one of the most skilful and sensitive; it is not easy to predict a good practitioner–client match, nor is it easy to monitor, during the unfolding of the process, the optimum kind and level of therapy for a particular person. Within the privacy of the one-to-one situation – and despite both training and experience – it can be hard to keep the necessary evaluative distance from a process to which both parties have become committed and attached, and on which one party's livelihood may depend. The opening up of the work to supervision can only in part redress this sense of 'privateness', for the 'at one remove' dimension is always present.

Yet psychotherapy has its public dimension, and (in my opinion) there have been and are something approaching creeds and sects among psychotherapists that partake of many of the characteristics and fallibilities of other secular and religious causes. Less extremely, it is possible for the body of psychotherapeutic knowledge and theory to lose its grounding in the – to an extent unpredictable – human exchange which is the essence of its practice, and gain a sort of life of its own. One consequence of this is that it can become impervious to challenge, modification or development. As in many disciplines the balance between lasting wisdom and a necessary openness to new thinking is difficult both to discern and to maintain.

Furthermore, until recently the practice of psychotherapy has been relatively unregulated. Currently, formal assessed training leading to qualification is becoming the norm, but it is not yet a statutory requirement and after it is completed there is no universal requirement for continuous peer feedback and scrutiny through consultation or supervision. In these circumstances the most potent instruments for both precept and regulation are the various professional bodies' codes of ethics and practice and their associated complaints procedures. This may have laid upon these instruments a weight they cannot bear and lead, as has happened with similar mechanisms in religious and other settings, to distortions in their form and in their use.

Dilemma and change in counselling and psychotherapeutic practice

Over time and the development of the professions the consensus of what constitutes good practice in counselling and psychotherapy, and thus the content of codes of ethics and practice, have changed and developed. Palmer Barnes, in her book *Complaints and Grievances in Psychotherapy* (1998: 34), draws attention to the need for practitioners to be aware of such changes as part of their professional responsibility to themselves.

In the field of counselling and psychotherapy one of the most prominent areas of questioning and development in ethical thinking has been in relation to boundaries. There are many instances but the following are exemplars. Is it or is it not ethical and good practice for a therapist or analyst to report on a trainee's therapeutic progress? Is there or is there not any place for touch in counselling and psychotherapy. Can a supervisor also be a person's line manager? There are issues about the when and how of the ending of therapy and who determines this, particularly when the work may seem to have got stuck and the parties are not in agreement as to what should happen. Guidelines on confidentiality have been greatly strengthened and now include, for example, much more that relates to contact between different professionals who may be involved with the same person. At the same time this is also being threatened by the rise, in the USA in particular but on the horizon in the UK, of the concept and practice of 'managed care' where reports are increasingly required to acquire access to more resources such as more sessions. This often seems driven by factors of economics and cost-effectiveness, but the substantive issue of research into clinical effectiveness can also present an ethical dilemma by its often inevitable intrusion into the counselling or psychotherapeutic work. This is true even of qualitative research such as the use of the single case. The writing of case histories is a valued and well-tried tool for informing the professional counselling and psychotherapy community. Yet an increasing number of practitioners are worried about the effect on the psychotherapeutic work of seeking the permission of the subject to write and publish. There is a perceived growing need to assess effectively the competence of trainees, yet the methods of direct observation and recording of sessions raise ethical questions in relation to boundaries and confidentiality.

The other area in which there has been much change is that of *contract*, including the requirement to seek informed consent for medical and other interventions. In the counselling and psychotherapy world there has been some move to favour written contracts, and in any case practitioners are asked to endeavour to give in advance of starting the therapeutic process as much information as is possible about the nature and terms of what is being offered and what may be expected during the process. The move is towards greater openness and transparency. This is easier said than done, however, for those therapeutic models that utilize the phenomenon of transference. The explanation and subsequent experience sometimes do not match up just because the transference relationship is very hard to explain in words in advance of the actual experience.

Almost all codes of ethics and practice state that practitioners should be careful not to go beyond the limits of their competence. Sometimes examples of this are gross, often due to lack of training and experience, but like many ethical points the issue is not so simple. A 'going beyond present competence' can creep up silently and insidiously in the unfolding of a particular piece of work and under its pressure; when this happens the solution is not obvious, and indeed there probably is no ideal way of dealing with it. Positive and continued learning or a messy and unsatisfactory ending are both possible outcomes. Or a more general complacency accompanied by a degree of omnipotence can set in – sometimes in very experienced practitioners. This is likely to be, at least at the start, unconscious and as such hard to recognize by a practitioner before some damage has been done. Traditionally, the counselling and psychotherapy professions have divided on the need for continued supervision or consultation; currently therefore some psychotherapeutic practitioners may work without it and therefore lack help in discerning a trend to 'beyond competence' or complacency in themselves or their work.

Ethical codes for counselling and psychotherapy have tended to be generic, in that they claim to serve all theoretical orientations. This is an inherently difficult enterprise by virtue of the substantive differences, amounting often to real conflict, between the various orientations on such issues as the existence, origin and maintenance of psychopathology, the recognition, management and/or fostering of transference, attitudes to dependence and to therapist self-disclosure. There has been and is a tendency for codes to proliferate and become ever more detailed in an attempt – vain in my opinion – to cover every possible contingency and each new one as it emerges. Furthermore, in so far as proliferation of codes of practice can come to be initiated when things have gone wrong, we may need to be reminded of the adage that 'hard cases make bad law'.

Changes in psychotherapeutic thinking and practice have not of course taken place in isolation, for change in ethical and moral thinking and practice also takes place in society at large. Nowhere has this been more true than in respect of attitudes to marriage and sexual behaviour in the second half of the twentieth century. Divorce, remarriage and cohabitation did of course happen before this, but have now been sanctioned by society as a whole even if not by all parts and factions within it. But there has been discrimination exercised in relation to change in this area rather than a blanket liberalization and endorsement of all behaviour. Adultery and promiscuity still receive a negative judgement and attitudes to homosexuality have been much slower to change than those in the heterosexual arena. Nearer home for the subject matter of this chapter, the maintenance of practitioner competence has until recently been located in the private realm of the personal individual responsibility of the professional. Well-publicized medical and other professional disasters and an increased emphasis, generally, on continuing professional development – with or without periodic re-scrutiny – have moved it much more firmly into the domain of public accountability.

However, in this chapter I am not interested in detailing or even listing, for their own sakes, the various changes and developments that are taking place in psychotherapeutic technique, psychotherapeutic ethics or the morality of society. I want, rather, to explore the underlying basis of society's discrimination in moral issues and how this relates to ethical change and development within the counselling and psychotherapy professions.

So I am concerned with two questions. First, what factors determine and discriminate ethical thinking and moral practice? Second, in respect of the counselling and psychotherapy professions how is such thinking best and most helpfully reflected in actual codes of ethics and practice?

Distinction between ethics and morality

I realize that in the above paragraphs I have been using the words 'ethics' and 'morality' and their derivatives as if they were interchangeable, whereas in fact I do not think they are. I think we get hints of the difference when we consider the usually accepted distinction between codes of ethics and codes of practice. Codes of ethics outline the broad principles that guide and underpin codes of practice. It should be possible to find the reasons for clauses in a code of practice in the corresponding code of ethics. In the examples that I gave earlier in relation to ethical development in the psychotherapy and counselling professions, I did not make a distinction, but lumped them all together. In fact, perhaps only the point about competence belongs in the broader realm of ethical thinking; the other points, about boundaries and contract surely belong in the area of practice or behaviour. As I write I am not sure even about this; is the need to remain competent really an ethical end in itself or does it serve a higher overarching value and derive its importance primarily from this? If so what is this higher value and how is it determined?

I think I am arriving at a way of expressing the distinction between ethics and morality. I could put it this way: the realm of ethics deals with the value systems and thinking which underpin moral behaviour. Ethics and moral philosophy are disciplines of the same order and dimension. Morality is their derivative and refers to the reflection of moral and ethical thinking in what people actually do.

Furthermore, morality – the word stemming as it does from the Latin *mores* or custom – has a social or consensual face. It usually reflects the consensus of how most or a majority of people are interpreting the ethical thinking of the time. As such morality cannot be absolute, because there will be others who will interpret the same ethical thinking differently. Minority interpretations can, of course, be disordered and represent the negative dimension of society, the antisocial, criminal or perverse. But they can also be a source of salvation for society as, for example, when individuals, such as Bonhoeffer in Nazi Germany, stand out against an oppressive and perverse state, or when Wilberforce challenged the status quo on slavery. But individuals or groups who hold a minority view that seriously challenges the ruling party can pay very dearly for their insight and courage – as did Bonhoeffer and Nelson Mandela. In less extreme situations minority interpretations can come to be the cutting creative edge for change and to be the growth points for the community.

One of the mistakes that I think we make all too easily is that in a search for certainty and security we may be tempted to reduce ethical thinking to morality, or codes of ethics to codes of practice. We quite often come across the phrase 'to do such and such is unethical'. But I think this is better understood as a shorthand for 'to do such and such is against that interpretation of ethical thinking and moral philosophy which reflects the current consensus'. Put this way the essential fluidity of the situation is revealed, for consensus can change. I do not want to divorce the words 'ethics' from 'action' for to do this is to risk making ethics solely a matter of thought and values without these being tested by actual reality, as indeed they must be, for 'you will know them by their fruits' (Matthew 7: 20). Values and thinking inform practice and vice versa. But I am concerned to let ethical thinking have first, as it were, a space to breathe so that it may then stay in dialogue and even dialectic with the morality of practice and not be absorbed into it. In fact, St Matthew's Gospel, the source of the above quote, provides a good example of what I mean. The quotation comes from what is known as the Sermon on the Mount (Matthew 5), but the first eleven verses (the Beatitudes: 'Blessed are the . . .') are of a different order of thinking from the rest. They represent overarching and general ideals, the ethical philosophy from which the rest, which consists of far more detailed prescriptions for behaviour and practice, flows. It is clear that the Beatitudes are indeed fleshed out in detail, but the point is that other prescriptions for practice could flow from the same Beatitudes; what actually follows in St Matthew is not the only and exhaustive possibility, and is likely to be temporally and culturally determined. Similarly, a belief in the supreme value of the soul, and in eternal life over our limited human lifespan, does not have to lead to persecution, the Inquisition or martyrdom, and has not in other times and in other places.

What determines ethical thinking and morality?

I now need to return to my fundamental question 'What determines ethical thinking and morality', though the question may in fact be two questions, in that the determinants for ethics and morality may not be identical. The question is as old as the hills. It features in Plato's dialogue *The Euthyphro* (Gallop 1997) which articulates and wrestles with the perceived dilemma that – within a theist worldview – either God commands a certain act because it is right or it is right because God commands it. If the former is true then there must be a fundamental standard of morality independent of God's will or commands and the question remains 'from whence does this come'.

From here we can have recourse to natural law theory whose essence is that human beings will reason out what is the correct course of action from a consideration of human nature and human needs. Thus ethical and moral thinking will identify such ethical determinants of morality – more fully explicated in other chapters of this book – as the need not to do harm, as in the Hippocratic Oath (Boyd *et al.* 1977); to try to ensure that the greatest good is achieved for the greatest number; that self-actualization, following Maslow ([1954] 1970), is maximized; that justice and autonomy are respected; that acts are judged as right or wrong or preferable by their consequences. But the questions obstinately remain. What governs our selection of these determinants? If any of them conflict, what determines the hierarchy of importance that we give to them?

In fact we do not extrapolate in a nice rational straight line from natural law to ethical and moral thinking. At least two other dimensions contribute to and confound the issues.

First, if we were each left to ourselves to formulate ethical principles and codes we would no doubt come up with different priorities. We do not need the subject matter of psychodynamic counselling and psychoanalytic psychotherapy to see something of why this should be, though it can certainly help to enlarge our understanding of why we come up with the ideas we do. Ethical thinking is not pure; it is dependent to an extent on our experience, on our less rational selves, on our prejudices and on our unconscious. It may well focus on particular areas and insights such as the need for counselling and psychotherapy to respect and facilitate autonomy and capacity for choice (see for example British Association for Counselling 1977: section 3.1). This insight has perhaps been emphasized in our time because the exploration of the issue of power and the exploitation of the imbalance of power within the helping professions had tended to be neglected. Other people writing codes of ethics for therapists and counsellors at other times might focus on other insights. Under these circumstances it has been claimed that the development of ethical and moral thinking can appropriately be undertaken only within communities and not by individuals in isolation, so that it can come to reflect the consensus of wisdom distilled from experience. But ethical and moral thinking in 'communities of faith', be it a religious, professional or political faith, can become enmeshed in those very faiths – and so not be able to evaluated by them critically. Therefore dialogue between individual and community and between different sorts of communities needs to be maintained.

The second dimension that can contribute is that of a powerful, coherent and apparently self-consistent worldview and value system such as religion. We see this strongly in the work of the thirteenth-century theologian St Thomas Aquinas (1964–81; see also McDermott 1989). Working from his vision of the final end (purpose) for humanity as the possession of the glory of God, Aquinas posits specific and interim ends for humanity – survival, reproduction, knowledge, ordered society, worship – which if sought and achieved will facilitate that final purpose. For Aquinas, ethics essentially flow from the theological vision of God the Creator. The vision is earthed in human life, but the progression from one to the other is, in an important sense, seamless. This view of the determinative contribution of religion when it is present should be contrasted with other views within Christianity most recently expressed by Richard Holloway (1999) in his book *Godless Morality* but not confined to him. To such thinkers theological thinking and faith are independent of ethics and morality; the latter do not necessarily flow from the former. The phrase 'Christian ethics' is a misnomer and can lead to ossifying practice bounded by immutable and detailed codes. The difference of opinion is clear and from time to time expressed forcefully. That this strong difference exists serves to reinforce the point I am trying to make, namely that ethical thinking is fluid and in my opinion is made up of far more than an orderly reflection on human nature.

There is a middle way. It may be that there are values that have overarching currency in both religious and non-religious thinking even though the explanations for their prominence may differ. I am thinking of the so-called Golden Rule of love, phrased in Judaism and Christianity as 'Thou shall love the Lord thy God ... and thy neighbour as thyself' (Deuteronomy 6: 4, Leviticus 19: 16, Mark 12: 29–31) and in the secular world represented by such characters as Mrs Doasyouwouldbedoneby and Mrs Bedonebyasyoudid in Charles Kingsley's *The Water Babies* ([1863] 1957). In both ways of thinking it is the relationship between self and others – not the self in isolation – that is emphasized as the determining principle for behaviour. But in the religious context and construct an additional layer of *explanation* is offered, the rooting of the precept in a superordinate relationship with God.

The problem with identifying an overarching ethical principle such as the prevention of harm or love of self and others is that it is then hard to define what is meant by those overarching words. Other layers of thinking have to be brought back to help, and then the old dilemmas are re-encountered. During the 1960s and 1970s, there came to be prevalent in Christian circles an approach to ethics known as 'situation ethics' (for an exposition see Fletcher 1966). In such 'situational' thinking the principle of love is exalted as in St Augustine's (1878–90: 2033) *'dilige et quod vis fac'*, but the normative approach to what constitutes loving behaviour across situations is minimized with the emphasis being on thinking anew what love demands or permits in a particular situation. The approach became vulnerable to extremes of interpretation partly perhaps (see Fletcher 1966: 79) through a tendency to mistranslate St Augustine as 'love and do what you like' rather than as 'love and then what you will do'. Nowhere have its pitfalls been more clearly depicted and explicated than in Susan Howatch's (1991) novel *Scandalous Risks*, in which in the name of love a priest denies the presence of adulterous sexuality and seriously abuses the boundaries of a pastoral situation. The possibilities for distortion and self-delusion and abuse in relation to the 'great' positive concepts of 'love', 'care', 'positive regard' and 'positive transference' are well known; it is all too easy for these concepts to become perverted and so turned, virtually, into their opposite. But this is not necessarily at all easy to discern, manage and resolve. Often the situation has arisen because all trust and emphasis have been vested in a single – often apparently entirely positive – overarching concept such as 'love' or 'care'. Other candidates such as respect, self-discipline and even self-denial have been suppressed or denied. Yet even if and when we accept that this is so, there arises a further problem: how are we to be able to be aware of, select and access the particular counterbalances necessary?

My own conclusion has to be that our ethical thinking and practice are necessarily the product of reflection on not one but several sorts of source material. These include the knowledge base of the discipline that is being considered, the communities of practitioners of that discipline, individuals internal and external to the discipline, current political and social thinking and consensus and overarching value systems such as religious faith and the various world religions. Ethical thinking and practice are also inevitably vulnerable to complication and distortion from each and all of these sources. We shall therefore in our ethical thinking have what we *currently* see as bottom lines and 'givens', but I think and hope that the preceding pages will have shown that it is not easy to discern our motivation in identifying these, or the mechanisms by which we arrive at them.

Ethical thinking in counselling and psychotherapy

I think it would be true to say that the current ethical bottom lines for counselling and psychotherapy centre on the need to protect from exploitation and harm those who seek help in a largely unregulated field. This is partly a reaction to the uncovering in the various helping professions of occurrences – sometimes sustained over a long period of time – of past and present harm and abuse.

In this sort of situation two reactions are likely. There may well be a flight towards the proliferation of more and more detailed codes of practice to tell practitioners what to do in every possible situation. It is almost as if the need is to provide a menu, which if followed will infallibly deliver the goods, in this case impeccable practice. We are likely to become more and more driven either by fear – fear of the other, fear of complaint or of litigation – or by an impossible quest for perfection. If this happens we find that ethical thinking has become to our professions what the Jewish Law became to St Paul – see his letters to the Romans (chs 2–7) and Galatians (chs 3–4) – namely an agent of holding back and oppression rather than a source of development and liberation.

Equally predictable is, I think, the rise of a counter-reaction against this and a return to the principle of needing to think our way though dilemmas. This, though, can also go into overdrive so that we can come to rely only upon the 'great' ethical principles and attempt to do without any practice norms or guidelines at all.

By temperament we shall, each and all of us, tend to veer towards one approach or the other; we shall tend to see most easily the apparent defects of the approach with which we are not comfortable. But each approach, if pursued to excess, can come to serve the profession ill.

I do not see an easy way to achieve the necessary balance. It surely is a matter of thought and counter-thought, assessing and reassessing experience. But in concluding this chapter I would like to offer a piece of further contributory exploration. Its primary source I have identified as being Christianity, though I am not claiming this as the only source. In all that now follows I would like it to be taken for granted that I entirely accept that the paramount ethical need is to protect from harm, and I would not wish to be seeming to compromise this. I am rather asking to be allowed to play – in the Winnicottian sense – not so as to water down or detract from this ethical stance, but to see if there is something that can be *added* that may *enrich* it. The theme I wish to explore is the place of forgiveness in psychotherapeutic ethics, morality and technique.

The place of forgiveness

I have argued in *Sin, Guilt and Forgiveness* that the most profound understanding of the word 'love' includes as primary ingredients the concepts and experience of forgiveness and compassion (Coate 1994: 206). In that book I attempted to justify this assertion on at least three different levels (Coate

1994: chs 4 and 5). On the level of human experience – pure and simple – it seems to be the case that it is forgiveness, rather than denial of hurt or revenge, that brings the sort of relief that allows people and situations to move forward, rather than be trapped in a stranglehold of the past. On the religious level, the Christian proclamation of salvation through the death and Resurrection of Christ is based not on the achievement of perfection, but on the acknowledgement of imperfection, sin, guilt followed through in trust of the possibility of forgiveness, redemption and reparation. I posited that on this point the religious and psychological stories correlate with each other. The religious experience of forgiveness correlates with that hypothesized (Klein 1935) threshold of psychological development known as the depressive position, which again is based not on perfection, but upon the 'good enough' experience and the toleration of both positive and negative experience of and feelings towards the same object. However, I further argued that it is possible for either the religious or the psychological experience to fall back from the threshold of the depressive position and become persecutory.

The question I want to ask is whether and how far ethical thinking, codes of ethics and practice and perhaps, above all, complaints procedures can come to reflect the maturity of the depressive position. And even if they can are they also vulnerable – and if so in what ways – to falling back into the paranoid schizoid position and so being experienced as persecutory?

I think that one of the danger points for ethical thinking and codes arises if they give the impression of claiming to set out perfect conditions for work, or that the ideal – in this case counselling or psychotherapeutic – experience can be guaranteed provided that the rules are followed. Injudicious and over-frequent use of the word 'ensure', as in, for example, 'ensure the well-being' – as if as human therapists we had the omnipotence to do this for another person – is one way in which such unrealistic expectations can be aroused. But the use of phrases such as 'all reasonable steps' can have the opposite and helpful effect. Furthermore, people – both practitioners and clients, consciously and unconsciously often hope that the answer to all possible ethical questions can be found written down in codes, and that all uncertainties could somehow be removed from the therapeutic process. Whereas perhaps it would be helpful if ethical thinking and codes were able to acknowledge more the inevitability of imperfect situations and ethical dilemmas, and that these may be the stuff of therapy and not constitute a defect.

Furthermore, ethical thinking and codes that are too close to perfection – even if not expressed in such bald and unvarnished terms – can, I think, give rise to a strange sort of parallel process. They can feed into a hope that the experience of therapy will itself be essentially a reversal and wiping out of an original bad or difficult experience, rather than a way of working through and moving on from that experience. In fact this therapeutic moving on often does involve being able to come to forgive those who perhaps intentionally or perhaps inadvertently may have been the source of pain and suffering. And in this process the inevitable failures and shortcomings of the therapy and the therapist will have their part to play.

I do not want this last paragraph to be misunderstood. I am not wanting to make excuses for poor practice nor suggesting that the therapist's mistakes and failures are somehow 'good'. I am trying, rather, to give expression to something more nebulous and harder to define, something about the *atmosphere and climate* in which ethical thinking takes place, and the *style* of the writing and codes which come out of that thinking. Can atmosphere and style come to reflect the depressive position?

Complaints procedures and processes are far more likely to be experienced as persecutory, however much the professional bodies may claim that they are meant to be educative. They are inevitably traumatic experiences for both plaintiff and defendant and will resonate on any weak chinks in a person's psychological make-up and development including those against which they may have been hitherto successfully defended. This is perhaps one explanation of why people sometimes do not and cannot behave well, and at times behave uncharacteristically badly, during a complaints procedure. Complaints arouse guilt and the guilt aroused may not be the mature depressive guilt that can feel concern and take responsibility, but rather the guilt that is born of a persecutory inner world (Coate 1994: chs 5–7). When we talk of supporting people through being complained against, I understand this to mean supporting them to take the appropriate responsibility, bear the pain and if possible move to the depressive level of functioning so that the process can begin to approach the fulfilment of its educative function. For the complainant I think the corresponding need would be to be able to give up the need for revenge or even the 'eye for an eye and tooth for a tooth' position however understandable these wants and need may be. The realistic position, however, for some people may be that the process cannot become educative. Their particular inner world, when functioning under this particular strain, is not such as to let education and reparation happen.

Beyond ethics?

There is a final question I want to articulate which perhaps belongs in the spirit of our current age. Over the last years there has been a turning of the tide. People have rightly become more aware of their rights; they have also been correctly less willing to condone poor practice by professionals and become more able to complain. Sometimes an apology is all that is wanted and needed, yet this is becoming harder to proffer because of the fear of the danger of seeming to be admitting liability in an increasingly litigious society.

There is need for justice, restitution – where possible – and compensation particularly for those who are perceived as vulnerable members of society. There is a necessary imperative that the profit motive shall not compromise safety. There is a need for professionals to be held accountable for their work. But there is also a danger of ours becoming an inherently blaming culture where the thought is that if something has gone wrong then somebody must be to blame and must be found to take that blame. We can also become driven by the revenge motive. When something does go wrong there is a narrow line between a necessary and transparent process of inquiry – one of whose primary goals is to minimize the likelihood of recurrence – and a witch-hunt that ends in scapegoating. How can we balance and reconcile the needs and the danger?

Perhaps what is missing here is the acknowledgement of the continued existence of *tragedy* and tragic circumstances. I find I am not sure to what order of thinking tragedy belongs; it belongs not with ethics, nor with philosophy nor with religion, nor with spirituality. Perhaps all we can say is that it is existential; it is part of the infrastructure of our human existence. It is a word and experience we might like to excise from our vocabulary partly because it often forces on us the sense of irreparable loss and feelings of helplessness. But I think we do so at our peril. There are things which happen for which nobody is to blame, or in which everyone did their best and the best was not good enough. There are also occasions when human error is manifestly paramount or when aspects of human nature such as greed or envy appear to dominate. These experiences and occurrences will need to be evaluated against ethical principles, morality and professional competence, but unless also the possibility of tragedy is accepted that evaluation may well go off key. There will be a layer and dimension missing, and so what might be recognized as tragedy will be explained, or indeed raged against, *solely* in terms of ethics, morality and competence. These will then be asked to bear a weight that does not belong to them, and in this their nature and purpose will become distorted.

The appropriate 'conversation' partners for what is recognized as tragic cannot be ethics, morality, competence, compensation or, I think, the psychological or psychoanalytic literature. Perhaps 'conversation' is not the right word, for tragedy by its nature often has no words and defies conversational exploration and rational explanation. Maybe the word is 'walk' rather than 'talk'. To walk with tragedy we have to go beyond questions of ethics, morality, competence and compensation into the realm of mourning, compassion, forgiveness and reparation. But unless we are prepared to acknowledge, confront, walk with and struggle to accept tragedy I do no think we can get the rest into a right perspective.

References

Aquinas, T. (1964–81) *Summa Theologiae*. London: Blackfriars.
Augustine of Hippo (1878–90) *In Epist. Joann. Hom vii. 8*, in J.P. Migne (ed.) *Patrologiae Cursus Completus, Series Latina*, vol. 35. Paris: Garnier.

Boyd K.D., Higgs, R. and Pinching, A.J. (eds) (1977) *New Dictionary of Medical Ethics*. London: British Medical Journal.

British Association for Counselling (BAC) (1997) *Code of Ethics for Counsellors*. Rugby: BAC.

Coate, M.A. (1994) *Sin, Guilt and Forgiveness*. London: Society for Promoting Christian Knowledge.

Fletcher, J. (1966) *Situation Ethics*. Philadelphia, PA: Westminster Press.

Gallop, D. (1997) *Plato, Defence of Socrates, Euthyphro, Crito, translated with an introduction and notes*. Oxford: Oxford University Press.

Holloway, R. (1999) *Godless Morality*. Edinburgh: Canongate.

Howatch, S. (1991) *Scandalous Risks*. London: HarperCollins.

Kingsley, C. ([1863] 1957) *The Water Babies*. London: J.M. Dent.

Klein, M. (1935) A contribution to the psychogenesis of manic-depressive states, *International Journal of Psycho-Analysis*, Vol XVI: 145–74.

McDermott, T. (1989) *St. Thomas Aquinas, Summa Theologiae, A Concise Translation*. London: Eyre & Spottiswoode.

Maslow, A. ([1954] 1970) *Motivation and Personality*, 2nd edn. New York: Harper & Row.

Palmer Barnes, F. (1998) *Complaints and Grievances in Psychotherapy*. London: Routledge.

13 And if not now, when? Spirituality, psychotherapy, politics

Andrew Samuels

Introduction

The latest hot topic of debate in academic philosophy revolves around the idea of 'vagueness' (Williamson 1994). Instead of moaning or making jokes about defining elephants, we take that kind of difficulty as our starting-point, rejecting the spurious precision that dominates the style and content of so many contemporary discourses, including psychotherapy. Spirituality is a vague thing.

Spirituality may be rooted in traditional, formal religion. Or it may be a highly idiosyncratic and personal affair. Or both.

Spirituality may be located above us, at ground level (even in the body) or below, in an underworld. Or on all three levels.

Spirituality may be understood as universal, comprehensive and catholic with a small 'c'. Or it may display a highly relativistic cast, being experienced and expressed radically differently according to time, place, age, sex, sexual orientation, ethnicity, class and one's physical and psychological health. Or both.

Spirituality may be regarded as fundamentally transpersonal, transcending the human realms of existence. Or it may exist only in a relational, inter-subjective, interactional setting. Or both.

Spirituality may be seen as a substance or essence – breath, *pneuma*, *ruach*. Or it may be more of a perspective on experience. Or both.

And how can something like spirituality be apprehended except in its relation to its opposite? But what is its opposite? Is it body, the social, the secular, the profane, the soul – or what?

This chapter interweaves spirituality, psychotherapy and issues of social justice. Its compactness means that there is less defining of terms and more naming of parts. Maybe this is a strength in that readers will have to ask

themselves whether they see what I am getting at as often as asking themselves whether they agree or disagree.

While approaches to psychotherapy and counselling that are specifically
and avowedly 'spiritual' certainly still exist, I think there has been a tendency in the 1980s and 1990s to evacuate and omit the spiritual dimension
from ordinary, mainstream, rigorous, thorough professional therapy work.
This renders spirituality non-ordinary and contributes to a further seques-
tration and ghettoization of those practitioners who want to integrate a
more spiritual *Weltanschauung* into their bread-and-butter work. After all,
the therapy relationship is a kind of covenant.

I shall begin by looking at different variants of spirituality because there
are no norms in this area. Then I move on to discuss a spiritually informed
transformative politics and make some suggestions about the role of psychotherapy therein. There follows a discussion about connectedness between
human beings and how this is both spiritual and political at the same time.
Finally, I show how psychotherapy is relevant to debates about social justice, themselves secretly spiritual as well as political.

I hope I will not be understood as collapsing spirituality, psychotherapy
and politics into each other because I have always argued against cheap
holism as a response to the complex problems of our time. But I do want to
challenge the way in which the borderlines and boundaries between spirituality, psychotherapy and politics have been positioned. For me Hillel, the
first-century Jewish sage, pointedly captured the urgency of this when he
wrote: 'If I am not for myself, who is for me? If I am only for myself, what
am I? And if not now, when?'

The plural spirit

There is a pluralistic diversity of spirit to consider and I shall focus in turn
on what I call social spirituality, democratic spirituality, craft spirituality,
profane spirituality and spiritual sociality.

Social spirituality

For me, social spirituality stems from Jewish traditions (just as psychoanalysis does). It is not just a question of discovering oneself as a spiritual
being and going out and meeting other people who are already spiritual
beings. It is a question of going out and meeting people and, together with
those other people, thereby becoming spiritual beings by doing something
together. That is what *Tikkun*, restoration and repair of the world, implies.
In this perspective, one achieves spirituality in part by being a certain kind
of human being in society. But we lack psychological underpinning for this
Jewish-inspired social spirituality. Here I turn to Jung, not so much for his

theories in the form he left them, but, as so often, for Jung's intuitive suggestions about *how* to start to do something, not what to do in precise terms.

Jung introduced the idea of the psychoid level of the unconscious. This is a level of the unconscious where psyche and matter are, in his phrase, two sides of a coin. I want to bring in a new notion of 'the spiritoid' to refer to a level of spiritual experience where the spiritual and the social are the two sides of another coin. What this means is that the transpersonal, spiritual dimensions of life have been staring us in the face all the time. We would not really need a separate strand of transpersonal psychology or transpersonal philosophy if the transpersonal is there always already in society at the spiritoid level, where spirituality and sociality merge. The problem, if there is one, is that we failed to notice this. As Charles Péguy said, 'Everything starts in mysticism and ends in politics'.

Clinically, too, the spiritual is often hidden in the open. Although case histories prove nothing except the desire of the clinician to be right, I would like to bring in here some work with a young mental health professional called Michael. He came to see me on account of his obsessive ruminative thinking about the nature of life after death. If there is nothing after death, then what possible joy or satisfaction could there be in life? And what I heard was that his father, and many other members of his family, were in a kind of spiritual void. They had come from religious backgrounds and all of them, not just the client, had lost contact with those. What was so interesting to watch and witness was not only the client engaging with neurosis by getting in touch with his own lost religious self (as Jung depicted it), but also his realization that his task was, with their active cooperation, to re-religionize or resacralize his family. He set out to do it – with, it has to be said, mixed results. He lacked appropriate rites and sacraments. But the task was perhaps the important thing for Michael rather than his success in achieving it.

Democratic spirituality

The second in this plurality of spiritualities is democratic spirituality. I have in mind here not only the challenging of the ever-upwards out-of-the-world move of the western spirit – the challenge which C.G. Jung and James Hillman have mounted. They have urged us to think about the downwards, darkening, deepening move into soul. But I have problems with both the upward (spirit) and the downward (soul) moves because both have become romanticized, both have become elitist. It is already the case that people feel they are supposed to move upwards or downwards, in certain prescribed ways.

Spirituality contains within it something crucial to democracy, something about equality and even the equality of potential (the last usually denied by contemporary social and political theorists on scientific grounds: genetics, IQ testing, the supposedly inevitable unequal distribution of ability). Spiritual potential is something quite other than educational potential or vocational potential or relational potential. As it is not susceptible to measurement, equality is its precondition, its *sine qua non* and not an outcome. There really is no spiritual equivalent to how many times a night you can do it or how many degrees you have or how much you earn. The notion of spiritual potential enables us to think in terms of equality of outcome.

Craft spirituality

The third spirituality is a craft approach to the topic, a craft spirituality. This is about locating holiness in the artificiality of the made world, in the manufactured world. The atelier or even the factory is the locus for what I have got in mind here. In modernity, whether it is late modernism, or postcapitalism, or Fordism, or whatever, the main strands are industrialization and technology: the making of things. This is still the case in the VDU world of postmodernity; things are made – even services are made. *In modern life, there is a holiness waiting to be released.* I think that the roots of holiness, on this reading of it, do not only lie in God, or in the transpersonal realm. They also lie in our making or manufacture of holiness: holiness as artifice. We make holiness all the time by conceiving of, designing and constructing sacred spaces, which used to be called temples. We make and manufacture holiness when we perform certain acts – sacred and, I suggest, profane acts – such as sacrificial acts, or acts of repentance, or acts of creativity, or even acts of bodily self-indulgence and self-abuse. Holiness can be made by humans, and hence be supremely artificial.

The notion that holiness is to be found in the material and social world is not a new one. For many people, whether religious or non-religious, the material world has long had this gleam to it. Since my childhood I have been completely fascinated and enthralled by God's detailed instructions to the Children of Israel about how to build the Ark of the Covenant and the Tabernacle (or Noah's Ark earlier on). I want to focus for a moment on the Ark of the Covenant, that portable sanctuary, symbol of holy manufacture, and allow it to become a usable metaphor for our discussions. In the divine detail of the construction of this Ark, what do we see? First of all, we see that God is the most tremendous obsessional fusspot. But we also see how ineffable holiness really does depend on every detail, every joint, every bevel, every dimension, and the kinds of materials that are used to make holiness:

And Bezaleel made the ark of shittim wood. Two cubits and a half was the length of it, and a cubit and a half the breadth of it, and a cubit and a half the height of it. And he overlaid it with pure gold within and without, and made a crown of gold to it round about. And he cast for it four rings of gold, to be set by the four corners of it; even two rings

upon the one side of it, and two rings upon the other side of it. And he
made staves of shittim wood, and overlaid them with gold. And he put
the staves into the rings by the side of the ark to bear the ark.

(*Exodus* 37: 1–5)

What happened to Bezaleel? Where is our Bezaleel consciousness today?
Why do we have so few portable tabernacles? Where is our capacity to
recognize that holiness is not only God-made, not only natural, and not only
made by us humans, but also there for the making? Idolatry lurks as the
shadow of craft spirituality but only things of substance cast a shadow.

Profane spirituality

The next category of spirituality is profane spirituality. Here is a short quote
from Zaehner's book *Mysticism Sacred and Profane*: 'There is no point at all
in blinking at the fact that the raptures of the theistic mystic are closely akin
to the transports of sexual union' (Zaehner 1957: 151). The idea that sex is
often numinous need not be dwelt upon too long; that sex is sometimes
frightening probably needs little explanation either. But what kind of sexuality lends itself to mysticism and spiritual projects? I want to talk a little
about *incestuous sexual fantasy*, to excavate the kind of spirituality locked
up in that problematic area. It is crucial for those of us who are working the
field of father psychology as we try to disclose the parameters of paternal
erotics: what is and is not going to happen in terms of what I have called
erotic playback between fathers and children.

Jung pointed out that for members of the same family to get into a certain
kind of relationship where the one cannot avoid coming into deep intimate
contact with the other, there has to be something that stops them from turning away from each other. There has to be something that makes it impossible for the people in the family to avoid one another. There has to be a
vehicle, a motor, a generator, for intimacy and love that is not found in intimacy and love themselves. According to my reading of *Symbols of Transformation*, volume 5 of Jung's *Collected Works*, Jung (1952) is claiming that
incestuous sexual fantasy holds some of the seeds for what it is that gets
people into a flowered relationship where they cannot avoid one another.
Inside and probably outside the family as well, this is what being 'turned on'
is about at a deeper level. In the family there is an appropriate dimension of
sexual excitation which leads to personality-enhancing interactions between
people. And out of these, spiritual connections are fashioned between them.

But, as I say, this perspective also applies beyond the family. Profane
spirituality implies that the purpose or aim of sexual arousal is something
more than reproduction or discharge of the drive. There is something else
here beyond the unending psychoanalytic exploration of the vicissitudes of
desire in the unconscious. There is a more teleological aspect to incestuous

sexuality than that and its *telos* is spirit. Hence, spirit also plays a part in bringing people into relationships where they cannot avoid each other: in the family, in sexual life generally, and also in therapy. The benign fetishism of human sexual arousal and excitation lies at the heart of what I am calling profane spirituality; when it has to be that one person, the special one, no other one will do.

Unfortunately, when one searches for the clinical response to ideas like these, one sees that some contemporary psychotherapy, especially when influenced by object relations theory, has gone in for a form of what I call 'safe therapy' or 'safe analysis'. Here we see sexuality (and therefore also spirituality) being repressed by the institutions of psychotherapy itself. We dissolve the exciting potential of our work into a bowl of milk by adapting a mammocentric worldview and ascribing to the therapist very little beyond a simulacrum of 'the mother'. And the patient or client becomes 'the baby'.

Clearly, there is a defensive, professional reason for this. It has to do with the need to avoid sexual misconduct. But there is a real tragic loss involved here as well. There has been a desexualization of psychotherapy by its own institutions. I mean more than just the professional organizations; I mean the books, the teachers, the hierarchies, the received wisdom, the consensus – all contribute to a spiritual abuse, when they turn away from adult sexuality. Hence, I want to speak out in public against the object relations hegemony, against maternocentrism, against that crude equation of psychotherapist and mother, against the moralizing that attaches to the depressive position, genitality or individuation. Spirituality also resides in immaturity, confusion and suffering. The gods have become symptoms, as Jung said.

To return to profane spirituality, there is more to it than sex, whether we think of incestuous sex or sex outside the family or sex in therapy. There are also questions of drugs and alcohol. I suggest here that we also look at these psychopathologies as spiritual matters. That is what Jung wrote to the founder of Alcoholics Anonymous. He made the point that there is an off-the-rails spiritual search in alcoholism. Similarly, there is a spiritual dimension to drug addiction, the use of tobacco and maybe also to shopping and consumerism, if one knows where to look for it.

Most important of all, though, is that profane spirituality is contemporary spirituality: popular music, sport, fashion. As I said, it is time to recognize that the spirituality in our world, our manufactured and made spirituality, our craft spirituality, is oozing out of the profane pores of contemporary life. It needs us only to recognize and name it. In Bani Shorter's (1995) words, everything is susceptible to the sacred.

Spiritual sociality

Lastly, I turn to spiritual sociality. Briefly, what I have in mind is the latent spirituality in organizations, whether community organizations or economic organizations, such as cooperatives, trade unions and the like, teams of all kinds, the manifold groupings and networks of civic society. All of these things partake in a certain kind of spiritualized ritual process. I would even suggest that there is a latent spirituality in professional psychotherapy and counselling organizations as well!

Transformative politics and psychotherapy

I shall move on to discuss the transformation and resacralization of politics: can psychotherapy make a difference here? Psychotherapy certainly cannot make a difference if it does not put its own politics in order. That is why it is so important to set up campaigns like those in existence to rid the psychotherapy world and its institutions of homophobia and racism and to open the profession up to people of low income, whether as practitioners or clients. No one who wants to work in the psychotherapy and politics fields can ignore the politics of psychotherapy. Hence, it is vital to challenge the absurd and offensive professional hierarchies and demarcations that are presently being deployed in seductive and/or authoritarian ways.

To return to politics as such, one of the things that has happened in western polities like Britain is that a huge divide has opened up between what we call political power on the one hand and political *energy* on the other hand. Political power is what you would expect it to be. It involves the control of resources such as water, or electricity, or information – because information and imagery are resources usually owned by the powerful. The people who have political power in western societies are the people who always have had it: the well off, men, whites. We should not believe what we hear these days about men as the new economic victims. This is simply not the case, although pockets of genuine male social and economic vulnerability do exist. Political power resides in its conventional homes: government, financial institutions and industry, the military establishment, patriarchal families and so forth.

Political energy is different in that imagination and a channelling of a spiritual drive are involved. We are witnessing in western society a veritable explosion of political energy in what academic political scientists call the new social movements. Without realizing it sometimes, most of us belong to one or other of the new social movements. In fact, all psychotherapists belong to one, because complementary medicine, alternative approaches to health, and therapy and counselling together constitute a kind of social movement with its own identifiable broad consensus of political and spiritual values. Other such movements are several aspects of feminism, animal rights, liberation theology, people working in the poverty lobby, lesbian and gay rights groups, environmentalists or ethnopolitical groups. What has taken place is a huge increase in (admittedly marginal) political activity at a high level of political energy. We are witnessing a conscious attempt to bring imagination to bear on political problems and this is happening in isolation from mainstream political institutions. If we start to look at the political map, the political ecology, of a western country with political energy in mind and not with political power in mind, then the shape of that map changes quite dramatically and radically. On the map of the distribution of political energy, we witness the location of these frank espousals of what I call trans-formative politics. This is a spiritual politics of resacralization in the sense that the inner–outer divide in our thinking is being disputed in a way that, for example, in the 1960s the New Left never managed to do.

For instance, it is said that we cannot achieve sustainable economic development without a shift in collective values. A shift in values not only is a spiritual issue but also would have to rest on a profound and collective psychological shift. Such a collective psychological shift in turn depends on shifts in each and every one of us. This kind of thinking is what informs transformative politics.

In the strange marginal eruption of political energy that is going on in new social movements of the kind I mentioned, there is something of interest to people whose primary fascination is either with the spiritual or with the psychological or with both. I hope that a new constituency is being born, wrought by a concern for all of these.

Where does this leave therapists? I have three suggestions. First, I want to suggest that, just as we can take a personal or family history, we can take both a spiritual and a political history of the client. Because of limitations of space, I shall focus on politics, although the suggestion that intake or initial interviews might go into the history of the client's relationship, or lack of it, with God is also a somewhat radical one.

There is a kind of political myth particular to each individual client (or indeed each therapist). What has formed a person's politics? What have been the *psychological* influences on their politics? Let me give a couple of examples of this. I invite my readers to think of their political attitudes, engagements and positions, today as they are now. And then think of those of their parents. What are the connections? Are you in identification with your parents? Are you in reaction to your parents? Or is it a bit of both?

My second suggestion concerns the 'primal scene', the term used in psychoanalysis to refer to the relationship in the mind between the man and the woman that created the subject. The primal scene is a mixture in most of us of memory and fantasy that gets elaborated and multilayered over a lifetime. Think about the intimate relationship of your parents or, if you grew up in a lone parent family, of the sexual life of the parent with whom you grew up. What are its characteristics? What is the image that comes to mind? What are the emotional themes of your primal scene? Is it harmonious? Is it vigorous? Is there a sharing of power, or is there an imbalance? Is the bedroom door closed? Primal scene themes are the most political themes in the internal family that one can imagine. Think of the child's sense of exclusion – and then think of political discourse about marginal, dispossessed and excluded groups in society. Or the child's curiosity – the first investigative journalism that we do. Then there is the question of who initiates and sets the manifesto for sexual behaviour.

The Midrash tells us that before Eve was created there was Lilith. God created Adam and Lilith from the same dust. And on their first night in the garden, Adam mounts her, to have sex with her. And she says: 'Get off me. Because why should you lie on top of me in the superior position when we were made at the same time, from the same stuff?' He rapes her. She cries out God's name, is drawn up into the stratosphere, and then enjoys a subsequent career as the stereotypical she-demon, responsible for stillbirths and wet dreams. She thereby becomes an emblem of that which most destabilizes traditional images of women (stillbirth) and traditional images of men (wet dreams, when the man loses control of his sexuality). But I do not want to focus on Lilith herself. What I want to underline is the idea that this version of the first couple's story shows how politicized the primal scene is. Not Adam and Eve and seduction but Adam and Lilith and the dominant–submissive politics of marital rape.

I suggest that the imagery a person has in them at this moment of their parents' intimate life and sexual relationship is an extremely useful indicator of their politicality, meaning their political values, desire and capacity to do politics. The primal scene moves between conflict and harmony, harmony and conflict. In particular, is it not about enjoying enough conflict, enough sense of vigorous in-and-out movement, to achieve a harmonious result, such as mutual sexual satisfaction or a baby?

The imagery people have in their hearts and in their mind's eye of their parents' sexual relationship tells them a lot about their political self-hood, provided they decode it that way. It is a self-administered diagnostic test of one's political potential to handle conflict creatively.

The third and final suggestion has to do with the ordinary economics of personal life. How do we handle money in our intimate relationships? And where did we learn to do that? And did we talk about these issues with our therapists? Although therapy is becoming much more of a place where client and therapist can talk politics, we lack books and papers that suggest how it can be done. Instead, what we hear more and more is: 'Yes, well, we certainly did talk about politics, but it was more of a chat as the session was winding down.' This is an awful misunderstanding because the so-called chat about politics may be the main thing of importance to the client at depth. The rules of the therapy game help to obscure this.

None of my theorizing would be possible without the huge expansion in the definition of politics that feminism brought about. 'The personal is political' are the words everybody knows. People often reverse it these days to say that the political is personal. We are in the process of refining our understanding that subjectivity, which is where a great deal of a person's spirituality resides, is irradiated by political, economic and social factors. No thoroughgoing psychotherapy today can ignore the concatenation of spheres that used to be kept thoroughly and virginally separate.

The hidden spiritual politics of primary human connectedness

Psychoanalysis has bequeathed to us a vision of how people relate to one another in society that reflects the culture from which it springs. Split-up and atomized individuals are supposed to get into relationships with each other via projective and introjective identifications. This implies that they are first positioned in empty space. Apparently there is nothing between us to start with. But there is. I shall use images here to get into what I want to communicate more quickly and directly. I wonder if we could imagine something like a 'social ether'. There would then be no empty space between people though it may look as if there is empty space. Physicists tell us that 98 per cent of the universe is composed of cold dark matter, which certainly exists, although no one has been able to locate or measure it. Apart from the fact that what the physicists say sounds mad, it is a reassuring statement from my point of view because it challenges the idea that people are physically separate. If this is so, then there is no need to struggle to achieve relatedness. Psychoanalysis would then be completely wrong about how object relations work. Moreover, there would be no reason or need to postulate a struggle to separate because being unseparate would come to be regarded as an ordinary state of affairs and not as a pathology where not phase-appropriate. This unseparateness I regard as quintessentially spiritual.

Psychoanalysis has encouraged us to place separation at the top of a hierarchy or scale of psychological values and, in this, it has traded off the western notion of an autonomous self. But being jointly immersed in the social ether, one with another, need not be an immature or neurotic or psychotic state. There is actually no basis on which to privilege the bloody struggle towards the kind of autonomous, atomized, despiritualized individualistic self that western societies have espoused, and which we now see as beginning to poison them.

Another heuristic image is that of a rhizome, the nutrient tube under the ground out of which separate stalks come up through the surface of the earth. In the garden, the stalks look separate. But our knowledge about what is going on below the surface tells us that there is a non-visible shared root-base for the separate stalks. One way of looking at formal psychological theories of connectedness, such as the collective unconscious, is to regard them as examples of a hidden, rhizomic, spiritual tradition of connectedness in western culture.

Once again, we find that feminism has contributed a lot here, albeit in a different language. Consider phrases that have come out of feminist psychotherapeutic and psychological thinking: Susie Orbach's 'separated attachment', for example (Eichenbaum and Orbach 1982). Or the title of a book of papers from the Stone Center in the USA: *Women's Growth in Connection* (Jordan *et al.* 1991). Or Carol Gilligan's (1982) work, where she disputes that all morality is principled and abstract morality, and writes about a morality of care based on relational values. These tags are further indications of a tradition so different from the individualistic version of humanity propounded by psychoanalytical theorizing. Yet the tradition of primary connectedness has somehow been suppressed or beaten and modern depth psychology has, for the most part but not completely, colluded in this.

Here we may find deeper spiritual and political significance of the countertransference revolution in psychoanalysis and psychotherapy. The fact that we take our subjective states also to be communications from our clients shows that, at a certain level, modern therapists are functioning on the basis of an idea of there being a primary human connectedness, an idea that is, as I have been arguing, a markedly spiritual one.

We can go on to politicize these thoughts further by saying that what an individual citizen experiences in their heart, body or dreams about the political and social world in which they are living tells us a great deal about that world. Just because it is hard to render such information into the language of formal and official political discourse does not matter. Just because a person does not know the statistics or the history, not being able to remember which president or prime minister preceded another, does not matter. If we are connected in the kinds of ways that I am suggesting, then, bearing in mind what we know about countertransference, what comes up in the citizen's subjectivity in relation to the political world in which he or she is situated is being communicated from that political world. It would then be possible to start to talk about citizens as therapists of the world, citizens-as-therapists. These citizens use their subjective responses to that world in a free and autonomous way, just as psychotherapists make use of their subjective responses to their clients in a free and autonomous way. And all of this stems from an apprehension that there is a hidden spiritual politics of primary human connectedness. Let me underscore the difference between this and most psychoanalytic theories of citizenhood that position the citizen as society's baby (or client) thereby avoiding the citizen's adult possessions of radical imagination and social responsibility.

Psychotherapy and the sense of justice

I conclude with some thoughts about justice, from a spiritual and a psychotherapeutic point of view. What is justice in this postmodern, multicultural, relativistic, socially constructed world, with no eternal or even humanistic values or grand narratives left? What is justice after the death of God? In Greek times even the gods were subject to justice which meant that justice had no location. Then the Judaeo-Christian tradition developed, and started to locate justice in heaven – somewhere else than in the social world here on earth. At that point, a split began to develop between spiritual values and what we can call social theory. I would like to try to heal that split by positioning psychology and psychotherapy somewhere between spiritual values, such as equality in God's eyes, on the one hand, and social theories of equality on the other. It is commonplace for social theorists to regard concepts such as equality in God's eyes as premodern and as justifying and stabilizing all manner of earthly inequalities. This is not utterly unreasonable, as the record shows. But it is an incomplete reading because even in modern accounts of social justice and equality, the idea of an ineluctable psychospiritual equality bubbles under as a kind of positive shadow. (The relationship between Christianity and socialism in a western country would be one specific example of the general pattern.)

Consider John Rawls's classic work on justice, *A Theory of Justice* (1971). This book has set the tone for most major debates about social justice ever since its publication. Without attempting to summarize Rawls's views in detail, I suggest that one of the most significant contemporary philosophers of social justice has pushed his thinking into the areas that spirituality and psychotherapy inhabit. It behoves us to listen to what the intersection of Rawlsian ideas about justice and our work might tell us.

Rawls is discussing the distribution of things in society, how it cannot be absolutely fair yet should be fair enough. He accepts that we can have an unequal distribution of things like money or power in society, provided that people who are less well off are specially catered for. By all means have inequalities, but they should be inequalities that are part of a greater move towards a general lessening of inequality.

Rawls then goes on implicitly to discuss self-esteem and mutual respect as goods that can be distributed within a society. So he would ask about the distribution of self-esteem: who *has* got self-esteem today? Rawls may be understood as reading self-esteem and mutual respect in an unusual way – not as psychological qualities present or not in and between individuals but as goods to be distributed in societies. We could then have a psychologically inflected debate about how we might distribute or redistribute self-esteem and mutual respect in western society. If that debate were to begin, psychotherapists could be, should be part of it. What we know about are the personal strain, delimiters and parameters on the growth of self-esteem and mutual respect. It is our stock in trade. Earlier, we saw that clinical work in psychotherapy may also be seen as secretly encompassing the political and social dimensions of experience. Recalling the earlier introduction of social spirituality, this further underscores the spiritual nature of the psychotherapy process. Now, we add in our observation of some secretly psychological and spiritual dimensions of social and political theory.

Grassroots activities

Several ideas introduced in this chapter were stimulated by recent grassroots developments with which I have been closely involved. I have carried out a number of consultations with politicians in Britain and the United States designed to explore how useful and effective perspectives derived from psychotherapy might be in the formation of policy and in new thinking about the political process. It is difficult to present psychotherapeutic thinking about politics so that mainline politicians – for example, a Democratic Senator or a Labour Party Committee – will take it seriously.

I have also been involved in the formation of three organizations whose objectives are relevant to the content of this chapter. Psychotherapists and Counsellors for Social Responsibility is a professional organization intended to facilitate the desire of many psychotherapists, analysts and counsellors to intervene as professionals in social and political matters making appropriate use of their knowledge and, it must be admitted, whatever cultural authority they possess.

The second organization is a psychotherapy-based think-tank, Antidote. Here, the strategy has been to limit the numbers of mental health professionals involved so as to reduce the chances of psychotherapy reductionism and foster multidisciplinary work in the social policy field. Antidote has undertaken research work in connection with psychological attitudes to money and economic issues generally, and is also involved in work in the area of 'emotional literacy' but expanding the usual remit from personal relationships and family matters to include issues in the public domain.

The third organization is a broad front based at St James's Church in London. The St James's Alliance consists of individuals from diverse fields such as politics, economics, ethics, religion, non-governmental organizations, the media and psychotherapy. It attempts to incorporate ethical, spiritual and psychological concerns into the British political agenda and to facilitate a dialogue which does not take place at present between non-governmental organizations, single issue groups and progressive political organizations. It is an experiment in gathering in political energy that is split up and dissipated under current arrangements.

Together with the thinking outlined in this chapter, these grassroots activities reflect the ways in which, in Giles Clark's words, 'the political world breaks out from inside us and shakes the walls of our consulting rooms, altering the tension between inwardness and social justice' (Clark 1995: 31). Hence the need to challenge the borderlines and boundaries that I mentioned at the outset: between public and private, political and personal, external and internal, activity and reflection, being and doing, extraversion and introversion, politics and psychotherapy, psychotherapy and spirituality, spirituality and politics.

Acknowledgements

This is an edited version of a talk given at the July 1996 conference of the Institute of Psychotherapy and Counselling on The Quest for the Heart of the Work: Spirituality and Psychotherapy.

I am grateful for the helpful comments on my first draft from John Lees, Fiona Palmer Barnes, Valerie Roach and Wendy Robinson.

References

Clark, G. (1995) Review of A. Samuels, *The Political Psyche* (1993), *Winnicott Studies*, 10: 17–39.
Eichenbaum, L. and Orbach, S. (1982) *Outside In . . . Inside Out: Women's Psychology: A Feminist Psychoanalytic Approach*. Harmondsworth: Penguin.
Gilligan, C. (1982) *In a Different Voice: Psychological Theory and Women's Development*. Cambridge, MA: Harvard University Press.
Jordan, J.V. et al. (1991) *Women's Growth in Connection: Writings from the Stone Center*. New York: Guilford Press.
Jung, C.G. (1952) *Symbols of Transformation*, in *Collected Works*, vol. 5. London: Routledge & Kegan Paul.
Rawls, J. (1971) *A Theory of Justice*. Cambridge, MA: Belknap Press.
Samuels, A. (1993) *The Political Psyche*. London: Routledge.
Shorter, B. (1995) *Susceptible to the Sacred*. London: Routledge.
Williamson, T. (1994) *Vagueness*. London: Routledge.
Zaehner, R. (1957) *Mysticism Sacred and Profane*. Oxford: Oxford University Press.

Index

SUPERVISION IN THE HELPING PROFESSIONS
Second Edition

Peter Hawkins and Robin Shohet

Praise for the first edition of *Supervision in the Helping Professions*:

The authors of this book really do know their subject well and have organised the presentation in a clear, systematic, readable style, refreshingly devoid of trans-atlantic jargon. It deals with all aspects of supervision and most importantly provides a meaningful blueprint about how useful and effective supervision can be. Let me recommend this book to you without reservation.   *Journal of the British Psychodrama Association*

The one really powerful book in this area, a book that fundamentally changed the way in which people think about supervision and training.
          Professor John McLeod, University of Abertay, Dundee, Scotland

A very readable book which is of immense help to anyone in a mentoring or supervisory relationship. It will appeal equally to educators, managers and students. All nurses will benefit from reading it. It is reasonably priced and well presented. Buy it.   Philip Burnard, *Nursing Times*

This timely book offers the reader a comprehensive and practical guide to the complex issues inherent in the supervision of health and social services personnel, from the students on field-work placement to the most experienced therapist.   *British Journal of Occupational Therapy*

If you are a supervisor in one of the helping professions, and particularly if you are responsible for training other supervisors, then this book is essential reading for you. It explores the purposes, models and different forms of supervision in counselling, psychotherapy, psychology, psychiatry, nursing, social work, community work, occupational and creative therapy, and the probation and prison services. Similarly, if you work in any of these professions and are interested in finding out more about how to obtain the support and supervision that you need, then this book will also be valuable reading for you.

The first edition was a 'ground-breaking book' in the development of supervision and supervisor training. This second edition retains the models for supervision in individual, group, team and organizational settings, but also contains new material including:

- an up to date review of the new literature, practice and training in the field
- a chapter on supervising across different cultures
- new models on supervising in groups
- ways of introducing better supervision into organizations.

256pp   0 335 20117 2 (Paperback)   0 335 20118 0 (Hardback)

QUESTIONS OF ETHICS IN COUNSELLING AND THERAPY
Caroline Jones, (contributing ed.) Carol Shillito-Clarke, Gabrielle Syme, Derek
Hill, Roger Casemore and Lesley Murdin

This book offers numerous questions and answers about ethics in counselling
and therapy, training, counselling supervision, research and other important
issues. The authors bring psychodynamic, person-centred, integrative or eclec-
tic approaches to their selection of questions and answers. They also bring a
variety of experience from independent practice, institutional and voluntary
agency settings. Between them they have experience as counsellors, psychotherapists, trainers, counselling supervisors and authors.

The questions cover a range of issues that practitioners need to consider including: confidentiality, constraints and the management of confidentiality; boundaries, dual and multiple relationships, relationships with former clients;
non-discriminatory practice, issues for individuals and agencies; competence
and the proper conduct of counsellors and therapists and the profession's
responsibilities to deliver non-exploitative and non-abusive help to clients.

Questions of Ethics in Counselling and Therapy also contains three appendices
offering useful information. It is written in a clear, accessible style and is aimed
at a wide readership in counselling and therapy, ranging from trainees to more
experienced practitioners.

Contents
*Introduction – Section 1: An overview of ethics relating to counselling and
therapy – Section 2: Ethics in counselling – Section 3: Ethics in training and
continuing professional development – Section 4: Ethics in counselling supervision – Section 5: Ethics in research – Section 6: Other important questions –
Appendices – References – Index.*

208pp   0 335 20610 7 (Paperback)   0 335 20611 5 (Hardback)

PSYCHOTHERAPY SUPERVISION
AN INTEGRATIVE RELATIONAL APPROACH TO PSYCHOTHERAPY
SUPERVISION

Maria C. Gilbert and Kenneth Evans

Maria Gilbert and Kenneth Evans have given us a beautifully written and richly illustrated account of psychotherapy supervision . . . Providing clear guidelines for effective clinical supervision, the book describes and vividly illustrates how the supervisor monitors, instructs, models, consults and supports the supervisee, all within the context of respect and empathy.

> Marvin R. Goldfried, Ph.D. State University of New York
> at Stony Brook, Stony Brook, New York, USA

Don't read this book if you have a well-worked-out, pre-determined model of supervision that you don't want to change . . . it will only disturb, distract and challenge you. If you would like to review your model of supervision, on the other hand, update it in the light of modern scholarship and insights, open it to 'manufactured uncertainty' so as to adapt it to the contemporary issues of the day, then it's a 'must' for you. It's a book of tomorrow in the light of the best of yesterday.

> Michael Carroll, Ph.D. Chartered
> Counselling Psychologist and BAC Fellow

Gilbert and Evans' book is sure to become a key text in the area of psychotherapy supervision from an integrative perspective . . . Gilbert and Evans draw much needed attention to the often neglected aspect of the contexts within which supervision takes place. Their focus on the multi-cultural aspects of supervision and their advocacy for anti-oppressive practices is of note . . . highly recommended to beginning supervisees and seasoned supervisors alike. This book will make a substantial contribution to the field for a long time to come.

> Gillian Straker, Professor of Psychology
> at the University of Sydney

Contents

Introduction – An integrative relational model of supervision – The model in practice – Creating an effective learning environment – The supervision frame: contracting and boundaries in supervision; styles and modes of psychotherapy supervision – Theoretical and research foundations for an integrative relational approach to supervision – Assessment, accreditation and evaluation in supervision practice – Developing personal style as a supervisor – Ethical decision making in supervision – Multicultural aspects and anti-oppressive practice in supervision and psychotherapy – Psychotherapy and supervision in the UK, in Europe and in the wider context – Resources for the supervisor – References – Index.

208pp   0 335 20138 5 (Paperback)   0 335 20139 3 (Hardback)